Part 5
Writing With Style

W9-CST-459

Forms of Writing

A Brief Guide and Handbook

Second Canadian Edition

Kay L. Stewart
University of Alberta

Marian E. Allen
Grant MacEwan Community College

Prentice Hall Canada Inc., Scarborough, Ontario

Canadian Cataloguing in Publication Data

Stewart, Kay L. (Kay Lanette), 1942– .
   Forms of writing

2nd. ed.
Includes index.

ISBN 0-13-518564-5

1. English language – Rhetoric.   2. English language – Rhetoric – Problems, exercises, etc.   3. Business writing.   4. Business writing – Problems, exercises, etc.   I. Allen, Marian, 1945– .   II. Title.

PE1408.S762 1997   808'.042   C95-933206-5

 © 1997 Prentice-Hall Canada Inc., Scarborough, Ontario
A Viacom Company

ALL RIGHTS RESERVED

No part of this book may be reproduced in any form without permission in writing from the publisher.

Prentice-Hall, Inc., Englewood Cliffs, New Jersey
Prentice-Hall International (UK) Limited, London
Prentice-Hall of Australia, Pty. Limited, Sydney
Prentice-Hall Hispanoamericana, S.A., Mexico City
Prentice-Hall of India Private Limited, New Delhi
Prentice-Hall of Japan, Inc., Tokyo
Simon & Schuster Asia Private Limited, Singapore
Editora Prentice-Hall do Brasil, Ltda., Rio de Janeiro

ISBN 0-13-518564-5

Acquisitions Editor: Rebecca Bersagel
Developmental Editor: Karen Sacks
Copy Editor: Chelsea Donaldson
Production Editor: Valerie Adams
Production Coordinator: Deborah Starks
Permissions: Marijke Leupen
Cover Design: Petra Phillips
Cover Image: The Image Bank/Steve Bronstein
Page Layout: Phyllis Seto

1 2 3 4 5   WC   1 00 99 98 97

Printed and bound in Canada

Every reasonable effort has been made to obtain permissions for all articles and data used in this edition. If errors or omissions have occurred, they will be corrected in future editions provided written notification has been received by the publisher.

We welcome readers' comments, which can be sent by e-mail to
collegeinfo_pubcanada@prenhall.com

CONTENTS

iii

PART 3: WRITING ESSAYS

9 Expository Essays

10 Other Types of Expository Writing

11 Persuasive Essays

PART 4: WRITING BUSINESS LETTERS, RÉSUMÉS, AND REPORTS:

21 Proofreading: Punctuation and Mechanics

APPENDICES

Appendix A: Quotations

Appendix B: Documentation

Appendix C: Format Conventions for Writing

Appendix D: Writing Essay and Short Answer Examinations

Preface
to the Second Edition

Our Approach

Our approach in the second edition of *Forms of Writing* rests on this assumption: that good writing results when you know your purpose, your audience, your subject, and the conventions of your chosen form. We focus on three main purposes for writing—to explain, to persuade, and to share personal experience—and show how your purpose influences the strategies you choose in writing for a particular audience. This emphasis on purpose and audience gives you a basic orientation that helps you to understand the conventions of a wide variety of forms, such as personal essays, research papers, and business letters.

Because of the wide variety of forms, this book works well in communications courses, introductory and advanced writing courses, and English courses with a writing component. Many students keep the text as a reference for writing in other courses and on the job.

This edition retains the basic organization of the first edition. We have updated the material and revised sections to make the book easier to use.

Features of the Text

- An overview of the writing process

- An extensive section on methods of developing paragraphs that will expand the range of your writing strategies

- Short chapters with easy-to-follow guidelines for many different types of writing, with samples

- Checklists for evaluating your own or your classmates' writing

- A section on Writing with Style that enables you to work independently to improve your word choice and sentence structure

- Explanations of sentence structure, grammar, punctuation, and mechanics with Exercises and Answer Keys.

Organization of the Text

- Part 1, *The Writing Process*, gives you an overview of all the steps in completing a writing assignment, from defining your purpose and audience to revising and proofreading.

- Part 2, *Writing Paragraphs*, introduces you to principles of paragraph structure and methods of developing paragraphs—such as analysis, definition, and evaluation—that you may use in many forms of writing.

- Part 3, *Writing Essays*, provides guidelines for the types of writing you are most likely to do in college and university courses, including essays on literature and research papers.

- Part 4, *Writing Business Letters, Résumés, and Reports*, covers the kinds of business writing that most people do, whatever their occupation—letters of application and ré-sumés, brief reports, and proposals.

- Part 5, *Writing with Style*, explains stylistic choices and accepted practices in grammar and punctuation so that you can meet your readers' expectations for clarity and precision in language.

- *The Appendices* cover material you may need to consult frequently: guidelines for using quotations, documenting sources, and formatting your writing. A glossary of grammatical terms is also included.

Changes in the Second Edition

This new edition includes

- Suggestions on using computers for prewriting, drafting, revising, and doing research

- Guidelines for writing interviews and opinion pieces

- More information on how to formulate a thesis for different types of essays

In addition, some sections of the first edition have been significantly revised:

- Steps in analyzing an argument now appear in a separate section (Essays Analyzing Nonfiction, 9e)

- Scattered sections on stylistic revision have been combined into one chapter at the beginning of *Part 5: Writing with Style.*

- MLA and APA documentation styles have been updated to include formats for citing electronic publications.

- About one third of the examples have been replaced.

Other Resources

- *Forms of Writing Workbook* provides additional exercises on sentence structure, grammar, and punctuation.

- *Instructor's Manual* includes suggested course outlines; classroom activities and exercises; teaching tips; and suggestions for further reading.

Good writing!

Acknowledgements

We wish to thank again all those who contributed to the first edition; this text also owes much to you.

Throughout, we have relied heavily on work done by students in various courses. Where we had permission to do so, we have named them. Named and nameless, we thank them all for entrusting their writing to us.

Special thanks to Diane Ewen, who prepared the index, updated the workbook, and transformed the Annotated Instructor's Edition of the first edition into an Instructor's Manual for this edition. Len Falkenstein researched and wrote a chapter that forms the basis for our remarks on using computers; Chris Rechner and Lois Drew also helped with research.

We would also like to acknowledge the assistance of several reviewers: Barbara Danbrook, Humber College; Francie Aspinall, Centennial College; Graham Frost, Capilano College; and Frank Daley, Seneca College.

At Prentice Hall, our longtime Acquisitions Editor, Marjorie Munroe, left the company and was replaced by Rebecca Bersagel; our thanks to both for their help along the way, and to Developmental Editor Karen Sacks and Production Editor Valerie Adams. Chelsea Donaldson's copy editing has been sensitive and thorough, and her patience remarkable. Sharon Kirsch's sharp eyes caught a multitude of typographical errors.

To colleagues, friends, and family who have offered encouragement and endured neglect while we completed this project, our heartfelt appreciation.

Kay Stewart
Marian Allen

Part 1

THE WRITING PROCESS
An Overview

As the Industrial Revolution marked the nineteenth century, so the Communication Revolution has marked the twentieth. New forms of communication, such as radio, film, television, and telephone, have made possible new ways of providing information and entertainment. We can pop a video into the VCR, download from a computer database, fax a document to its destination in seconds. These new technologies, far from reducing the need for good writing skills, have increased them. Someone, somewhere, must write the script for the video, the entries in the database, the important letter or report. And someday that person may be you.

Writing, in some form or another, is likely to play a significant role not only in your education but also in your professional life and your personal life. In our changing world, the demands made upon your writing skills will be varied and changing. You can more easily meet these demands if you understand the basic steps that many successful writers take in the process of completing a piece of writing.

What we offer is a blueprint: you may find your writing process much less clearcut and tidy. You may discover that you spend more time and energy on some steps than on others, depending on the writing project and your creative style. The writing process is not a rigid structure for you to impose on your writing but a general plan to help you shape an idea into a written piece. Use the steps to guide you; make the process your own.

Chapter 1

Identifying Your Purpose and Audience

Before you begin to write, you need to define your purpose and audience. Otherwise, you may stare blankly at your piece of paper or keyboard, unsure of how to start; or you may plunge blithely ahead, only to discover that you have misunderstood your writing task.

1a Defining Your Purpose

In this book, we will focus on three broad purposes for writing: to explain, to persuade, and to share ideas and experiences. The first purpose leads to **expository writing**, the second to **persuasive writing**, and the third to **personal writing**. Your understanding of your purpose and audience will influence your choice of form and methods of development, your relationship to your readers, and your choice of language and style.

Expository Writing

Your writing is expository whenever your main purpose is to provide information, to explain how something works or how something is done, or to explain the meaning of concepts, historical events, works of art, and so on. As these examples suggest, in expository writing your emphasis is on your subject, rather than on your audience or on you as a writer. You and your readers are like observers peering through a microscope and trying to see the same thing on the glass slide.

Persuasive Writing

The central question of all persuasive writing is, *What is good?*— good for one person, a group, a nation, humanity, or the planet. Your purpose is to convince others of your vision of what is good.

You may want to persuade your readers to share your attitudes and beliefs or to act on those beliefs. To accomplish this goal, you have to consider how to appeal to your audience. In the interplay among writer, subject, and audience, the emphasis in persuasive writing shifts towards the audience.

Personal Writing

Personal writing gives you the chance to discover what you think and how you feel about ideas and experiences, and to share these discoveries with others. However, your subject is not always something that happened to you—you may also write about your reactions to the world around you. Nor does personal writing always have to be the serious business of revealing your innermost thoughts and feelings. You, the writer, are on centre stage, and you may therefore choose to present yourself as comic or tragic, satiric or romantic, serious or slightly mad.

Examples

To illustrate differences in these types of writing, we will consider three paragraphs on the same subject, shoplifting. The first comes from an expository essay on what causes people to shoplift.

Sample Expository Writing—Purpose: To Explain

Knowing what is stolen and where it is stolen from does not answer the most basic question about shoplifting: why do people steal? According to a security guard for Sears, the reason is not need: "In all the time I've worked here, and of all the arrests I've made, and I've made over 400 arrests, not once, not once was it out of need." Most shoplifters who are caught have more than enough money with them to pay for the item and many have credit cards as well. So why do they steal? According to Bill Cheung at Eaton's, the peak seasons for shoplifting are September and January-February, when new school terms begin. Presumably, at the beginning of the term, students look at the clothes or toys their peers have and want them. Children and adolescents, it seems, shoplift to fit in.

—Amanda Thompson

4

This paragraph illustrates the principal features of much expository writing. The writer explains why some people shoplift without stating her opinion about the behaviour. She presents her information and analysis as objectively as possible, referring to shoplifters as *people* and *students*, for example, not as *thieves* and *juvenile delinquents*. In this way, she keeps the focus on her subject, not on her opinions about the subject or on her own personality.

Sample Persuasive Writing
Purpose: To Change Opinion or Behaviour

Contrary to the popular view, most shoplifters do not steal because they are poor. A longtime security guard for Sears, who has arrested more than 400 shoplifters, points out that "not once" had the person stolen out of need. Shoplifters usually have more than enough money with them to pay for the stolen goods, and they often have credit cards as well. They may tell themselves that the stores are so rich they will not miss this little eraser/tube of lipstick/make-up case/radio/stereo/jacket. But it is not the stores that pay; honest customers pay through higher prices. There is thus no reason to be lenient with shoplifters. They are as guilty of theft as the person who steals a wallet from a locker room or a tape deck from a car, and should be treated accordingly. If we turn a blind eye to shoplifting, we are not only condoning a crime, but also sentencing ourselves to pay the penalty.

Here the writer's purpose is not to explain some possible reasons for shoplifting but to persuade readers to change their attitude, and possibly their behaviour, towards shoplifters. In contrast to the neutral language of the expository paragraph, the writer uses emotionally charged words and phrases (*honest, guilty, lenient, condoning, sentencing*). This language focuses attention on the attitude that the writer wants readers to adopt.

Sample Personal Writing
Purpose: To Share Personal Experience

I was thirteen at the time, in a new school, and desperate to make friends. For the first few weeks, everyone ignored me. Not that all my classmates were friends with each other. At lunch hour and after school they divided into groups and alternately ignored and insulted each other. I was afraid that if I didn't make friends soon, they would stop ignoring and start insulting me. So one day, I followed a gang of five or six into the mall at lunch. As they straggled through Eaton's, I kept several feet behind, stopping every now and then to gaze intently at leather briefcases or umbrellas so they wouldn't think I was being pushy. When they clustered around the jewelry counter, I ducked down the next row. And there in front of me were bags and bags of candy, ready for Hallowe'en. Without thinking, I grabbed one and stuffed it under my jacket.

This writer invites us to share the isolation, fear, and desire to belong that lead to shoplifting a bag of candy. The story carries us along and makes us part of the events. Even though we may disapprove of the theft, we are drawn into the writer's subjective experience.

The first question to ask yourself about any writing situation, then, is *What is my purpose?* In some writing situations, you may be free to choose your own purpose. If you wanted to write an article on grizzly bears for a general interest magazine, for instance, you could choose to explain the grizzly's habits, to argue for better protection for this endangered species, or to share your own adventures in grizzly country.

In many school and work situations, however, your purpose will be given or implied. An assignment that asks you to write a persuasive essay on capital punishment defines your purpose. A manager who asks you to write a report on the branch office assumes that your report will be expository, not a personal account of your frustrations in trying to compile the data.

1b Defining Your Audience

Defining your purpose is the first step in writing; the second is defining your audience. Just as your style of speaking changes as you move from the poolroom to the classroom, so your style of writing changes with your audience. Are you writing for readers who already know a great deal about your subject, or for those who know nothing at all? For educated adults, or for elementary school children? Considering the needs of your audience will help you decide what to explain and what you can take for granted, for instance, or whether to use a formal or an informal style.

Making Reader Profiles

You can develop a clearer sense of your audience by asking yourself these questions.

1b

Defining Your Audience

1. Who will read this piece? A specific person, such as a supervisor? A group of people with similar interests, such as *Star Trek* fans? A group of people of varying ages and backgrounds, such as newspaper readers?

2. What attitude will my reader(s) likely bring to this piece of writing? Interest and enthusiasm? Hostility and defensiveness? Critical detachment?

3. How much knowledge will my reader(s) already have about my subject? What information do I need to provide?

4. What expectations will my reader(s) have about the way this piece is written? Is there a specific format I should follow?

Answering these questions will give you a **reader profile:** a general sense of your audience's needs and expectations. Keeping this reader profile in mind as you write or revise will help you communicate more effectively. If you give some thought to what a potential employer looks for in a letter of application, for example, you can tailor your application to match those expectations.

Chapter 2

Gathering Material

Garbage in, garbage out *is a favourite saying of computer programmers. What's true of computers is also true of writers. If you don't give yourself good material to work with, your writing will be weak in content. The following techniques will help you generate ideas, collect information, and find a focus.*

2a Brainstorming

Brainstorming allows you to capture your spontaneous responses to your subject. Put a key word from your writing task in the centre of a blank page. Allow yourself to free-associate—what ideas, examples, questions, memories, or feelings spring to mind? Surround your key word with notes, without rejecting anything. If you were preparing a report on the need for life skills courses in high school, for instance, you might end up with a brainstorming diagram something like this:

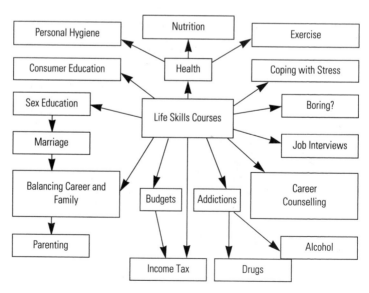

8

With so many ideas to consider, you can find a fresh angle on your subject or choose material of special interest to your readers. And brainstorming guarantees that you won't run out of things to say.

2b Freewriting

Asking
Discovery
Questions

Many people discount their most creative ideas, intuitions, and memories before they start. To get around this internal censor, try **freewriting**. Write continuously about your subject for five or ten minutes, without stopping to correct or criticize. If you run out of things to say, write something like "I can't think of anything to say" and keep writing. Do not hesitate over words, make corrections, or stop to think. After ten minutes, look over what you've written and sum it up in a sentence. If your summary suggests new ideas, freewrite for another ten minutes.

2c Asking Discovery Questions

There are two ways to use this technique.

1. *Start with the journalist's five W's and an H: Who, What, When, Where, Why, and How.*

   Answering these questions will give you information that your reader is likely to need in any situation. If you were writing a letter of complaint about a garment that had been damaged at the dry cleaners, for instance, you might ask these questions: What is the garment? Where did I take it? When did I take it in and pick it up? Who wrote up the order? What is the damage? How did the damage occur? What do I want the company to do?

2. *Ask questions based on the methods of developing paragraphs.*

   (Eight methods—analogy, analysis, classification, comparison, definition, description, evaluation, examples, narration—are discussed in detail in Chapter 5.) Examples (discussed in Chapter 4) give substance to paragraphs developed in many ways. For an essay on drug addiction, for instance, you might ask questions like these:

   • What is taking drugs like? [analogy, comparison]

   • What are the stages of addiction? [process analysis]

- What functions do the addict's relationships serve? [systems analysis]

- What are the causes? the effects? [causal analysis]

- Is it possible to classify addicts? [classification]

- How is addiction defined? [definition]

- How would I describe an addict's behaviour? [description]

- How could I assess the strengths and weaknesses of a drug addiction treatment program? [evaluation]

- Is there a story I could tell about drug addiction? [narration]

- What examples can I give? [examples]

2d Keeping a Journal

Keeping a **journal** can be an excellent way of gathering ideas and information for a long-term writing project. Use your journal entries to reflect on issues, respond to your reading, collect relevant newspaper or magazine items, note questions to pursue, and record your progress. When the time comes to write your essay, you will have lots of material and original insights.

2e Prewriting on the Computer

If you work on a computer, you can use it for gathering material long before you start to write your first draft. Brainstorming may be easier with pen and paper, but the computer is ideal for freewriting, asking discovery questions, and keeping a journal. For example, you can create a file (called *Notes,* for example) where you can take notes on your reading, copy down quotations, compile references, and jot down ideas as they come to you. Print out and review this material before you start to write.

The computer can also help you avoid the temptation to correct typos or make other changes as you freewrite. Try darkening the monitor with the contrast control or covering the screen with a blanket or towel. (If you are working in a computer lab, you may get some odd looks, but the results should make it all worthwhile.)

2f Finding a Focus

You have defined your purpose and audience. You have gathered ideas and information about your subject. But you have so many ideas and so much information that you don't know what to include and what to leave out. You need a focus.

To define a focus for your writing, link your purpose—explaining, persuading, or sharing personal experience—with one or more aspects of your subject. For a short piece, you may choose to discuss one aspect in detail. For a longer piece, you may include several. Suppose, for example, that your subject is car auctions and your purpose is to explain some aspect of this subject. For a short piece, you could focus on what a car auction is. For a longer piece, you might also explain how cars are sold at auctions and why people buy or sell cars there.

Writing your focus at the top of your paper when you begin your draft will remind you of what to cover.

Chapter 3

Drafting, Outlining, and Revising

Once you have defined your purpose and audience, and have some material to work with, it's time to think about giving your material a form.

Strategies for drafting, revising, and editing vary from form to form and writer to writer. For a brief letter, you may simply type out your request, proofread for mistakes, and seal the envelope. A letter of application, a report, or an essay will require a more careful consideration of content, organization, and style.

Strategies for drafting and revising vary with these longer writing tasks as well. Some writers discover their main point in the process of writing a draft, and then make substantial changes in content and organization. Others plan what they want to say, either in their minds or in an outline, and so their first draft has a main point and a clear pattern of organization. Revision for these writers is largely a matter of smoothing out sentences and improving word choice.

We will illustrate both ways of getting started so that you can choose the method that best suits you and your writing task.

3a Fast-Drafting

If you decide to write a fast draft to help clarify your thinking, set a fixed period—usually an hour or two—and don't let yourself get bogged down. Write a complete draft within this time. If you have trouble with the introduction, for example, either leave some space and come back to it later, or write something like *What I want to do in this paper is* _____ and go on from there.

When you reread, you may find that your main point has surfaced near the end and that you need to restructure. Making an outline of your draft will help you decide how to reorganize your material.

3b Making an Outline

An outline shows you at a glance the main divisions of your paper and the relationships among major points, minor points, and details. Making an outline thus helps you to classify your material and detect gaps in it.

There are several points in the process of drafting and revising where you might find an outline useful. Some writers like to make an outline before they write a first draft. For this kind of preliminary outline, use your statement of focus as a guide to your main points. Under each main point, jot down the details you will need to include.

Other writers use a revision outline to clarify the organization of their ideas. After writing a draft, they make an outline showing the main point and supporting details in each paragraph. You can use this outline to evaluate the structure and completeness of your piece.

You can also make a formal outline of your final version to accompany a lengthy report or research paper. Put your thesis, the main point of your piece, at the top of the page. List your major points with Roman numerals, your subpoints with capital letters, and details with Arabic numerals. The format of your outline should resemble the one below.

Thesis: Because shoplifting has become so widespread, methods of identifying and apprehending shoplifters have changed.

I. Extent of the problem
   A. Type of goods stolen
      1. From novelty stores
      2. From department stores
   B. Amount stolen annually

II. Types of shoplifters
   A. Professionals
   B. Amateurs

III. Some reasons for shoplifting
   A. Need
   B. Desire to fit in
   C. Thrills

IV. Methods of detection
   A. Following suspects
   B. Using one-way mirrors and closed-circuit television

13

As you can see, each level of the outline (Roman numerals, capital letters, Arabic numerals) represents a division of the level below. For this reason, you should have at least two items at each level (if you have an A, you must have a B; if you have a 1, you must have a 2). Each item at a particular level must be an equivalent subdivision of the level above. For example, *Need*, *Desire to fit in*, and *Thrills* are equivalent items under *Some reasons for shoplifting*. This equivalence will be more obvious if you make items at each level grammatically parallel (see 17e, Faulty Parallelism).

3c Revising and Proofreading

When you have written a draft, evaluate it according to one of the checklists provided in this book. (For paragraphs, see page 18; for essays, p. 66; and for business letters, résumés, or reports, see page 178.) Make any necessary revisions in content, organization, style, and format. If possible, give your work to someone else to read. If that is not possible, try reading your work aloud to get a better sense of how it sounds to another reader. If some sections seem wordy, monotonous, or stilted, see the pointers in Chapter 16, Improving Your Style.

Revise your draft over and over until you are satisfied, or at least until you run out of time. (Revision is usually the most time-consuming part of the composing process.) Then give your next-to-final version a careful going-over to check for errors in grammar and punctuation and for misused words. For more information on the mechanics of writing, see Part 5: Writing with Style.

3d Drafting and Revising on the Computer

Most word-processing programs make drafting and revising on the computer quick and easy, allowing you more room to experiment. You can insert, delete, and move text until you are satisfied with the result. If you and your classmates are linked by e-mail, you can share drafts of your work and post editing suggestions to one another electronically. E-mail also provides a forum for collaborative writing. You and others can log on simultaneously and attempt to write or edit a document collectively. This process can provide you with insights into how others write as well as give you helpful feedback on your own work. Although you may make many changes onscreen as you write, it is a good idea to print hard copies to help you revise. One reason is that your monitor displays only a small section of your document. A hard copy will give you a better grasp of how well your material is organized and whether you've been enticed into wordiness by an empty screen. Another advantage is that you can circulate a hard copy to others for feedback.

To aid in editing, many word-processing packages include a built-in thesaurus, spell checker, and grammar and style checker. Although you may find these options helpful, you need to be aware of their limitations. A thesaurus, whether in print or on disk, cannot tell you whether a listed synonym is appropriate in a specific context. Spell checkers only recognize words that have been entered into their memories; they may tag as errors acceptable variations in the spelling of certain words (*analyse/analyze*, for example); and they will not catch properly spelled words used incorrectly (*there* for *their*, for example).

Grammar and style checkers have similar limitations. They may help you recognize grammatical and stylistic problems such as sentence fragments and convoluted sentences. But they cannot distinguish between an outright error and a choice you've made for stylistic or rhetorical effect. Like spell checkers, they are best used to supplement your own proofreading skills.

Word-Processing Guidelines

- Whenever you write on the computer, remember to save your work every fifteen minutes or so, and always keep two copies of your work in electronic form (normally one on your hard drive and one on a disk) in case one gets lost or damaged.

- If you work with more than one system or software package, make sure well before your due date that the various components are compatible, or make contingency plans in case they're not. You will avoid the grief and frustration of discovering, for instance, that your friend's printer garbles your document.

15

- If you share disks, use your disks in other computers (including those in computer labs), or download material from the Internet, install a memory resident virus checker to protect against viruses.

The Journal Writer—includes guidelines for journal writing and journal writing exercises

http://www.rio.com/%7Ewplace/journal.html

The Joys of Journaling—Dennis J. Cleary

http://www.cwo.com/%7Ezenden/journal.html

Handout on brainstorming by consultants at the Undergraduate Writing Center at U.T. Austin.

gopher://gopher.utexas.edu:3003/00/pub/uwc/ Handouts/brainsto.txt

York University Computer Assisted Writing Centre— Strategies—Techniques for Generating Ideas for Your Essay

http://www.writer.yorku.ca/strategies/contents.html

Writers on the Net—Classes, Tutoring and Mentoring, Writers' Groups

http://www.writers.com/

Writer's Resources on the Web—good extensive range of links

http://www.interlog.com/~ohi/www/writesource.html

Canadian-Based Publications Online

http://www.cs.cmu.edu/Web/Unofficial/Canadiana/ CA-zines.html#Magazines

Part 2

WRITING PARAGRAPHS

CHECKLIST

Paragraphs

	OK	NEEDS WORK
1. Is your purpose clear?	☐	☐
2. Is the paragraph a readable length (not too long or too short)?	☐	☐
3. Have you chosen an appropriate method of development?	☐	☐
4. Does the topic sentence state the main point?	☐	☐
5. Are the details adequate?	☐	☐
6. Are the details relevant?	☐	☐
7. Have you used effective transitions?	☐	☐

Chapter 4

What Is a Paragraph?

*Although you have probably been writing paragraphs
for years, you may not be sure exactly what a paragraph
is. Here is a useful definition to keep in mind: a paragraph is a unit of writing that makes a clear point about
a subject and includes information directly related to
that point.*

Paragraphs are the building blocks of writing. Introductory
paragraphs lay the foundation; concluding paragraphs provide the
capstone, or finishing touch. In between are the middle paragraphs, each one discussing one aspect of your subject (one
point in an analysis, one step in a process, one event in a narrative). Each middle paragraph is thus both a self-contained piece
of writing and a part of a larger structure. In this chapter we
focus on middle paragraphs as self-contained pieces of writing.

4a Paragraph Divisions

By dividing your material into paragraphs, you signal that all the
information in a particular paragraph relates to one aspect of
your subject. In this way, you help your reader to understand
how you have organized your material. Paragraph divisions that
seem random—because paragraphs run on for pages or consist
of only a sentence or two—will confuse your reader.

Readers find excessively long paragraphs difficult to understand and uninviting to read. Normally, you should be able to
discuss one aspect of your subject adequately in about half a
page. If you need more room to develop your ideas, subdivide
your paragraph. Instead of trying to discuss several effects of
taking a summer school course in one paragraph, for example,
focus each paragraph on one effect, such as the effect on your relationship with your family.

You may occasionally use a one-sentence paragraph to signal a transition or to emphasize a point. But a series of short
paragraphs can confuse readers; they lose the sense of how the
paragraphs relate to each other and to the piece of writing as a

whole. If several short paragraphs discuss only one aspect of your subject, you can simply combine them. More often, however, paragraphs are short because they do not provide enough reasons, details, and examples to explain one aspect of your subject. You will find many methods of developing paragraphs discussed in Chapter 5.

4b Topic Sentences

A topic sentence does not merely state the topic or subject of the paragraph; **it states your main point about that subject**. After you have read through your draft, ask yourself: what's the main idea in this paragraph?

To answer this question, you need to make a clear distinction between your subject and the point you meant to make about that subject. For example, if your subject is how taking a summer school course affected your relationship with your children, your main point might be "Surprisingly, I found that going to school gave me more time with my children than I had anticipated" or "Predictably enough, my children outdid themselves in bids for the significantly reduced time I was now able to spend with them."

A good topic sentence exercises control over the content of a paragraph by clarifying what belongs and what doesn't. Suppose your subject is your experiences working the night shift in a convenience store. If you merely restate your subject with a topic sentence like "I work nights in a convenience store," neither you nor your reader has any sense of what to expect in the paragraph. The topic sentences below give a much better sense of what the paragraph will be about.

> Working nights in a convenience store almost eliminated my social life.
>
> Working nights in a convenience store introduced me to a side of my neighbourhood I hadn't known before.
>
> Working nights in a convenience store became an increasingly terrifying experience.

Exercise 4.1

Consider the following statements as possible topic sentences for a paragraph. If you think the sentence makes a point that would control the content of the paragraph, put C beside it. If you think it doesn't, rewrite the sentence.

1. Last summer I climbed a mountain.

2. Hospitals can be bad for your health.

3. Canada is a member of NATO.

4. Watching a movie in a theatre is a more intense experience than watching it at home on television.

5. Nearly 20% of high school athletes take steroids.

4c The Body of the Paragraph

As we have seen, topic sentences state an idea that you can then develop through more specific details. If you attempt to support your topic sentence with other generalizations, rather than specific details, you will have trouble explaining your ideas and convincing your readers that the ideas are valid. Consider the following example.

> **Because most cyclists ignore the rules of the road, they are a danger to themselves and others.** Most motorists hate and fear cyclists. When I see how cyclists ride anywhere they want on the road, I wonder what they are protecting inside their helmets.

This paragraph consists of three topic sentences, so it's not really a paragraph. If it seems uncomfortably familiar, pay particular attention to this section of the text where you will find a variety of methods to develop the body of a paragraph. You will learn, for instance, what kind of details to put into a paragraph you are developing through description or causal analysis and how to organize them most effectively. You will also learn how to combine methods of development to increase the clarity and impact of a paragraph or a longer piece of writing. For example, you might begin a research paper on why small businesses go bankrupt with a narrative paragraph or two about the collapse of a local business.

The Importance of Specific Details

Whether you are developing your paragraph through definition, comparison, process analysis, or some other method, you will probably need to provide examples (specific instances) to support your point. You can use examples more effectively by following these guidelines.

- *Include an example to support any important general point.*
Consider these two versions of a paragraph on the Marxist definition of violence. The first is a series of general statements.

> The Marxists maintain that an act of violence is quite different from a violent act. An act of violence is an act that causes harm and suffering whether or not it is done violently. This distinction between an act of violence and a violent act allows the Marxists to point out that acts of violence do not necessarily involve physical force.

In the second version, examples illustrate the main points.

> The Marxists maintain that an act of violence is quite different from a violent act. Stirring a cup of tea, for example, can be done violently and therefore could be described as a violent act. An act of violence, on the other hand, is an act that causes harm and suffering whether or not it is done violently. Such acts do not necessarily involve physical force. To illustrate this point, one need only envision a situation where urban terrorists poisoned the air, with the result that citizens died quietly in their sleep. No physical contact was made, but no one could say that violence did not occur.

Without the **examples**, the specific instances used to explain the general statements, it is difficult to grasp the distinction between an act of violence and a violent act.

- *Make sure your examples are typical.*
Suppose, for instance, you were arguing that mandatory retirement is unfair. You might want to support your position by giving the example of your mother, who was not eligible for a full pension when she was forced to retire at sixty-five because she did not begin to work full-time until she was forty. If you used only this example to support your argument, readers might object, saying that your mother's case was not typical and therefore was poor evidence. This example would be effective, however, if you could show that many women are in the same situation. You would also want to use examples of other people, such as those who change employers or careers.

- *Explain the meaning of your examples.*
An example seems puzzling when its relation to a general statement is unclear.

> Advertisements make life easier in some very basic ways. A good example is the commercials that play a few bars of many songs included on a tape.

How can playing snippets of songs "make life easier"? A sentence or two of explanation would make this connection clear. Explain your point first and then give your example:

> Advertisements make life easier in some very basic ways. One way they do this is by offering the consumer an opportunity to sample products before buying. A good example of this is the commercials for musical compilation tapes that play a few bars of many songs.

Where there are several steps in the argument, as here, you may need to add another sentence after the example to remind your reader of your main point. The paragraph on advertising ends with this sentence showing how the commercial makes life easier:

> These snippets give the consumer a fairly good idea of whether or not the tape suits his or her taste in music and is thus worth buying.

- *Integrate your examples smoothly.*

If you haven't had much practice using examples, you may be tempted to introduce them with awkward phrases such as *An example of this is when....* (see Mixed Constructions, 17g). You can integrate your examples more smoothly by using constructions such as these: *for example, a further example, is exemplified by, for instance, an instance is, such as, this point is illustrated in, an illustration of this point is.*

> Another instance of this government's indifference to the needs of ordinary people is the plan to tax basic foods and children's clothing.

> The adolescent's need to conform is best exemplified by the popularity of a few kinds of designer jeans.

> The half-hour line-ups in the cafeteria are further evidence of the need for more staff.

Exercise 4.2

List several examples you could use to illustrate each of the following ideas.

1. Families planning to eat out will find a variety of restaurants offering nutritious food at reasonable prices.

2. My home town's points of interest are waiting to be explored.

3. Many Canadian writers are highly regarded in other countries.

4d Structuring a Paragraph

There are two basic ways of organizing information in a paragraph. You can begin with your topic sentence and then fill in the reasons, examples, and other details that provide evidence to support it, or you can begin with these details and examples and gradually lead your reader to the main point you want to make about them. The first method places immediate emphasis on your main point, whereas the second emphasizes the process of thinking and feeling that led you to it. You can see the difference between these two basic ways of organizing information in the following two examples.

4d

Sample Paragraph: Topic Sentence First Arrangement

Working nights in a convenience store introduced me to a side of my neighbourhood I hadn't known before. One surprise was the discovery of nocturnal neighbours who emerged from their homes only after midnight, but the night lives of people I had met before were also surprising. I discovered that old Mr. Jones, with whom I had exchanged perhaps twenty sentences in the past ten years, was a talkative insomniac, addicted to corned beef sandwiches at 3 a.m. He had been an intelligence agent with an amazing career, which he unfolded in successive nightly installments. And then there was Mrs. Anderson. I had always imagined her to be one half of a happily married older couple, but twice in the first month I worked at the store, Mrs. Anderson met a man (who was definitely not her husband) and disappeared into the night. I was beginning to see new meaning in the term "convenience store."

Sample Paragraph: Details First Arrangement

Before I started working in one, a convenience store was just a place to go when you ran out of milk late at night. I hadn't realized that I had many nocturnal neighbours who emerged from their homes only after midnight. More surprising, however, were the night lives of people I knew. Old Mr. Jones, with whom I had exchanged perhaps twenty sentences in the last ten years, turned out to be a talkative insomniac, addicted to corned beef sandwiches at 3 a.m. In nightly installments he unfolded his amazing career as an intelligence agent. And then there was Mrs. Anderson.

I had always thought of her as one half of a happily married older couple, but twice in the first month I worked at the store she met a man (who was definitely not her husband) and disappeared into the night. Working nights in a convenience store was introducing me to a side of my neighbourhood I hadn't known before.

4e Transitions

Transitions are words and phrases (*on the other hand, for example, as a result, similarly*) that help a reader to move from one sentence to the next in your writing. If you compare the following paragraphs, you will see how transitions can dramatically increase the clarity of your ideas and the flow of your writing.

Draft Paragraph Without Transitions

I had been working as a carpenter for five years. I injured my back. I needed to find a different sort of job. I had always been interested in starting my own business. I decided to take business courses at a community college. I was uneasy about taking college courses. My writing skills needed work. I got a D on my first essay. I was discouraged and considered dropping the course. My instructor asked me to speak with her. She explained how I could improve my essay and gave me a chance to revise it. I decided to stay in the course and pursue my dream of a new life.

Revised Paragraph with Transitions

After working as a carpenter for five years, I injured my back. **As a result of this injury,** I needed a different kind of job. I had always wanted to start my own business, **so** I decided to take some business courses at a community college. I was, **however,** uneasy about taking college courses. English, **for example,** scared me **because** I knew my writing skills were weak. **When I** got a D on my first essay, I was discouraged and considered dropping the course. Then my instructor asked me to come in and speak with her. **During this interview,** she explained how I could improve my essay and gave me a chance to revise it. **Because of this encouragement,** I decided to stay in the course and pursue my dream of a new life.

In the revised paragraph, sentences are linked by transitions showing time relationships and causal connections. You will find information on transitions to use with a specific method of development, such as description, narration, and causal analysis, in the appropriate section of Chapter 5, Methods of Developing Paragraphs. For more information on transitions, see Chapter 16, Improving Your Style.

Exercise 4.3

4e

Transitions

Write a paragraph on any subject that interests you. Begin with your topic sentence. Then rewrite the paragraph, putting the details first and ending with your topic sentence. Underline your topic sentences and circle all transitional words and phrases.

Chapter 5

Methods of Developing Paragraphs

5a Narration

When you narrate, you give an account of an action or a sequence of events. Narrative is the basis of fiction and films, but writers also tell stories in many forms of nonfiction: autobiographies, biographies, case studies, historical writing, personal essays, scientific observations, sports reporting, travel writing, and so on. Although there are many differences in the narratives you may find in these forms, they share a central similarity: they recount a series of actions that take place over time.

Short personal narratives are often used to enliven other kinds of writing. An article criticizing cuts to health care, for instance, may begin with a story about a patient who died while awaiting surgery. It is these personal narratives we will focus on in this section. You will find examples of narration combined with analysis in the samples that illustrate causal analysis (5e), plot summaries (10c), expository essays (9b), and project reports (15g).

Narrating in Personal Writing

Telling stories is one of the main ways we make sense of our lives for ourselves and share our world with others. Funny stories, heroic stories, romantic stories—they all have something to say about who we are. The stories we keep hidden—stories about our fears, our failures, our struggles—are often the ones that, when told, connect us to others. Here are some suggestions for writing personal narratives:

- *Choose a single meaningful event with a definite beginning and end.*

The event may be part of a larger story that you could write about in a personal essay. For instance, you might write a narrative paragraph about one adventure with a friend that could later form part of a longer essay exploring your relationship with this friend more fully.

- *Decide what point you want to make about this event.*

Did your adventure, for example, teach you something about taking risks—or about taking precautions? about trust—or about self-reliance? You could state this point explicitly in a topic sentence, or you could allow it to emerge implicitly from the way you tell the story.

- *Decide how to organize your paragraph.*

To heighten suspense, you can give events in chronological order, with your point emerging at the end. Or, if you want to emphasize your reflections on the incident, you could begin with your point and then tell the story.

- *Use transitions to help your reader follow the sequence of events.*

Show how events are related in time by using terms such as *first, next, then, last; in the beginning, in the end; soon, later, as soon as, meanwhile;* and by referring to specific times, days, months, seasons, and dates.

- *Select details that will create in readers a response similar to your own.*

Recording small details is one way to individualize your stories. In writing about a familiar situation such as attending a circus, for example, you might make the experience fresh for your readers by comparing the fake tears of a clown with the real tears of a child who drops an ice-cream cone.

- *Choose words that make the experience vivid for your reader and convey your attitude towards the event.*

For more on word choice, see Chapter 16, Improving Your Style.

- *Include your thoughts, feelings, and judgments about the event.*

Direct statements about thoughts, feelings, and judgments help readers understand the significance of details. For example, you might begin or end a series of seemingly random and contradictory ideas with the statement *I was confused.*

Sample Personal Narrative

This narrative paragraph creates suspense through its precise details, expressions of feeling, and chronological arrangement of events. The image in the last two sentences implicitly makes the

writer's point about overcoming fear. These two sentences therefore serve as the topic sentence for the paragraph. A paragraph
such as this would make a good introduction to a personal essay.

Others have ascended the incredibly high platform, seemingly thousands of feet above the pool. More than one has returned by the wet
ladder, a sensible choice in my mind. Why then is my foot on the
first rung? It is colder and slicker than would appear. My feet leave
the safe ground and propel me towards the high roof of the pool.
Part way up I consider turning back. Yes. But another below has decided to follow, and I must reach the top before turning around. Half
way up, I guess, but I dare not look down lest my arms and legs
freeze in terror. I keep my eyes focused on the ladder, only inches from
my nose. The last step comes into view. With dangerously stiff muscles
and complete lack of grace or courage, I plant my feet on the concrete
slab. I see my wet footprints and decide to look at nothing else. With
the slap of feet an older boy makes his entrance onto this platform in
the sky. He passes, grinning at me, and in one quick fluid motion he
disappears over the edge. I hear nothing, nothing, then a faint splash.
Something deep inside me snaps and I follow suit. Crazy. Stupid.
Stop! I'm in the air, hand clasped tight over my nose as I shut my
eyes. Dear God, I'm drowning. I must be at the bottom of the pool.
Frantically kicking, I break the surface. It's hard to wipe this maniac
smile off my face. Perhaps once more.

—Ken Miller

5a

Narration

In this passage from a personal essay about confronting death,
a small incident—a glimpse of crumpled metal—triggers the
writer's memories of an accident years earlier. The topic is stated
in the first sentence. Note the transitions that help to create a
smooth flow from one event to the next.

A flash of crumpled metal catches my eye, and for an instant I'm drawn
back to a scene with bodies and bikes strewn about like dice on a crap
table, images that I thought I had wiped from my mind. I'd been over-
taken by a biker on a Yamaha and another on a Suzuki with an ac-
companying passenger. At the Yamaha driver's prompting they began
to race, much to my disgust. Shortly afterwards, the Suzuki driver and
his passenger were lying on the median, the driver with a compound
leg fracture and back lacerations, his passenger with what appeared
to be a broken neck. The driver of the Yamaha was even less fortunate.
As the smoke from the crash cleared, it revealed the man lying in the

29

centre of the three-lane highway, his bike a heap of crumpled junk in the right-hand lane. His breathing was laboured and shallow as I stopped to help him. A few seconds later he was dead.

—Chris Paterson

Exercise 5.1

Identify a quality you particularly like or dislike in yourself or someone else. Then write a narrative paragraph about an incident that reveals this quality.

Example: a roommate's stinginess—refusing to share chips and salsa while we watched the Grey Cup.

Exercise 5.2

Choose a significant experience in your life (such as a birth, death, marriage, divorce, move, an accident, achievement or failure). Use brainstorming to help you recall the small but meaningful incidents you associate with the experience (such as riding in an ambulance). Choose one of these incidents with a definite beginning and end and write a narrative paragraph that shows its significance.

Example: Experience—changing schools in the middle of grade four. Event—failing a math test on my first day. Significance—always feeling an outsider at school.

5b Description

When you describe people, places, or things, you attempt to translate into words how they look, sound, feel, smell, move, or taste. The language you use to describe something will depend upon your purpose and audience. A geographer writing a scientific article about the Canadian Shield would describe Northern Ontario differently from a real estate agent selling holiday properties. Someone writing a personal essay about growing up in the bush would offer a third perspective on the same landscape, one coloured by the intensity and selectivity of childhood memory.

You will have a chance to practise the kind of description called for in scientific and technical writing in the section on systems analysis (5e). Here we will focus on description in personal writing.

Description in Personal Writing

In personal writing, you want your reader to share experiences—such as your father's delight in reading bedtime stories, your fear as you walk down a deserted street at night, your love-hate relationship with an unreliable car. As these examples suggest, descriptions are like snapshots of significant moments in which you capture your attitude towards a person, place, or thing. You convey your attitude by selecting details that work together to create a dominant impression of your subject. If you wanted to show your father's delight in bedtime reading, for example, you would ignore the note of exasperation that crept into his voice if you interrupted too often, and instead describe his excitement as he became different characters in *Peter Pan*.

Personal essays often contain vivid descriptions of people, places, and things. You will also find that a descriptive paragraph makes a good introduction or middle paragraph in expository and persuasive essays. For example, you might begin a persuasive essay on the importance of parental involvement in children's learning to read with a paragraph describing your father reading. A descriptive paragraph like this adds human interest to discussions of general issues. For an example, see the sample expository essay on child poverty (9b).

Follow these guidelines for writing descriptive paragraphs:

- ***Choose a subject that you are very familiar with or that you can observe while you write.***
It is surprisingly hard to remember the kinds of details that will bring your paragraph to life—the colour of a friend's eyes, the sound of wind through trees, the smell of a schoolroom. If you choose to describe something from memory, try closing your eyes and putting yourself into the scene before you write about it.

- ***Decide what dominant impression you want to convey about your subject.***
A good description is not merely a catalogue of features: "My cat is a Siamese with the usual blue eyes and dark grey ears." It creates a *dominant impression* by giving details that convey a particular quality of your subject: a kitten's playfulness, an aunt's stubbornness, the peacefulness of a landscape.

31

- *Focus your paragraph.*

For example, describe your subject at a particular time or performing a particular action. This focus will help you to *describe* rather than give examples. For instance, you could vividly *describe* a kitten's playfulness—how it looks, moves, sounds—by focusing on how it acts in front of the mirror. Without this focal point, you might give many examples of a kitten's playful behaviour without describing any of them in enough detail to be interesting.

- *Select details that contribute to the dominant impression you want to convey.*

Include a broad range of sensory details—not just how something looks but also how it sounds, feels, tastes, smells, moves.

- *Arrange the details in a spatial order with the most important detail last.*

Choose an arrangement that reflects how you as an observer would perceive your subject: in a panoramic sweep from left to right; from close up to farther away, or vice-versa; or from the most obvious feature to the least obvious.

- *Show how objects are related in space.*

Use transitional words such as *nearer, farther; on the right, on the left; at the top, at the bottom; to the east, to the west.*

- *Begin or end with a point about the person, place, or thing you are describing.*

"My cat is very playful" is a descriptive generalization, but it is not an interesting point about the kitten's behaviour. You could make a more interesting point about the transitory nature of youth and playfulness. You could state this point explicitly in a topic sentence: "Watching my kitten play, I remember how I used to make faces at myself in the mirror, not realizing that the scowls of childhood would settle into the lines of middle age." Or you could let it emerge implicitly through your description: "Each day the kitten tires of the game more quickly, and soon we will both pass the mirror without a glance."

In the following paragraph from a personal essay, the writer tells us almost nothing about the physical appearance of a teacher who "shocked me so much that I experienced a marked change in my attitude towards school and the subject of English." Instead he chooses details that show how Mr. Wellington's surroundings reflect his vulnerability, and then makes this point in a topic sentence at the end.

Sample Personal Description

Mr. Wellington was neither neat nor tidy. The chaos of his room seemed to echo the sound of someone saying, "Hang on, it's in here somewhere. I just put it down yesterday. I'll find it." The walls were covered from top to bottom with posters, but not a single one was hung straight. His desk was inhabited by masses of paper that had somehow gathered there as if attracted by a "paper magnet." Surrounding his desk was a whole herd of dictionaries, including a condensed version of the *Oxford English Dictionary*, which required a magnifying glass to peer into the depths of its compiled wisdom. He would frequently consult these books in efforts to stop the arguments waged against him about the meanings of words in the poems we analyzed in class. Throughout all this activity, his coffee cup was never to be seen detached from his hand. I cannot blame him for needing a cup of coffee to carry him through to the next period. It was his coffee cup that made him look human, vulnerable—not like the other teachers, who were not human but "teachers." Perhaps it was his vulnerability that inspired confidence, even though he was surrounded by what looked like ineptitude.

5b

Description

—*Steve Marsh*

Exercise 5.3

Make a list of the sensations you experience as you eat something, such as an ice-cream cone or a slice of pizza. Use all of your senses. Arrange your list so that a point emerges from your description.

Exercise 5.4

Write a descriptive paragraph about one of the following:

• a person who has had an impact on your life.

• a place where you feel safe (or unsafe).

• an ordinary object to which you have a strong attachment.

Exercise 5.5

Sit for half an hour in a public place—on a bus, in a mall, in church, at a hockey rink—and make notes about what you see, hear, and smell. Then write a descriptive paragraph about the place as a whole, one or more people in it, or a particular object. Be sure to select details that convey a dominant impression and make a point about your subject.

5c Classification

When you classify, you organize facts and ideas into categories and subcategories. That means you start with a general category, such as "customers," and divide the category into specific types or kinds. You might, for instance, divide "customers" into these types: the impatient, the rude, the apologetic, the business-like, the indecisive. These subcategories allow you to explain the general characteristics shared by many individual people. You can also classify abstract concepts. For example, you could divide the category "effects of unemployment" into subcategories such as economic effects, social effects, and psychological effects.

If you were writing an essay, you could make classification your principle of organization and devote a paragraph or more to each of your subcategories as shown in the diagram below.

Classification can also provide a systematic method of organizing material as you move from generalizations to specific details in individual paragraphs. If your classification is easy to follow, you can present a great deal of information in a short space.

For this reason, classification paragraphs make good overviews of material you will then explain in more detail, and good summaries of material you have already covered. They are also handy for making humorous points and points that don't need much development, as in the sample paragraph below.

Here are suggestions for writing classification paragraphs.

- Choose a general category that you know enough about to divide into two to four subcategories (For example: customers, coffee bars, musicals, Stephen King novels).

- Decide on a principle of classification, and state this principle at the beginning of your paragraph.

A principle of classification tells you how to divide things into groups. For instance, you could group restaurant customers

34

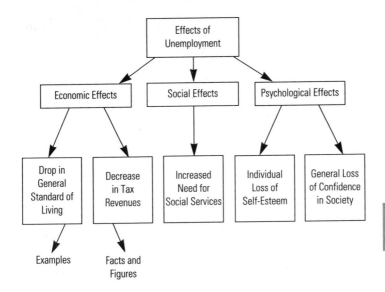

according to age groups, or attitudes towards staff, or eating habits. Each of these is a principle of classification.

- Make a list of the *types* represented by your principle of classification. If you chose "eating habits" as your principle of classification, for example, you might come up with types such as these: the bottomless pit, the doggie-bagger, the gushing gourmet, the constant complainer, the garbage collector, the reluctant sampler.

- Describe two to four types, depending upon how much you need to say to explain each type. Use actual examples (the man who made seven trips to the salad bar) or hypothetical examples (the kinds of complaints various customers make, all attributed to the constant complainer).

- To signal your shift from one subcategory to another, use parallel sentence structure and/or transitions that indicate enumeration (*first, second, next, finally*).

- Begin or end your paragraph with the point you want to make.

  For example, "As I snicker or groan at the eating habits of my customers, I wonder how I appear to those who serve me when I go out to eat."

The following paragraph classifying people by the way they walk is taken from an essay on the importance of first impressions. The writer makes the point of the paragraph explicit in the topic sentence. Notice how she uses parallel sentence structure ("if" clauses) and transitions to guide readers through her four types of walkers.

Sample Classification

The way you walk tells others a lot about what type of person you are and how you feel about yourself. Fast-moving, hard-stepping, and arm-swinging, you look straight ahead and give the impression that you have something very important on your mind. It is an aggressive, no-nonsense, watch-out-world walk that usually signifies to others that you are quite confident (maybe too much so?). Your walk can intimidate most mere mortals. If you are the "floater" walker, you take itsy-bitsy steps, barely hitting the ground, creating a kind of an airy flutter. You walk in a childlike, somewhat unconfident manner, which speaks of innocence, sweetness... and a touch of silliness if you are over age five. If you are a "shy" walker, you have little confidence. Your shoulders are slumped forward, your head is bowed down, your feet are turned in slightly, and you move quickly, almost noiselessly, hoping no one will notice you. The message is clear: please do not bother me, just let me be miserable in peace and quiet. Finally, you could be a person who walks with your shoulders back, chest high, spine stretched from the waist and straight, displaying comfortableness and confidence when you walk.

—Brigitte Berube

Exercise 5.6

Complete the following diagram with appropriate categories. What is the principle of classification for each subject? Can you figure out two other principles of classification for each subject?

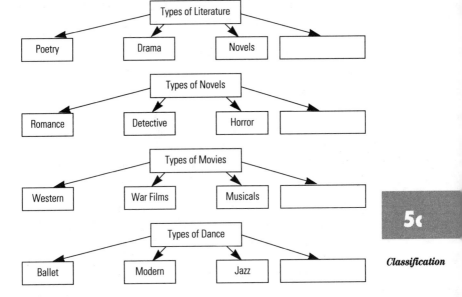

Exercise 5.7

Choose one of the following subjects and make a four-level diagram showing how you could divide your subject according to two different principles of classification. Use this model:

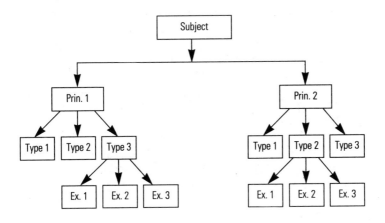

- music
- clothing
- living accommodations
- vacation spots
- crimes

Exercise 5.8

Write a classification paragraph based on one of the principles of classification you developed for the diagram above.

5d Definition

"There's glory for you!"

"I don't know what you mean by 'glory,'" Alice said.

Humpty Dumpty smiled contemptuously. "Of course you don't—till I tell you. I meant 'there's a nice knock-down argument for you!'"

"But 'glory' doesn't mean 'a nice knock-down argument,'" Alice objected.

"When I use a word," Humpty Dumpty said in a rather scornful tone, "it means just what I choose it to mean—neither more nor less."

—From *Through the Looking-Glass* by Lewis Carroll

Humpty Dumpty may get away with arbitrarily deciding what words mean, but most of us cannot. If we want to communicate, we have to use words in ways that others will understand. Thus when you use words unfamiliar to your readers, or use familiar words in an unfamiliar way, you need to provide **definitions**.

In examinations and other kinds of academic writing, you may be asked to define terms to show that you know what they mean. In most writing, however, you provide definitions not to demonstrate your own knowledge but to help your reader understand what you are talking about. Depending on what kind of information your reader needs, you may use a synonym, a class definition, an extended definition, or a stipulative **definition**.

Synonyms

A **synonym** is a word that means the same, or nearly the same, as another word. Use synonyms, set off by commas or enclosed in parentheses, to define slang expressions, specialized terms of trades and professions, regional and dialect usages, and foreign words and phrases. These examples illustrate how to integrate synonyms smoothly into a sentence:

At the heart of a microcomputer system is the central processing unit, or microprocessor, as it is also known.

—*Bernard Doering*

As we entered the Air India 747, the steward clasped his hands and said, "Namaste" ("greetings to you").

—*Vijaya Rao*

Class Definitions

If a synonym cannot provide enough information, give a **class definition**. A class definition explains a term by saying what kind of thing it is (its class) and how it is different from other members of its class. Cats, for example, are a kind of feline (the class), but so are lions, tigers, cheetahs, leopards, and cougars. To distinguish cats from other felines, you might mention that cats are small and commonly kept as pets.

This is the standard form of the class definition:

An X is a member of the class Y with the characteristics A, B, C ....

Plagiarism [term to be defined] is the act [class] of presenting someone else's words or ideas as your own [distinguishing characteristics].

A bailiff [term to be defined] is a person [class] who performs limited functions within a judicial system, such as having custody of prisoners in court, serving warrants, or serving as magistrate for minor offences [distinguishing characteristics].

You can sometimes integrate a class definition more smoothly by using it as a modifier:

Crustaceans—**arthropods with bodies covered by a hard shell or crust**—were the subject of a recent television special.

Extended Definitions

Unless you are a biologist, you may still be unsure what crustaceans are because you are unfamiliar with the word *arthropod*. When a class definition does not offer enough explanation, you will need to use an **extended definition**. Some writers take a paragraph, or even a whole essay, to define a term. In a

5d

Definition

persuasive essay, for example, you might give an extended definition of the word *violence* to show that it can legitimately be applied to the destruction of the environment.

Here are three ways to expand definitions.

1. Add examples.

   By crustaceans I mean such things as lobsters, crabs, barnacles, and wood lice.

2. Give negative examples—that is, words or things that might seem to be included in the class but are not.

   Oysters and clams also have shells, but they are not arthropods because they do not have jointed legs.

3. Use an analogy to compare your term with something more familiar. (For more on analogies, see Analogy, 5h.)

   To understand the function of crustacean shells, we might think of the way the armoured steel of a tank provides shelter, both from the elements and from enemy attack, for the more vulnerable people inside. Similarly, the crustacean's shell protects it from the environment and from its enemies.

How often will an extended definition be needed? Don't insult your readers by defining words they know, but never assume your subject is as familiar to them as it is to you. Try to read what you've written with their eyes. Would a brief phrase explain basketball lingo for non-sports fans? Could you clarify what you mean by *oral literacy* by giving an example of storytelling in traditional Inuit families? Would an analogy help to explain the principle of indeterminacy to a nonscientific audience?

Stipulative Definitions

Our understanding of words, especially of abstract terms such as *violence, loyalty, pornography,* and *censorship,* is shaped by our own experiences, and we bring these personal connotations to what we read. You can make sure that you and your readers are talking the same language by using a **stipulative definition**.

To stipulate means to specify conditions or terms, as in an agreement or contract. A stipulative definition specifies which meaning, from a range of possible meanings, a term will have within a particular context. Stipulative definitions allow you to limit your treatment of your subject. You may consider various meanings of the word *censorship,* for example, and then stipulate that you will use the word to mean the passage of laws designed to prevent the publication of certain material. Accordingly, your readers cannot expect you to discuss other actions that they might consider censorship, such as withdrawing books from libraries. As this example suggests, stipulative definitions are particularly necessary when the meaning of a term is controversial.

Because they establish common ground with readers and mark out the territory you will discuss, stipulative definitions make good introductions. Suppose, for example, you were writing a research paper on the question of intelligence in chimpanzees. If you launched into an analysis of chimp behaviour without saying what you meant by *intelligence*, your readers might object to your argument on the grounds that intelligence in animals cannot be measured. You would therefore want to introduce your essay with a paragraph something like the one that follows.

Sample Stipulative Definition

Intelligence is sometimes defined as what intelligence tests measure. If we want to consider the question of intelligence in chimpanzees, we obviously cannot simply administer the Stanford Binet or other commonly used IQ tests. But we should be able to determine whether experiments with chimpanzees demonstrate elements of intelligence considered important by psychologists: the capacity for abstract thinking or reasoning, problem-solving, acquiring knowledge, and adapting to one's environment; memory, mental speed, and linguistic competence (Snyderman & Rothman, 1987).

By using this stipulative definition of intelligence as a thesis, you would establish a basis by which you and your readers could discuss the intelligence of chimpanzees according to specific behaviours.

Sources of Definitions

When you need to define a word, begin with a standard dictionary such as those published by Gage, Random House, and Oxford. For more detailed information about specialized meanings, changes in meaning over time, and current usage, consult works such as the following. You should be able to find them in the reference section of your library.

- Unabridged dictionaries. The *Oxford English Dictionary* provides a history of each word's use and changes in meaning.

41

- Specialized dictionaries. Available for many professions and academic disciplines. Examples: *Dictionary of Business and Economics, Dictionary of Philosophy, A Handbook to Literature.*

- Etymological dictionaries (word origins). Example: Ernest Klein, *A Comprehensive Etymological Dictionary of the English Language* (Elsevier, 1971).

- *Dictionary of Slang and Unconventional English* and similar works.

- Books on regional dialects. Example: Léandre Bergeron, *The Québécois Dictionary* (Toronto: Lorimer, 1982).

- Books of quotations, such as *Bartlett's Familiar Quotations* (often indexed by key words).

Exercise 5.9

Give a synonym or class definition that would explain each of these terms to readers unfamiliar with your subject.

1. rap music
2. black hole (or other scientific term)
3. hotdogging (or other slang expression)
4. winterize
5. blacksmith

Exercise 5.10

Write an extended definition of one of the following terms for a persuasive essay defending or attacking the concept.

- marriage
- patriotism
- equality
- masculinity or femininity
- charity

Exercise 5.11

Write a paragraph defining what one of the terms below means to you.

- childhood (or adolescence/maturity/old age)
- discrimination
- friendship
- spirituality
- the dark

42

Exercise 5.12

Write a paragraph of stipulative definition for one of the following terms.

- literacy
- sexism
- equal opportunity
- qualified applicant
- human being

5e Analysis

Analysis is a way of explaining a subject by dividing it into its parts and showing how the parts relate to the whole. **Systems analysis** shows the relation of parts in space; **process analysis** shows the sequence of parts in time; **causal analysis** shows the relationship between causes and effects; and *textual analysis* shows how the parts of written works (and performances) relate to the whole. Here we will discuss systems, process, and causal analysis. You will find information on textual analysis in Essays Analyzing Literature (9c) and Essays Analyzing Nonfiction (9e).

Dividing up a complex or unfamiliar task, situation, or idea into smaller units often makes it easier for readers to grasp what you are saying about your subject. For particular writing assignments, you may use these four types of analysis alone or in combination. In writing a how-to article on making knives, for example, you would use process analysis to develop your material. But in writing an expository essay on knife-making, you might include sections on the process, on the effects of changes in technology, and on the marketing system consisting of suppliers, knife-makers, dealers, and collectors. Or in writing a review, you might discuss the process of making a film as well as analyzing the final product.

Systems Analysis

We tend to think of a system as a physical object with working parts, such as a car engine or the body's immune system. But more abstract phenomena also operate as systems, such as systems of government and philosophical systems. When you explain how such abstract systems "work" by showing how the parts are related to the whole, you are also engaged in systems analysis.

A systems analysis is like a blueprint. You give an objective general description of your subject rather than a subjective particular description. If you were analyzing the functions of the Cabinet, for instance, you would discuss the role of the Minister of Defence, not the personality of the current minister.

Usually you begin by identifying the system and explaining its purpose in a topic sentence. Next you describe the most obvious or most important part of the system, such as the Prime Minister, and show how other parts function in relation to it. Then you explain the function of each part in relation to the whole. Use appropriate transitions to show how the parts are related.

Sample Systems Analysis

In the following example, the writer describes stereo systems in general (not his particular system with its scratches and coffee stains) and explains the function of each component.

A stereo system consists of a varying number of individual components, grouped in such a way as to give the audiophile a choice of musical reproduction. The heart of the system is the receiver, which takes the electronic impulses from the other components, amplifies them, and sends the signals on to the speakers. It is the job of the speakers to transfer these impulses back into sound, by means of an electromagnet. The original music may be recorded in a number of different ways, the most popular means being on record, tape, or compact disk. Each of these types of recording has a specific type of playback machine which, when hooked into the stereo system, allows for the reproduction of the original sound. To produce sound, the record turntable, cassette tape player, or compact disk player passes the vibrations or electronic pulses created by the recording on to the receiver for amplification and playback.

–Jim Griffin

Process Analysis

Process analysis has one of two purposes: to explain how something happens ("How Airplanes Fly") or to explain how to do something ("How to Fly an Airplane"). In each case, you emphasize what happens (or should happen) every time the process is repeated ("How to Develop Film"), rather than what happened during one particular instance ("How I Ruined My Sister's Wedding Pictures").

Begin with a topic sentence that identifies the process and its major stages. Then discuss the stages, and the steps within each stage, in the order in which they occur.

The amount of detail you include about each step will depend on your purpose and audience. When you explain how something is done but not how to do it, focus on the major stages so that your readers get a sense of the whole process; avoid giving detailed information about individual steps. On the other hand, when you give directions for readers to follow, discuss each step in detail, drawing your readers' attention to potential problems.

Use transitions indicating time relationships (*next*, *after*, *then*) or enumeration (*first*, *second*, *third*) to signal when you are moving from one stage or step to the next.

Both the following excerpts explain the process of making Ukrainian-style Easter eggs. The first is designed to give a general understanding of the process; the second is a more detailed set of instructions that would allow the reader to actually perform the process.

Sample Process Analyses

The three major stages in creating an Easter egg are mixing the dyes, waxing, and dyeing. First, the dyes are prepared. Then, a special stylus with a cup-like reservoir is used to cover all the areas of the pencilled-in design that are to remain white in melted wax. The egg is then submerged in the lightest colour dye. After several minutes, the egg is removed with a spoon and wiped to remove any excess dye. All areas that are to remain yellow are then covered in wax, and the egg is placed in the next darker shade of dye. The waxing and dyeing process is repeated until the design is complete and all the desired colours have been used.

The three major stages in creating your Easter eggs are mixing the dyes, waxing, and dyeing. First mix the dyes according to the instructions on the packages. Now the waxing and dyeing can begin. Light the candle and heat the tip of the stylus in the flame. Scrape some wax into the cup-like reservoir of the stylus. Using the design you have made as a guide, proceed to cover with wax all areas that are to remain white. If the wax in the stylus hardens, remelt it by placing the tip in the candle flame. Then place the egg in the lightest dye, usually yellow, and let it remain for several minutes so the colour will have time to set. When the time is up, remove the egg with a spoon and wipe off any excess dye with a paper towel. The next step is to cover with wax all areas that are to remain yellow. Now place the egg in the next darker shade of dye. Repeat this waxing and dyeing process until the design is complete and all desired colours have been used.

—Laurel Kiehlbauch

5e

Analysis

Causal Analysis

The analysis of causes and effects is basic to much of the writing you are likely to do in school or at work. You may write a research paper for a history course on the causes of the War of 1812; a lab report for botany on the effects of varying the amount of daylight received by tomato plants; or a letter to your insurance agent on the causes of a traffic accident.

Most actions or events worth writing about have multiple causes and effects. Brainstorming, asking discovery questions, and researching will help you avoid oversimplifying your analysis.

For a research paper on the effects of cutbacks in government spending on education, for instance, your first response might be to focus on the financial strain students are under because of higher tuition fees. You would gain a broader perspective, however, by brainstorming about other effects on students and reading about the effects on schools and post-secondary institutions. Your final essay might examine the effects of funding cuts on students, teachers, and institutions. For suggestions about the kinds of causes and effects you might consider, consult Evaluation (5g). For an example of an expository essay developed through causal analysis, see "The Effects of Child Poverty" (9b).

If you are explaining causes or effects that are independent of each other, arrange your material in an order that suits your audience. You might discover, for example, that the three main causes of traffic accidents are poor road conditions, impaired driving, and mechanical failure. There is no causal connection among these three factors (drinking too much doesn't cause the roads to be icy or the car to break down). If you were writing an essay, you would decide which cause to emphasize and discuss it last. If you were writing a report for the city transportation department, on the other hand, you would discuss the most important factor first.

If you are discussing a chain of causes and effects (A causes B, B causes C, C causes D), make sure that your topic sentence focuses on the most significant cause(s) and effect(s). Arrange your material in chronological order, but to make it clear that you are writing a causal analysis rather than a narrative, choose words and expressions that emphasize causal connections (*a major effect, a second cause, one consequence; caused, resulted, affected; as a result, because, consequently, moreover, therefore, thus*). Suppose you were writing an essay on the effects of the Riel Rebellion on federal politics. Your notes for one paragraph might read as follows:

1. Riel's execution **caused** a renewed demand for rights by French-speaking Québécois.

2. These demands alarmed the federal government; **as a result**, it abolished French language rights in Manitoba.

3. This action **resulted** in loss of support for the Conservative Party in Québec.

4. This decline in support **caused** the party to lose the next federal election.

5. Québec's pivotal role in federal politics is a continuing **effect** of its position as the sole defender of the rights of French-speaking Canadians.

In writing your paragraph, you would add a topic sentence emphasizing the most significant effect (the increased power of Quebec). You would also fill in additional details, while keeping the focus on the chain of causes and effects, as in the paragraph below.

Sample Causal Analysis

Although the failure of the Riel Rebellion weakened the position of French-speaking Canadians in Manitoba, it had the enormously significant effect of strengthening the power of French-speaking Canadians in Québec. Before Riel was executed in 1885, Québec had ignored the struggle of the French-speaking Manitobans to maintain their cultural identity. As a result of his execution, Riel became a martyr to the cause of rights for all French Canadians and the focus for a renewed demand for French rights in Québec. Alarmed, the federal government abolished French education rights in Manitoba in 1890; Québec

5e

Analysis

47

thus became the only province where provincial rights guaranteed the survival of French culture in Canada. The consequence of this action, it soon became obvious, was that no federal government could remain in power if it lacked Québec's support. The Conservative Party, weakened by MacDonald's death in 1891, lost the election in 1896 mostly because it had offended Québec by abolishing French rights in Manitoba; the Liberals, led by Wilfrid Laurier, gained power by securing a large majority in Québec. Since that time, no federal government has been able to ignore the French province.

Exercise 5.13

5e

Analysis

Which form of analysis (systems, process, or causal) would you use to develop each of the following topics?

1. Explain how to transact a cash sale using a computerized cash register.

2. Discuss the effects on the environment if the Amazon rain forests are destroyed.

3. Explain the Canadian military ranking system.

4. Briefly outline the reasons for the failure of Allied forces during the Dieppe Raid, August 19, 1942.

5. Describe how to charge the battery in a car.

6. Describe the human circulatory system.

7. Explain how to warm up the muscles before exercising.

8. Explain the impact of a person's emotional state on his or her well-being.

Exercise 5.14

Write two separate lists of causes explaining why your provincial government is popular (or unpopular). Make one a list of independent causes; present the second list as a chain of causes and effects.

Exercise 5.15

Write a paragraph explaining a process. Choose one of the following topics.

• how to tie-dye a sweatshirt

- how to operate a piece of equipment

- how to teach a child good table manners

- how to train your roommate to assume his or her share of the household responsibilities

- how to study for an exam

- how to buy a car

- a topic of your choice

5f *Comparison*

When you compare, you match similarities and differences in two or more subjects. **Comparison** may be your primary method of development in a piece of writing, as in the sample research paper, *"Tom Sawyer* and *Anne of Green Gables:* Two Models of Heroism" (12f). Or you may combine comparison with other methods of development. The author of the sample narrative essay, "Rookies (8b), for example, compares her attitude towards playing hockey with that of her sister.

To compare subjects effectively, you need a basis of comparison. A basis of comparison tells you which similarities and differences to focus on. For example, if you are asked on a biology exam to compare the fertilization process in mammals and amphibians, you have been given a basis of comparison: the fertilization process. In other writing situations, your purpose and audience will suggest an appropriate basis of comparison. If you are comparing two cars for your company, for instance, your basis of comparison will be determined by the purpose of the report. Is your company thinking of leasing one of the cars? Establishing a dealership? Paying insurance claims? Each of these purposes would lead you to choose a different basis of comparison, such as cost effectiveness, marketability, and amount of damage.

In other writing situations, the basis of your comparison may not be so obvious. Suppose that you were writing an essay comparing the roles of the North West Mounted Police and the U.S. Cavalry in the settlement of the west. You would need to consider many facts and opinions about these forces before deciding on a general similarity or difference to use as a basis of comparison.

When your basis of comparison is not obvious, follow these steps, each of which will be discussed in detail.

49

Step 1: Make parallel lists of the similarities and differences in your subjects.

Step 2: Decide which general similarity or difference most of the items on your list illustrate and use it as your basis of comparison.

Step 3: Formulate a point about your basis of comparison and use that point as your main idea. In a paragraph, this main idea will become your topic sentence; in an essay, it will become your thesis.

Step 4: Decide whether to use the block method or the point by point method to organize your material.

Step 1: Listing Similarities and Differences

Although making lists may seem time-consuming, you will discover that it is time well spent. Your lists will serve three purposes: they will ensure that you have lots of material, that you compare equivalent aspects of your subjects, and that you provide the same information about both. Let's take an example.

In writing about her trip to South America, one student wanted to make her impressions more vivid by comparing one aspect of life in Bolivia with its Canadian counterpart. Deciding to compare plumbing in the two countries, she compiled these lists:

Plumbing in Canada	**Plumbing in Bolivia**
—drinking water from kitchen tap	—water carried from square; boiled before drinking
—bath at any temperature	—water must be heated
—flush toilets	—often hole in backyard

Notice that the columns present matching points of contrast. These three differences provide material for a substantial paragraph.

Step 2: Choosing a Basis of Comparison

The next step is to decide what your similarities or differences have in common. From her lists comparing plumbing in the two countries, the student could have chosen any one of several points, such as health concerns, standards of hygiene, or availability of water. Each of these points would have provided a general difference that her examples would have illustrated. She chose to make the availability of water her basis of comparison.

Step 3: Formulating a Main Idea

The crucial step, too often overlooked, is to decide what point to make about your basis of comparison. In an expository essay or report, your main idea might simply be a statement of your comparison: "In Bolivia, water is much less readily available than it is in Canada." In personal or persuasive writing, however, you want to convey your attitude towards the subjects you are comparing, not merely to report on their similarities or differences. Your reflections might lead you to a main idea such as the one the student traveller chose: because of its easy availability, Canadians may take water for granted, whereas for most Bolivians, water is a luxury.

Step 4: Organizing Comparisons

Block Method

The simplest way of organizing a brief comparison is the **block method**. In this method, you mention both subjects in your topic sentence, but then say everything about one subject before saying anything more about the other. When you are ready to discuss the second subject, you signal the shift by a transitional word or phrase. Organizing her material on plumbing in Canada and Bolivia by the block method, the writer created the following paragraph.

Sample Comparison: Block Method

Although most Canadians take hot and cold running water at home for granted, indoor plumbing is a luxury for most Bolivians. When we want a drink, we merely turn on the faucet and fill our glasses. If we decide to have a bath, we just run the taps and adjust the water to whatever temperature we desire. We even have the comfort of toilets that flush. But few Bolivians have the luxury of indoor plumbing. Many have to stand in line at one tap in a central square at certain designated hours to fill their containers with water. This water must then be made to last for the remainder of the day. It must be boiled before it can be drunk and heated before it can be used for washing. A flush toilet is also not a feature in every Bolivian home. Toilet facilities usually consist of a hole dug in the back corner of the lot and often must be shared by several families.

—*Wendy Amy*

If the material is too long for one paragraph, you can easily start a new paragraph when you shift to your second subject.

Point by Point Method

The **point by point method**, in which you shift back and forth between subjects, is sometimes more effective than the block method when you are organizing a longer piece of writing (see Patterns for Comparison Essays, 7c). At the paragraph level, however, shifting between subjects can produce an annoying or confusing "ping-pong" effect, as you can see in this version of the previous example:

Most Canadians take hot and cold running water at home for granted. Many Bolivians do not have the luxury of indoor plumbing. When we want a drink, we merely turn on the faucet and fill our glasses. Many Bolivians have to stand in line at one tap in a central square at designated hours to fill their containers with water. If we decide to have a bath, we just turn on the taps and adjust the water to whatever temperature we desire. Many Bolivians....

Normally, you would wish to avoid this rapid shifting back and forth between two subjects, but sometimes a paragraph that "ping-pongs" may be effective for special emphasis or for humour, as in the following example.

Sample Comparison: Point by Point Method

Yesterday my housemate behaved very strangely. In the morning he bounded into the kitchen, a cheery smile on his face. In the evening he dragged himself through the front door, muttering curses at the neighbour's dog. In the morning he enthusiastically described his great plans for the day as he cooked and consumed great quantities of eggs, bacon, and toast. In the evening he stared glumly into the cabinets, the fridge, the cabinets again, before settling silently in front of the television with a slice of cold pizza. In the morning he dressed with care and brushed his hair until every strand was in the right place. In the evening he slopped around barefoot in a T-shirt and ragged pair of jeans. But then yesterday was his first day at his new job, and he hated it.

Exercise 5.16

Choose two topics from the following and list the similarities and differences between the subjects being compared.

- camping in a motor home and roughing it in the bush with a tent

- having a permanent, full-time job and working part-time

- watching a sport and playing a sport

- an old friend and a new friend

- drawing and painting

- reading and travelling

- watching movies at home on television and watching movies in a theatre

- some aspect of life in Canada and the same aspect of life in another country

Exercise 5.17

Find a basis of comparison for each of the two topics that you chose in Exercise 5.16 above.

Exercise 5.18

Choose the strongest list (similarities or differences) from one of the two topics that you chose in Exercise 5.16 above. What point would you make about your subject based on the information in this list?

Exercise 5.19

Select a method of organization (block or point by point) and write a comparison paragraph based on the topic that you selected in Exercise 5.18.

5g Evaluation

Analyzing something—such as an event, a text, a system, or a process—is often a step towards evaluating it. When you evaluate, you answer questions like these: Was the event a success or a failure? Is the film good or bad? Is the system working effectively or not? What are the advantages and disadvantages of using this process? Your analysis is the basis for the judgment you make about your subject.

Asking Evaluative Questions

There are many perspectives from which to make judgments. When you analyze nonfiction (see 9e), you try to determine, among other things, the perspective(s) the author brings to bear on the subject. You can make the basis of your own judgments clearer to your readers by identifying your own perspective(s). Are your objections to a film, for instance, aesthetic (the acting is bad) or moral (it glorifies violence), or both?

Here are questions to ask about your subject from five of the most widely applicable general perspectives.

1. Aesthetic

Is it aesthetically pleasing? What are its strengths and weaknesses? Do the parts make a satisfying whole? Is the form suited to the content or function? Is it well-made? Is it appealing to its intended audience or users? For an example of evaluation from the aesthetic perspective, see the sample book review (11i).

2. Moral

Is it morally right or wrong? Why? Who does it help or harm? Is it ethical? Does it promote values I accept or reject? What are they? Why do I accept or reject them? For an example, see the sample opinion piece, "Why I Won't Buy a New Car" (11c).

3. Logical

Is it true? What are the arguments for and against it? Is the reasoning logical? Is the information accurate and complete? Does the evidence justify the conclusions or recommendations? For a more extended discussion of how to evaluate the logic of an argument, see Essays Analyzing Nonfiction (9e).

4. Legal

Is it legal? What are the conditions and limitations of the law? Whose interests does the law serve?

5. Practical

Is it practical? What are its advantages and disadvantages? Will it work? Is it cost-effective? Is it useful? For an example, see the sample reading report (15d).

You can clarify your thinking about your subject by considering each set of evaluative questions. You might use brainstorming diagrams or make parallel lists of good and bad points.

Suppose, for example, that you were writing a persuasive essay on whether pornography should be banned. You might begin with these points.

5g

Evaluation

	Against Banning	**For Banning**
1. Aesthetic	Some "pornographic" works have literary and artistic merit	Most pornography is crude and boring
2. Moral	Right to freedom of expression	Contributes to violence against women and children
3. Logical	Difficulty of defining "pornography"	Research studies suggest social harm
4. Legal	Infringement of legal rights	Precedent in banning hate literature
5. Practical	Difficult to enforce	Protect children from from sexual exploitation

Deciding Which Questions to Answer

Often your subject or your form will limit the range of evaluative questions you answer. Truth may be irrelevant if you are reviewing a children's movie about talking dinosaurs. Similarly, if your purpose is to compile a report on existing pornography laws in Europe, it would be inappropriate to condemn the laws on moral grounds. Your schedule and the availability of material will also determine how many questions you answer. If you are writing a short essay, it is better to consider one set of questions thoroughly than to skim through them all. You could write a paragraph or an essay on any one of the points in the chart above, for instance. For a longer essay, you may appeal to more readers and do more justice to your subject by considering two or three aspects—the aesthetic and moral dimensions of a book, for example, or the moral, legal, and practical issues facing the health professions.

Whether you consider both sides of a question or only one depends on your purpose and audience. In expository writing, you give readers a balanced perspective by considering both good and bad points. In personal and persuasive writing, you may emphasize either the good or the bad, but if your judgments are too one-sided, you are likely to bore or alienate your readers.

Suppose, for instance, you were writing about hiking in the Laurentians. If you were writing a trail guide, hikers would want to know that on a particular trail they could expect both spectacular views and treacherous rock slides. In a personal or persuasive essay, however, you could emphasize either the pleasures or the pains of hiking. But if the picture you paint is too rosy (or too gloomy), readers may reject it as unrealistic.

Writing Evaluative Paragraphs

When you evaluate, you not only state your opinion about your subject but also support that opinion by giving reasons, examples, and other kinds of evidence. This paragraph, taken from a research paper on acid rain, focuses on the economic benefits of reducing sulphur emissions.

Sample Evaluation

Curbing acid rain has advantages besides clean air. Recovering sulphur, rather than releasing it into the atmosphere, is economically beneficial. Sulphur has a world-wide market as a fertilizer. It has also been used as part of asphalt road fill. According to an industry report, stockpiles of sulphur will be depleted quickly if the current growth rate continues (Rankin and Rowland 1982). Some companies are actively searching for sour gas so that they can extract not only the natural gas but the sulphur, too. Plainly, more extensive sulphur recovery holds out the possibility of creating new jobs as well as cutting down on acid rain (Rankin and Rowland 1982).

Exercise 5.20

On what grounds (aesthetic, moral, logical, legal, practical) would you evaluate each of the following? Several of the topics can be approached from different perspectives.

1. A city council decision to expand a major residential street to three lanes in each direction

2. A community theatre production of *Miss Saigon*

3. A school board decision to integrate special needs children (such as the hearing impaired) into regular classrooms

4. The exercise classes at a local health club

5. A proposal to designate a building as a historic site

6. A country singer's latest recording

7. A city bylaw banning the consumption of food and beverages on public transportation

8. An educational institution's decision to raise admission standards

9. An application to build a convenience store in your neighbourhood

5g

Evaluation

Exercise 5.21

State your position on one of the subjects in Exercise 5.20. List the arguments you would use to support your position.

Exercise 5.22

Write a paragraph based on your list of arguments in Exercise 5.21.

5h Analogy

Analogies compare a concept or situation that is difficult to understand with something more familiar. One science writer, for instance, explains the diffusion of gases by comparing the behaviour of gas molecules in a container to the behaviour of people in an elevator—both spread out to fill the available space. Analogies are not always true (couples often cling together in elevators) or necessary (some readers are knowledgeable about science). But they enable you to draw upon knowledge that you and your audience share in order to communicate new information, describe uncommon experiences, or convert readers to your point of view.

Using Analogies in Expository Writing

When you are writing for readers who know less about your subject than you do, analogies will help you to define terms and to explain situations. For instance, if you wanted to explain random sampling to readers who were not social scientists, you might use the analogy of pulling a handful of assorted candies from a jar. Or, if you wanted to make sure high school students understood the concept of random motion, you might use the following analogy.

Sample Analogy: Expository Writing

The movement of molecules is referred to as *random motion*. Random motion is defined as "the movement of the smallest possible physical unit of an element or compound, composed of atoms." This definition may seem puzzling. However, if you think of a molecule as a billiard ball, and random motion as the movement of billiard balls, the meaning becomes much clearer. Picture in your mind the green top of a pool table with billiard balls scattered upon it. Each ball represents a molecule. If you close your eyes and push a single ball on the table with a strong degree of force, it will eventually hit another ball and send it into motion. This ball will strike another, and so on, with no set pattern or order. Just as billiard balls move within the boundary formed by the edges of the pool table, so molecules move within the boundaries of the element or compound of which they are a part. This is random motion.

—Kim Felske

Using Analogies in Personal Writing

Analogies also create vivid images that allow readers to share your thoughts and feelings. In the next sample the writer compares her disastrous marriage to an ill-fated voyage.

Sample Analogy: Personal Writing

In the beginning, being married to him was like taking a long-awaited voyage on a luxury liner. I had all the care, attention, and comforts I had dreamed of. I said to myself that I was on the best ship in the world and I felt lucky to be there. After a while, though, being married to him was more like being in the lifeboat with just enough rations for survival. But by that time, I had forgotten what life was like on the luxury liner. I said to myself that I was on the best lifeboat in the world and I felt lucky to be there. Finally, being married to him was like clinging to a paddle in the sea. But by that time, I had forgotten what life was like on the lifeboat, and I told myself that I had the best paddle in the world and felt lucky to be holding on to it.

5h

Analogy

Using Analogies in Persuasive Writing

Forceful analogies have a strong emotional appeal. The following analogy between the behaviour of a rich family and the behaviour of rich nations appeals to the readers' emotions.

Sample Analogy: Persuasive Writing

Picture a rich family living on a hill in splendid luxury. Look down on the plains around the hill and see the people in shacks, starving; hear the children cry. The rich family sends down a bit of food and clothing once a year, but otherwise they live as always. "We have the right to enjoy our wealth," they say. "We cannot feed and clothe and care for all those people," they explain as they add another foot of barbed wire to the fence around their property. Meanwhile the anger and frustration of the poor grow against them. The rich western nations are very much like this family. An early 1970s estimate numbered 420 million starving people on the plains of the world spread at our feet. Like the rich family, we send bits of food and clothing. Like the rich family, we make it harder and harder for the poor to get in. Meanwhile the anger and frustration of the poor grow against us.

—Ken Ainsworth

Two cautions about using analogies in persuasive writing:

1. Do not use analogies to make unfair emotional appeals—ones that arouse prejudice. For example, smearing an opponent's reputation by charging that "Voting for X would be like voting for the Devil" might appeal to some voters, but would likely alienate many more.

2. Analogies do not provide strong logical support for an argument. Because you are comparing things that are basically different, your analogy may break down if it is pushed too far. Readers who spot weaknesses in your analogy may reject your argument.

Writing Analogies

5h

Analogy

If you decide that an analogy would give your piece of writing the clarity that it needs, follow these steps.

Step 1: Make a list comparing your subject with a variety of things that are different in appearance, form, or kind but similar in behaviour.

Living next door to the United States is like

- having the Friendly Giant for a brother

- sleeping with an elephant

- living under a volcano

Step 2: Choose the simile that best fits your purpose and your readers.

✗ • having the Friendly Giant for a brother [some readers would not be familiar with the television show]

✗ • living under a volcano [suggests too hostile an attitude]

✔ • sleeping with an elephant

Step 3: Develop your simile into a paragraph by exploring the similarities it suggests. What would sleeping with an elephant be like? If the elephant rolls over, there's the obvious danger of being crushed without the elephant's noticing. You might also fear getting a tusk in the back or being strangled by the trunk if the elephant tries to snuggle up. These characteristics suggest that because the United States is much more powerful than Canada, it is a potentially dangerous, even if well-intentioned, neighbour.

Exercise 5.23

Complete each of the following similes.

1. Being out of work is like _____.

2. Being unable to read is like _____.

3. An old pair of jeans is like _____.

4. Starting a new friendship is like _____.

Exercise 5.24

What analogy would you use to explain war to a child?

Exercise 5.25

Make a list of the similarities suggested by one of the following analogies.

• Raising a family is like managing a business.

• Looking through the family photograph album is like travelling in a time machine.

• People addicted to food can be like junkies addicted to drugs.

• Throwing all of our garbage into dumps is like stockpiling dangerous weapons.

Exercise 5.26

Choose one of the comparisons in Exercise 5.23, 5.24, or 5.25 above and write a paragraph developing that analogy.

5i Combining Methods of Development

Knowing how to use different methods of development, as we have seen, gives you more to say about your subject. So far, we have concentrated on writing paragraphs that employ a single method, such as analysis or definition. You can also combine methods of development within a single paragraph. In a paragraph analyzing the effects of alcoholism, for instance, you might find that you needed to define the term *fetal alcohol syndrome*. In the following paragraph, the writer makes her classification of track and field events more interesting by embedding it in a brief narrative.

Sample Paragraph:
Combining Methods of Development

It was one of the first track meets I attended with my family, and as usual my dad had wandered off. Mom was amazed at the level of activity on the track and in the field and asked me to explain some of the logistics. The first thing she needed to know was the difference between track events and field events. I explained that track events are run on the track, whereas field events are held in the field in the centre of the track. Track events can be separated into two further groups: the sprints and the long distance events. Sprints are short races, generally 400m or less, while long distance races start at 800m and generally go up to 3000m. Now that she understood the track side of things we turned to the field. The easiest way to divide field events is into throwing and jumping events. The throwers have a choice of what they wish to throw: javelin, discus, or shot put. The jumpers have choices to make as well, among pole vaulting, high jump, triple jump, and long jump. Mom was shaking her head and saying, "All this is wonderful, but I still can't see your dad." I let out a sigh and decided to go find some friends and warm up for my 400m. After I was ready for the 400, I went to see if Dad had found his way back yet. Sure enough he had. "This is great, but how do you know what goes on in all of the events?" he asked. I shrugged and told him to ask Mom!

—Laura Magowan

Exercise 5.27

Here are several suggestions for combining methods of development in a paragraph. Choose the one that most appeals to you and write a paragraph of about 200 words.

1. Provide a narrative framework for a definition.

2. Compare an analogy and a description (for example, the analogy "life is like a prison" and a description of life in prison).

3. Classify the causes or effects of domestic violence.

4. Evaluate two definitions of a word such as *masculine* or *feminine*.

5. Add descriptive details to a process analysis (try a subject like how to plant a garden or how to go broke).

5i

*Combining
Methods
of
Development*

Resources for Writers and Writing Instructors

http://www.english.upenn.edu/~jlynch/writing.html

University of Victoria—Excellent Writer's Guide

http://webserver.maclab.comp.uvic.ca/writersguide/ paragraphsTOC.html

Part 3

WRITING ESSAYS

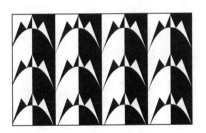

CHECKLIST:

Essays

	OK	NEEDS WORK

Purpose and Audience

1. Does the essay have a clearly defined purpose (to explain, to persuade, to share your personal experience)? □ □

2. Does the essay meet the needs of your intended reader? □ □

Thesis

1. Does your thesis state a specific idea that the rest of the essay develops? □ □

Development

1. Is all the material in the essay relevant to your thesis? □ □

2. Are you satisfied that you have adequately supported your thesis? □ □

3. Are the connections among your ideas as clear as possible? □ □

Essays that Begin with the Thesis

1. Does the introduction identify your subject and the range of material you will cover? □ □

2. Does the introduction end with your thesis? □ □

3. Do your paragraph divisions indicate the major sections of your essay? □ □

4. Does each topic sentence clearly state the main point of the paragraph and show how the paragraph relates to the thesis? □ □

5. Do transitions help your reader to follow the connections among your ideas? □ □

6. Does the conclusion restate the thesis, sum up the main points, and suggest a broader context or implications of your subject? □ □

Essays that Lead Up to the Thesis

1. Does the introduction identify your subject, arouse the reader's interest, and suggest the structure of your essay? □ □

2. Are your paragraphs arranged in order of increasing importance? □ □

3. Do transitions help your reader to follow the sequence of ideas, events, or details? □ □

4. Does the conclusion sum up the ideas, events, or details by stating or clearly implying your thesis? □ □

Comparison Essays

1. Have you used either the block or point by point method of organization effectively? □ □

Research Essays

1. In a research essay, have you included appropriate and correctly documented secondary sources? □ □

2. Is this material relevant to your thesis? □ □

3. Have you explained why you agree or disagree with this material? □ □

6a

Identifying your Purpose and Audience

Chapter 6

The Key to Writing Essays: The Thesis

6a What Is an Essay?

"Write an essay," your instructor says. But what, exactly, is an essay? The term *essay* can be applied to a wide variety of non-fiction writing: light newspaper columns and impassioned letters to the editor; thoughtful magazine articles and scathing movie reviews; academic articles and the research papers you write in many of your courses. These pieces are all essays because they have a thesis, a main point to make about their subject.

6b What Is a Thesis?

A thesis states an idea or an opinion about a subject and presents one or more reasons to support it. In an expository essay, this opinion is the overall point you want to explain: "What this means is... ." In a persuasive essay, this opinion is the argument you want to convince your readers to accept: "What you should think (or do) is... ." In a personal essay, this opinion is a generalization based on your personal experience: "What this means to me is... ."

A good thesis does more than state an opinion. It also gives one or more reasons to support the opinion: "You should do this for these three reasons... ." As this example suggests, setting out your reasons allows you to control the content of the essay. Of all possible reasons for holding a particular opinion, you will discuss only those you have mentioned. Your thesis thus tells both you and your reader what you intend to cover.

You can formulate a better thesis if you follow these guidelines.

• **State an opinion rather than merely restating your subject or essay topic.**

Suppose, for example, that your subject is *group homes for the mentally disabled* and you have narrowed this subject to the topic of *licensing regulations*. You will not have a thesis if you merely restate your subject: *This essay is about group homes for the mentally disabled.* Merely repeating your topic is no more useful: *This essay will discuss the licensing of group homes for the mentally disabled.* A thesis that states an opinion will give you a much clearer focus for your essay: *To prevent the exploitation of clients, social services should tighten regulations governing the licensing of group homes for the mentally disabled.*

- **State an opinion rather than a fact.**

Factual statements provide little focus or control over the content of the essay. You could turn a fact such as *Satellite dishes give Canadians access to hundreds of foreign television channels* into a thesis by stating your opinion of the effects of this situation: *By giving Canadian viewers access to hundreds of foreign channels, satellite dishes will threaten the Canadian television industry.*

- **Make sure your thesis states your opinion, not the writer's.**

When you are analyzing a piece of writing, you will include the writer's main point about his or her subject somewhere in your analysis, but it will not be your thesis. Your thesis will explain *your* interpretation of the piece or evaluate its strengths and weaknesses. For example, the thesis of a newspaper editorial might be that Canadian judges should allow trials to be televised. After analyzing the editorial, you might arrive at a thesis stating that the writer's reliance on American examples weakens the argument.

- **Make the thesis as precise and specific as possible.**

If you state a well-defined opinion with one or more reasons to support it, you will know exactly what points to develop in the body of your essay. Avoid vague generalizations: *These stories have a lot in common* or *the Second World War had a big impact on Canada.* Instead, state the most important similarities in the stories or the most important social, political, or economic effect(s) of the war: *The diversification of manufacturing brought about by the Second World War transformed the Canadian economy.*

There is no one right thesis about a subject. Your thesis will reflect your unique way of looking at your material. It will be shaped by your purpose, your audience, your chosen essay form, and your methods of development.

Exercise 6.1

Consider the following sentences as thesis statements for an essay. If you think the sentence makes a clear point that would control the content of the essay, put **C** beside it. If you think it doesn't, explain how it could be improved.

1. There is at least one television set in 97% of Canadian homes.

2. Science fiction is popular because it gives readers the opportunity to explore new ideas.

3. This essay will analyze Canadian foreign policy during the 1950s.

4. Between 1950 and 1990 the depiction of women in films changed enormously.

5. In the essay "My Wood," E.M. Forster argues that owning property damages a person's moral and spiritual health.

6c Discovering Your Thesis

Don't feel discouraged if you don't immediately know what point you want to make about your subject. Normally you will need to gather some material or even write a first draft before you can figure out your thesis. In fact, if you formulate a thesis first and then look for information to support it, you are likely to distort your subject.

To figure out your thesis, follow these steps.

1. *Gather information about your subject. Use one or more of these methods—brainstorming, freewriting, asking discovery questions, keeping a journal, conducting interviews, or doing library research.* See Part 1: The Writing Process: An Overview for more information on the first four of these. See Chapter 10 for information on interviews and Chapter 12 for information on how to use library materials.

2. *Group this material into two or three categories.* For ideas on how to divide your material, see the sections in Chapter 5 on specific methods of development, such as classification (5c), analysis (5e), comparison (5f), and evaluation (5g).

3. Formulate a thesis that focuses on the meaning of these broader categories.

Suppose, for example, that you have been asked to write an essay on your first job. If you have come back to school after a career as a nurse, you might write a personal essay on the satisfactions and frustrations of nursing when you began work twenty years ago; an expository essay explaining working conditions then; or a persuasive essay arguing that working conditions for nurses have not improved much over the twenty years. Whatever your focus, you would begin by jotting down information about various aspects of your job.

Nursing twenty years ago

1. Earned $275/month with reasonable rates for room, board, and laundry in nurses' residence

2. Advancement by seniority

3. Good job security

4. Not many chances to develop new skills

5. Performed menial and routine tasks, no clinical specialization

6. Worked 40-hour/5-day week; split shifts and short changes (e.g., work 3:30 p.m.-midnight, then 7:30 a.m.-4 p.m.); understaffed

7. Nurses supervised or administered, little nurturing or ministering to patient

8. Nurses expected to follow doctor's orders, not to make independent decisions

9. Basic level of technology

10. Doctors viewed nurses as subordinate

11. Little interaction with management

12. Education required: basic 3-year diploma; training based on practice

6c

*Discovering
Your
Thesis*

You would then group these aspects of nursing into more general categories, such as these:

- financial dimensions of employment (1,2,3,6)

- professional responsibilities (4,5,8,9,12)

- possibilities for emotional satisfaction (7,10,11)

To work out an overall statement about nursing twenty years ago, you would first need to decide what point you could make about each of these dimensions of the job. You might choose the following points: *Twenty years ago, nurses worked long hours with strenuous shift changes for low wages but their jobs were relatively secure. Their opportunities to show initiative and develop new skills were quite limited. The emotional satisfactions of nursing were also limited by lack of direct contact with patients and their subordinate position to doctors and hospital administration.* The main message that seems to emerge is that twenty years ago nursing was a secure job but one with limited opportunities for intellectual growth and emotional satisfaction.

The way you formulate your thesis depends on the kind of essay you are writing and the emphasis you want to give to each of your points.

The Personal Thesis

Whether a personal essay is narrative, descriptive, or reflective, your thesis should make a point about what your experience *meant* to you. Often this is a point about what this experience taught you about yourself, about others, or about life itself.

As a young woman seeking independence, I was attracted to the job security offered by nursing despite the limited opportunities for intellectual growth and personal satisfaction.

The Expository Thesis

The thesis for an expository essay is the generalization that emerges from your analysis of your material. The thesis explains the significance of your subject by telling your readers *what* its parts are, *how* it got that way, *why* it has the nature it has, or all three. This thesis explains *why* nursing twenty years ago was as it was.

The relative abundance of health care dollars meant that nursing jobs were secure; however, the hierarchical nature of the system meant that nursing provided limited opportunities for intellectual growth and emotional satisfaction.

The Persuasive Thesis

The thesis for a persuasive essay tells readers *what* they should think or do and *why*. You reach your thesis by evaluating the strengths and weaknesses of your subject (see Evaluation, 5g). Your thesis may focus on strengths ("Nursing was a good career choice twenty years ago because of the job security it offered") or weaknesses ("Nursing was a bad career choice because of the limited opportunities for intellectual growth and emotional satisfaction"). On most issues, however, readers are more likely to be convinced by a thesis that gives a balanced perspective.

> Although nursing offers less job security than it did twenty years ago, it is still a good career choice because of the many opportunities it offers for intellectual growth and emotional satisfaction.

The Comparative Thesis

When you are comparing, whether in a personal, expository, or persuasive essay, your thesis should do more than state the most important similarities and/or differences in your subjects. It should also explain how or why they are similar or different. If you were comparing working conditions in nursing twenty years ago and today, for instance, you might discover that opportunities for intellectual growth and personal satisfaction have increased, but job security has decreased. Your thesis might explain the reasons for these differences in this way:

> Changes in medical technology and in the structure of the health care system make nursing more intellectually and emotionally satisfying than it was twenty years ago, but cuts in health care spending make jobs less secure.

Exercise 6.2

Choose two of the following subjects. For each subject, develop a thesis for a personal, expository, persuasive, and comparison essay.

1. consumerism
2. student loans
3. professional sports
4. your favourite book or film
5. immigration

Chapter 7

Essay Structure

Essays, like houses, come in a variety of shapes, but they all have a structure—a principle of organization that binds the parts together. The structure serves two purposes: to show your readers how parts of your essay relate to each other and to create interest. Your choice of structure for a particular piece of writing will depend upon which of these purposes is more important.

The overall structure of your essay is determined by where you put your thesis—near the beginning or near the end. Since most essays for academic courses begin with the thesis, we will discuss this method in detail. Ending with the thesis is most effective for some kinds of personal and persuasive essays. You will find three patterns to follow when you choose this method.

Comparison essays present special problems of organization. We offer two possibilities, the block method and the point by point method. For suggestions about how to organize specific kinds of essays, see the appropriate section.

7a Beginning with Your Thesis

When you put your thesis in the introduction, it provides a framework for the rest of the essay. This pattern emphasizes the results of your thinking.

Advantages and Disadvantages

The main advantage of this method is its immediate clarity. By stating your main point first and then providing the evidence to support it, you never leave your reader wondering about the relevance or significance of your material. This method is particularly effective when you are discussing a complex or technical subject at some length, for most readers will have trouble following several pages of specific detail if they don't see how your evidence connects with your main point. For this reason, you will probably organize most of the essays you write for academic courses with the thesis first.

Beginning with your thesis may not be the best strategy, however, if you are writing on a controversial subject or on a topic that is unfamiliar to your readers. You may alienate readers who feel forced to agree or disagree with your conclusions before they have had time to consider the issue.

The Basic Components

Thesis and Topic Sentences

Your thesis, you will recall, gives your opinion about your subject and your reason(s) for holding that opinion. By giving your reasons in the order you plan to discuss them, you create a map to guide your readers through your essay. To show them where they are along the way, you use topic sentences that restate your reasons as points you will develop in your middle paragraphs.

In the following example, you can see how the thesis and topic sentences create a structure that focuses the reader's attention and controls the content of the essay.

Essay Topic: Are fairy tales suitable for children? Write a 1000-word essay in which you defend your position.

Thesis: By providing models of hope, courage, and determination, fairy tale heroes help children to see the value of developing these virtues in their own lives.

Topic Sentences:

– From the story of Jack and the magic bean seeds, children learn that even seemingly foolish hopes can lead to success.

– Children who have felt abandoned like Hansel and Gretel can learn the value of courage in adversity from Gretel's brave rescue of her brother.

– Cinderella has been criticized recently for waiting passively for Prince Charming to rescue her, but a closer reading of this tale shows that she, too, uses hope, courage, and determination to solve her own problems.

Giving an essay such a clearly defined structure is not easy; you won't achieve a perfectly worded thesis and matching topic sentences on your first try. In the process of gathering material, you may discover a tentative thesis and major categories (such as courageous characters and hopeful characters). These categories—or the thesis—may change when you write an outline or a draft, since your ideas will usually become clearer and so will your understanding of how they relate to each other. Then, when you revise, you can rewrite your thesis and topic sentences so that they provide a clear, logical framework.

The Introduction

In this type of essay structure, the opening sentences define the range of material you will cover and provide a context for the thesis, which ends the introduction. The opening sentences thus act like the framing shots of a movie, setting the scene and introducing the characters before the action begins.

Your introduction can be based on any of the methods of developing paragraphs discussed in Chapter 5. In academic essays, for example, you may classify the material you plan to discuss (such as types of fairy tales), define a key term from your thesis (such as autism), or sketch the development of a current situation (such as previous attempts to amend the Constitution). For a more general audience, you may want to create interest by giving a vivid example, telling a relevant anecdote, or describing a scene.

Whatever the method you use, be sure to give your readers all the background information they need, including authors and titles of works, and dates and places of events.

Remember the following points when you are writing your introduction:

- *Avoid making large claims that the rest of your essay does not support.* Do not, for example, begin by saying "Children are not really frightened by fairy tales" unless you can (and will) provide hard evidence to support the generalization.

- *State your thesis, not your topic.* You do not need to include a sentence that merely repeats the assigned topic, such as *In this essay I will discuss the suitability of fairy tales for children.* The title of your essay should make the topic clear.

- *Focus on the big picture, not the details.* While you may choose to open with an example or incident that captures the essence of your argument, be wary of including detailed information that belongs in the body of the essay.

Sample Introduction

In the past, fairy tales were criticized as too unrealistic to provide suitable models for children. Recent critics are more likely to condemn fairy tales as too violent and/or too sexist. A closer examination of three popular fairy tales, *Jack and the Beanstalk*, *Hansel and Gretel*, and *Cinderella*, shows that this criticism is unjust, for these tales provide vivid examples of hopeful, courageous, determined characters who solve their own problems. Fairy tale heroes thus help children to see the value of developing these virtues in their own lives.

Middle Paragraphs

Sometimes, such as when you are tracing the development of a concept or analyzing a chain of causes and effects, your material will determine the order of your middle paragraphs. Usually, however, you will have to decide how to arrange your points. Consider how you can best keep your audience interested. You might begin with the point that your readers will find easiest to understand and end with the most difficult. Or you might build interest by beginning with your least important point and ending with the most important.

To see how you would decide which point is most important, consider the structure of the essay on fairy tales. The thesis and topic sentences suggest three blocks of material: Jack as a model of hope, Gretel as a model of courage, and Cinderella as a model of hope, courage, and determination. Because *Cinderella* has been most criticized (in *The Cinderella Complex*, for example) and there are more points to make in its favour, it makes sense to put this tale at the end.

You can't always cover a block of material in a single paragraph. To support the point about *Cinderella* with adequate examples, for instance, you would need several paragraphs. Whenever your discussion of a point takes up more than half a page (typed, single spaced), divide your material into subpoints, each with its own topic sentence. Use an umbrella topic sentence to tie the block of material together and show how it relates to the thesis.

UMBRELLA TOPIC SENTENCE

Cinderella has been criticized recently for waiting passively for Prince Charming to rescue her, but a closer reading of this tale

7a

Beginning with Your Thesis

shows that she, too, uses hope, courage, and determination to
solve her own problems.

Topic Sentence: SUBPOINT 1	Because Cinderella never stops hoping that she can go to the ball, she makes every effort to accomplish the difficult tasks her stepmother sets. [Examples]
Topic Sentence: SUBPOINT 2	When she is returned to her rags and cinders, Cinderella is still brave enough to demand to see the Prince. [Examples]
Topic Sentence: SUBPOINT 3	Far from waiting passively to be rescued, Cinderella makes a determined effort throughout the tale to solve her own problems. [Examples]

Conclusion

7a

*Beginning
with Your
Thesis*

Your conclusion should draw together the evidence you have
presented to reinforce the main idea of the essay as a whole.
Instead of merely summarizing your main points, you emphasize their implications. While you don't want to raise new issues
that should have been discussed earlier, you do want to show
how your essay fits into a wider context. Your conclusion should
have three basic components: a restatement of your thesis, a
brief explanation of the significance of the major points, and a
suggestion of the broader implications of the subject. You can
present this last element in three ways:

- Move from the specific to the general to suggest that the material you have covered is part of a larger issue.

  *Thus in a world too often disrupted by dislocation, divorce, and
  death, fairy tales offer children a hope of happiness.*

- Compare your subject with another subject with which your
reader is likely to be familiar.

  *And, whatever the critics say, fairy tales are much less violent
  and sexist than the television programs most children watch
  every day.*

- Stress the significance of your subject by emphasizing its
causes or effects.

Children may learn these moral values elsewhere, but nowhere else will they experience so satisfying an entry into the magic of reading.

Sample Conclusion

Children, like adults, learn who they are and what they can be through the examples of others. The hope, courage, and determination modelled by Jack, Gretel, and Cinderella show children that these virtues can help them to create happier lives for themselves. In doing so, these tales add an ethical dimension to children's education, a dimension that is too often missing in modern life.

For examples of essays beginning with the thesis, see the sample essay analyzing literature (9d) and the sample literary research paper (12f).

7b Leading Up to the Thesis

If you choose this method, your thesis may appear in the middle of your essay or at the end, or it may be implied rather than stated directly. This pattern emphasizes the process of your thinking rather than your conclusions.

Advantages and Disadvantages

By delaying the presentation of your thesis, you can create suspense and interest. This approach is particularly effective in personal essays, where you share with your readers the process by which you have come to an insight about your experience. Leading up to your thesis is also useful in a persuasive essay when you want to convince your readers to consider a potentially controversial point of view or to think in new ways about an old problem.

The danger with this method is that you may end up with a lot of details but no main point. You can prevent this problem by structuring your essay according to one of the three patterns discussed below.

Pattern 1: Questions and Answers

In this pattern, you ask a question in your introduction that the rest of the essay will answer. You may consider and reject possible answers until you conclude with one that seems satisfactory; or you may give a series of partial answers that add up to a comprehensive one.

Introduction: The introduction sets out the problem or issue and asks the question to be answered.

Middle Paragraphs: In the body of your essay, you examine possible answers in detail. Each answer forms a major section of the essay, composed of one or more paragraphs. You can help your readers follow the structure of your essay by repeating key terms and using parallel sentence structure in each answer. Arrange your paragraphs in a sequence such as simplest to most complex or weakest answer to strongest answer.

Conclusion: In the conclusion, you present the best or most comprehensive answer as your thesis. You can signal that you've reached your thesis by repeating the question from the introduction or by summarizing previous answers.

The following example demonstrates how the question and partial answers pattern can work.

INTRODUCTION: [Question]	How can teachers help reduce fighting in school?
MIDDLE PARAGRAPHS: [Topic Sentences]	We can watch for signs... .
	We can discuss the issue with students... .
	We can also teach students ways of resolving arguments... .
	Most important, we must model good problem-solving behaviour in our conflicts with students... .
CONCLUSION: [Thesis]	To reduce fighting in school, we must educate both ourselves and our students about the uses and misuses of power.

The sample non-literary research paper, "Whose Turn Is It to Clean Up This Garbage?" (12g), displays elements of this pattern. Note that the question to be answered is raised in the title.

Pattern 2: Specific Details to General Meaning

In this pattern, you begin with particular details and end with a thesis, either stated or implied, about the meaning of the experience as a whole.

Introduction: The introduction plunges your reader into the subject of your essay and arouses interest through narrative or descriptive detail. It gives a sense of structure by suggesting the final event of the narrative (*We wouldn't rest until we found the lost treasure of the Incas*) or the scope of the description (*The old neighbourhood was unrecognizable*).

Middle Paragraphs: In the body of the essay, fill in the specific details. As units of thought, your paragraphs will correspond to units of your narrative (*first week, next day, that afternoon, the moment had come*) or description (*the streets, the houses, our house*). Arrange your paragraphs in a chronological or spatial sequence that will lead naturally to the generalization in your conclusion. Foreshadow this generalization by references to thoughts and feelings (*I wondered whether we were on a fool's errand*) or by choice of diction (*narrow streets, cracked sidewalks, shabby houses, our house shrunken and decayed*).

Conclusion: In the conclusion, you sum up the meaning of the experience, either through explicit commentary (*The real treasures were those we had left behind: family, friends, and country*) or through an image that makes the point (*Staring back at me was the image of a white-haired old man, his face deeply creased by sorrow and worry. Several moments passed before I recognized my own reflection in the glass*).

For an example of this pattern, see the sample descriptive essay, "Smokey Mountain" (8d).

Pattern 3: Rearranged Chronology

When you write about events that took place over a long period, you don't have to present them in chronological order. You can rearrange the chronology to increase interest or to show the workings of thought and memory. You can begin in the present and flashback to the past, as in the sample narrative essay, "Rookies" (8b). Or you can move between different points in past and present, as in the sample reflective essay, "A Language of My Own" (8f). This technique is useful for exploring past causes of present situations, reflecting upon changes, and bringing new understanding to old events.

Introduction: Your introduction establishes tone, atmosphere, setting, and your past or present point of view on your subject.

Middle Paragraphs: In the body of the essay, you explore the links between present and past through methods such as narration, description, definition, analysis, evaluation, and analogy. Arrange your paragraphs in order of increasing importance, letting your thesis emerge at an appropriate point in your middle paragraphs or in your conclusion.

Conclusion: Your conclusion links your understanding of past and present.

7c Patterns for Comparison Essays

You can use either the block or the alternative method to develop a comparison essay. We discussed both of these methods in detail in Chapter 5, when we described how to arrange material in paragraphs developed through comparison. Both methods have advantages and disadvantages.

Block Method

When you use the block method, you cover all the aspects of one subject before you discuss the other.

Advantages: Clarity and Simplicity

The block method gives you a chance to develop all of your ideas on one subject before you turn to the other. It is therefore simple to work with when you don't have much time to organize an essay—on exams, for instance. The block method can work well for short essays on familiar subjects, as in comparisons of places you have lived or people you have known. It is also effective when you are using a brief treatment of one subject as a basis for a more lengthy treatment of another. Finally, if you are comparing more than two subjects, you will probably need to use the block method to avoid fragmenting your material.

An important advantage of the block method is that you are less likely to distort your material by trying too hard to find similarities or by exaggerating the importance of one aspect of a subject. The sound patterns in one poem, for example, may contribute much less to the meaning than do the sound patterns in another.

Disadvantages: Repetition and Loss of Focus

One disadvantage of the block method is that readers may forget what you have said about your first subject by the time you make similar points about your second subject. For this reason, you may have to repeat points. Another danger is that you may lose your focus on the basis of your comparison: the common element you are discussing (such as the setting of the two stories or the economic effects of two policies). As a result, your reader may decide that you have discussed both subjects but never actually compared them. To avoid this problem, make sure your analysis focuses on the same element(s) of both subjects.

Sample Outline Using the Block Method

If you were using the block method to organize an essay comparing the advantages of working with the advantages of going to school, your outline might look like this.

I. The advantages of working
   A. Friendships with co-workers
   B. Money
   C. Free time

II. The advantages of going to school
   A. Friendships with other students
   B. Learning new ideas and skills
   C. Achieving goals

III. Working compared with going to school
   A. Friendships at work and school
   B. The immediate rewards of money and free time compared with the long-term rewards of learning and a sense of achievement

Notice that this structure leads naturally to putting your thesis at the end, where you draw together your comparisons.

Point by Point Method

Here you deal with one aspect of both subjects before moving on to another aspect of both subjects.

Advantages: Focus and Conciseness

An important advantage of the point by point method is that it helps your reader to grasp the most important similarities and differences by bringing specific points about your subjects closer together. It thus avoids one of the main disadvantages of the block method: repetition. This emphasis on points of similarity and difference also keeps you focused on the task of comparing. For these reasons, this method is often better for organizing a lengthy and complex comparison.

Disadvantages: Complexity and Fragmentation

With this method, you have to identify all the points of similarity and difference you plan to discuss before you begin writing. For this reason, it is difficult to use for in-class essays. Another disadvantage is that if you don't have much to say about each point, your essay may ping-pong rapidly from one subject to the other. You can correct this problem by gathering more material or by combining subpoints so that you can write separate paragraphs on each aspect of each subject, as illustrated in the outline below.

Sample Outline Using the Point by Point Method

Thesis: Both myths and fairy tales can give us insights into cultural values, but fairy tales provide more useful role models for children because they portray more realistic characters who manage to solve their problems.

    I. Cultural values in myths and fairy tales
        A. Cultural values in myths
        B. Cultural values in fairy tales

    II. Characters as role models in myths and fairy tales
        A. Nature of characters
            1. Superhuman characters in myths
            2. Realistic characters in fairy tales
        B. Ability of characters to meet demands
            1. Failure of characters in myths
            2. Success of characters in fairy tales
        C. Fate of characters
            1. Unhappy endings of myths
            2. Happy endings of fairy tales

You will find an example of the point by point method of organizing a comparison in the sample literary research paper (12f).

Chapter 8

Personal Essays

When you write personal essays, you share your thoughts, feelings, and experiences with your readers. But since you are writing an essay, your readers will also expect you to say what your experience means. As we consider three kinds of personal essays (narrative, descriptive, and reflective), we will discuss how to fulfill your readers' expectation. Since most of your personal essays are likely to be based on events in your life, we will examine narrative essays most closely.

8a Narrative Essays

Like other essays, **narrative essays** must have a point, a main idea. To see why a main idea is important, let's consider an example.

Suppose you decide to write about "My Canoe Trip." The title, as you can see, doesn't suggest any point about the trip. It offers no principle to help you select which events to include and which to leave out or how to arrange them effectively. So you might begin at the beginning, go on to the end, and stop. But would all the events of your trip, presented in that manner, interest anyone except your best friend?

Imagine, then, that you decide to focus on one incident and write about "A Frightening Canoe Trip." You would now have a way of deciding what to include in your essay, and you might even think about how to present your material—such as describing your nervousness as you approached a patch of white water and then flashing back to the events that led up to that moment. Readers interested in canoeing might find your experience thrilling to read about. But what about readers who never canoe and will never find themselves in a similar situation?

Think about your harrowing experience. What did you learn from it? There are many possible lessons that you might have learned—the dangers of over-confidence, for instance, or the power of nature, or the joy of unexpected courage. Most of us learn these lessons at some time or another. A main point about what you learned, if it is true to your experience, will give your readers a second level of interest. They can read your essay not only to find out what happened, but also to discover what your experience meant to you. This meaning will be the thesis that you state or imply through the telling of your story.

What you have learned should not be a moral tacked on to the end—*From this incident I learned never to kill frogs.* It should emerge from the way you present the concrete details of the experience. You render not only the events themselves but also your thoughts and feelings through specific details. Writing *I was frightened* depicts your state of mind much less vividly than writing *Whenever I see little ripples in the river I think of the powerful currents beneath the surface, and my mouth goes dry with fear.* When you convey the unique quality of your experience through details such as these, your readers will understand more readily the meaning of the experience for you.

Writing a Narrative Essay

Follow these guidelines when writing a narrative essay.

8a

Narrative Essays

1. Focus on a single experience; you will then have room for the wealth of detail you need to make your essay interesting.

2. Make a central point about the meaning of this experience. You may discover this point in the process of writing.

3. Include only events and details relevant to the central point.

4. Provide enough specific details about *who, what, when, where, why,* and *how* for a reader to understand how events and actions relate to the central point.

5. Create interest through vivid, concrete diction (16c), figurative language (16d), varied sentence structure (16e), and other devices.

6. Put your thesis at the beginning, at the end, or at the point in the narrative where the meaning of events becomes clear to you.

7. Within this overall structure, arrange your material to create a specific effect, such as suspense, humour, or pathos.

8. Make the sequence of events clear to readers by using transitional words and phrases (*the next morning, now that I look back*).

8b Sample Narrative Essay

Kathy Reiffenstein uses vivid language to carry her readers with her through the buildup to a hockey game. She clearly indicates shifts from the present to the past and back by phrases such as I *remember, our first game, tonight*. What is her thesis? Do you agree with it?

Rookies

by Kathy Reiffenstein

Garters, hip-high stockings, lace-up boots, gloves. They sound like the clothing of a seductress, until we add to the list shin pads, plastic helmets, and jumbo shorts with suspenders. The medley of twisted straps and hard plastic and thick padding is a confusing jumble to the first-time hockey player, who may not realize that if you don't put your shin pads on before your socks, you'll end up having to undress and start all over. As a female, brought up as a female, I have no memories of Mom dressing me at early morning games. I have only the routine I memorized just last year—garter, then shin pads, stockings, pants, shoulder pads, elbow pads, skates, jersey, helmet, and finally the gloves.

The boys I know who play hockey wear only their underwear beneath their equipment, since they like to stay as cool as possible. We girls are envious, but we don't have our own equipment—we borrow from Campus Rec. The thought of all the anonymous bodies who have oozed sweat into the padding is enough to prompt us to wear leggings and T-shirts underneath and endure the extra warmth. We arrive at our games 45 minutes early, because we must wait in line for equipment, then struggle through the routine of dressing, then wait for our coach to tape us up. The equipment is meant for husky, muscular males; apparently it has been assumed that small-boned, puny people just don't play hockey. So our coach tapes our pants around our waists, he tapes our elbow pads onto our arms to prevent them from sliding down around our gloves, and circles our socks with tape to keep our shin pads in place. "Tape me, I need

tape!" we cry, as we seem to be unable to tape ourselves or even each other—not that we've tried. We
would rather harass our coach and interrupt him in
the daunting task of dressing the goalie. The goalie
lies face down on the floor while we take turns
buckling up the multiple straps that cross the backs
of her legs, holding her enormous leg pads in place.
Each pad is about a foot across, and on her short
body, extends from her ankle to her hip. Someone
grasps her arms and hoists her up, since she can't
get up on her own. Unless standing, she is like an
upturned turtle—without the sturdy goal posts to
cling to, she would never get back up if she fell
down during a game.

Our coach, who wears a tie in accordance with our
half-serious attempts to be a "real" hockey team,
doesn't say much to us before the game. No strategy
advice, no motivational speeches. He is silent in
the noisy, nervous babble of the dressing room. We
worry because we see that some of the girls from the
team we'll be playing have brought their own equipment (which means they must be good), or we think we
might have played them last year and lost. Then one
of the girls announces that she saw that most of the
other team have figure skates, not hockey skates,
and with this we console ourselves. After all, tough
girls don't own figure skates. We hobble around the
dressing room on our skates like clowns on stilts,
our movements stifled by the bulky padding. We are
instantly fat and tall. No wonder hockey players are
fierce and aggressive—in all this equipment it's
impossible not to feel huge and invincible. We
anticipate and dread the game at the same time; we
are confident, worried, excited, afraid. The clock
counts down the seconds of the game in progress;
while we wait for it to end, we joke, giggle loudly,
take helmets on and off. We mill around anxiously,
our bodies tight and tense.

I remember watching my younger sister play hockey
when we were in high school, thinking I had never
been so entertained in my life. The puck would shoot
down the ice, and the skaters would follow slowly

and carefully while the puck waited patiently in the corner. Their coach would shriek hysterically, "Skate! Skate! Skate!" over and over while the players glided serenely down the ice. At least seven of the players would reach the puck and mob around it, fighting their own teammates for it, slamming into the boards and each other until someone shot it back down the ice again, and once more they would follow it. My sister looked like a fool, but nevertheless, I admired her. I never thought that I would have the courage to try something that I knew I wouldn't be successful at, right out in public, without caring what people thought of me. But a year later, I signed up for a girls' hockey team and prepared to become a spectacle.

Our first game was a circus. Not one girl on our team had ever played hockey, other than casually on an outdoor rink, or worn hockey equipment before. The strange sensations of heavy, restricting padding and stiff gloves made skating awkward, although it was a pleasant surprise to learn that falling down is painless when you're wearing hockey equipment. And fall down we did—we seemed to fall whenever we came into contact with anything else. We collided with the other team's players and with our own players, and after the tooth-jarring impact, we fell. We skated too quickly towards the puck, smashed into the boards, and fell. We reached too far with our sticks when the puck floated by, and plummeting forward, fell. One girl made a desperate attempt at a slapshot, missed the puck, and fell.

Not only were we uncoordinated, we were completely ignorant of the rules, written and unwritten. The whistle that constantly stopped the game perplexed us; not one of us knew what it meant to be "offside," and our coach's attempts to explain that we weren't allowed to be inside the blue line while the puck was outside the blue line only confused us more. We hovered uncertainly and reluctantly around the blue line. No one knew how to play a position—when we weren't busy worrying about the blue line, we were chasing the puck wherever it happened to go.

8b

Sample Narrative Essay

89

Unfortunately, by the time I got near the crafty chunk of rubber, it was usually racing smugly down the ice, eluding us once again.

Tonight, we file on to the ice to warm up. My equipment is still a bit damp from the previous wearer's exertions, so it is chilly, and a cold layer of air seems to rise from the ice. The rink's surface is powdery with a fine snow of ice slivers, sliced up by someone else's skates. My skate blades, wobbly and teetering on the rubbery floor of the dressing room and hallway, are stable on the slippery sheet of frozen water. I glide around the outside of the rink, trying several cautious stops, testing my edges. I check the stands to see if any friends have come to watch our game and cheer us on. Some of the boys we know cruelly remind us of our ineptitude after the game, as if we have no right to be playing hockey. But at least they come; a substantial number of fans can intimidate the other team. Perhaps we are no better than a team of six-year-old boys, but we don't expect to be: as women, this supposed Canadian institution of hockey is new to us. It is foreign and fascinating. After years of watching from the stands, now I am a part of the action. The sweat, the thirst, the thrill—suddenly I understand why almost every Canadian male loves this game.

Hockey is sweat. Faceless enemies racing. My coach's voice. Frantic scrambles. Split-second decisions. Instinct. Sweat plastering my T-shirt to my back, trickling from my forehead. Heat exudes from every pore, and my padding seems to absorb it, holding it next to my skin. I stuff the straw of a water bottle through my mesh mask and accidentally spill some on my chinpad. Now it reeks of the sweat of multitudes of past hockey players; my own drips down to join theirs. I realize that I am one of them—I am a savage, aggressive opponent, I am a part of the game. So what if I fall sometimes, so what if I don't make perfect passes, so what if the blue line confuses me? I cheer my teammates and hug our goalie when she lets the puck through. I apologize to players on the other team when we accidentally run into one another, but shove them back when they hit me on purpose. I don't know if these dynamics are the same when boys play hockey, but it doesn't matter. We have taken a sport that men seem to need to be proficient at if they are truly Canadian, and are trying it for ourselves. And we've discovered what we have been missing all of these years. I've already decided—if I ever have a daughter, she's not taking figure skating lessons. She's playing hockey.

8c *Descriptive Essays*

If the unifying principle of narrative essays is *what happened to me*, the unifying principle of **descriptive essays** is *what I saw*. Keep this distinction in mind because narrative essays may include descriptions of people, places, and objects, and descriptive essays may include accounts of things happening. In a descriptive essay, however, the focus is on rendering your impressions of some part of the physical world and its meaning for you.

Subjects for Descriptive Essays

You can write descriptive essays about places, people, or other animate and inanimate things. You might write, for example, about the town or neighbourhood in which you grew up to show that the community was either close-knit and friendly or alien and frightening. You might write a character sketch of a coach who taught you the importance of dedication, or you might focus on a family heirloom to explain its meaning in your life.

Image and Meaning in Descriptive Essays

As in narrative essays, concrete images create meaning more effectively than direct statements do. Specific images of people, places, and objects allow your reader to see through your eyes and thus to understand the basis of your thoughts, feelings, and judgments. In the paragraph that follows, taken from the sample descriptive essay, "Smokey Mountain" (8d), the writer uses repeated images of water, culminating in the reference to the hurricane, to convey his complex attitude towards the scene.

8c

Descriptive Essays

91

These were the fringe dwellers of Manila, people who survive on an industry brutally isolated from the rest of the population. As I looked down from the safety of my perch high above the swarming crowd, the garbage appeared as faint streams spread across the valley. Bits of tin foil and splintered glass sparkled like breaking waves in the sunlight. The smear of black smoke rising out of spontaneous combustion appeared like thick steam from the water's surface. From where I stood, the whole scene had a certain beauty about it... but then, from the right distance, so does a raging hurricane.

This passage emphasizes the way a Canadian observer might feel safely distant from this scene of poverty and squalor. But it also conveys, in the image of the hurricane, the writer's recognition of the potential for violence and upheaval. Because we are encouraged to "see" this meaning for ourselves, the images are more effective than a direct statement of the author's reactions would be.

Organizing Descriptive Essays

For short descriptive essays, such as "Smokey Mountain" (8d), it often works well to allow the meaning of the whole to emerge gradually from the accumulation of details. But to maintain readers' interest in longer descriptive essays, you may need to state your main point near the beginning and bring in other methods of development—such as a comparison of one person with another, for example, or an analysis of the effects of a shifting population on a town.

Whatever overall structure you choose, arrange the parts of the essay by an appropriate principle of organization, usually spatial. This spatial organization may be literal (you could move from one part of the town to the next) or figurative (you could move from what is "easy to see" about a person to what is "hard to see"). Most important, your method of organization should culminate in an image that conveys the dominant impression you want to create.

8c

Descriptive Essays

8d Sample Descriptive Essay

Smokey Mountain

by Bill Howe

The young boy struggled up the side of the hill. His legs were straining under the weight of the sack he had slung over his shoulders and his one arm was flailing to catch his balance as he teetered over the narrow path. His shirt and trousers were soiled with sweat and dirt, and his legs were buried deep inside his oversized rubber boots. A floppy cap sagged over the side of his blackened face, hiding the scowl of dignified scorn he directed at the intruders. He quickly turned away and made off towards a sculpture of bed springs, tires, and scrap metal.

The hill I was standing on is known to the Filipinos as Smokey Mountain. It has been built up over many years from garbage deposits delivered from the streets of Metro Manila. Over eight million people contribute every day to this towering masterpiece, but its dismal appearance has not discouraged the poor who find their home within its refuge of waste. A population of some 15 000 squatters has developed into a thriving community, complete with a division of labour natural to such territory. There are people who sort through the garbage for cherished bits of plastic and metal, people who work in the distribution centres selling salvaged goods to local recycling plants, and people who go out into the streets at night to collect the garbage from the richer districts before it is diluted by the rest of the collection.

Most of the people migrated here to escape the hopeless life in the remote provinces, only to find the economic depression of their new surroundings worse than what they had left behind. The putrid smell of rotting debris wafting through the air continually reminds them of their own decay. The villagers are plagued with diseases contracted in their own backyard. On a good day, their labour might earn them only two or three dollars, but still they consider themselves fortunate to be able to earn money at all. The people appear proud and content with their life, and the children play in the garbage pile as if it were a giant sandbox filled with buried toys.

From where I stood, I had a panoramic view of the flow of garbage below. The convoy of tawny yellow dump trucks formed a brilliant streak which faded into the distant skyline of Manila. As the trucks dropped off their loads, people eagerly surrounded the untouched deposits, in hopes of discovering some carelessly discarded treasure to take home to their families. Tin cans, tires, wooden crates, plastic bottles, discarded clothing—nothing was overlooked for its value on the salvage market.

Attacking the hill from below was a huge bulldozer burrowing into the debris like a huge mechanical mole. As it lurched forward, it uncovered a trail of pristine spoil, its huge rutted tracks quickly filling with pools of mud freshly squeezed from the rubble below. The people followed the beast as though it was their master. As their bent frames waded slowly through the soggy mess, they seemed enslaved to the garbage beneath their feet, imprisoned by their own poverty.

These were the fringe dwellers of Manila, people who survive in an industry brutally isolated from the rest of the population. As I looked down from the safety of my perch high above the swarming crowd, the garbage appeared as faint streams spread across the valley. Bits of tin foil and splintered glass sparkled like breaking waves in the sunlight. The smear of black smoke rising out of spontaneous combustion appeared like thick steam from the water's surface. From where I stood, the whole scene had a certain beauty about it… but then, from the right distance, so does a raging hurricane.

One of the dump trucks passed me as I was leaving the smouldering mountain. I grinned to myself as I read the words inscribed across its side boards—"Manila on the Go!"

8e Reflective Essays

If narrative essays present a person acting, and descriptive essays present a person perceiving, **reflective essays** present a mind thinking and feeling about a particular subject. The emphasis shifts from the outer world to the inner world.

Subjects for Reflective Essays

Reflective essays allow you to explore the meaning of your experiences through methods other than narration and description. You might define what friendship means to you, for instance, by discussing the qualities and behaviour that characterize relations between friends. Or you might explore the meaning of friendship by classifying your friends, by comparing friends and acquaintances, or by developing an analogy such as "a friend is like a favourite pair of shoes." Or you might evaluate your own behaviour as a friend.

Another way of reflecting upon your experience is to focus upon causes and/or effects: what causes you to be a good/poor student or employee? what causes you to act outrageously or timidly? what are the effects in your life of being native, white, Sikh, Asian, black, French-Canadian? of being Catholic, atheist, Jewish, Muslim? of being an immigrant or Canadian-born? of growing up in a certain time, place, family, social class? of having your particular body, mind, temperament?

Organizing Reflective Essays

Because the emphasis in reflective essays is on thinking and feeling, you may find yourself shifting back and forth between making generalizations and giving specific details. To give the sense of a person thinking and feeling, you may allow the structure of your essay to mirror the sometimes unexpected movements of your mind. The trick is to find a balance between too loose a structure that lets the essay fall apart and too tight a structure that stifles your personal voice. Try using one of the patterns for leading up to your thesis (7b), the block or point by point method of organizing comparisons (7c), or the weighing of alternatives characteristic of evaluation (5g).

8f Sample Reflective Essay

In this essay (a shortened version), the writer reflects upon the effects of living with—and without—a diagnosis of a disability. As she searches for a language for her experience, she moves back and forth between past and present. Transitions guide readers through these shifts in time.

A Language of My Own

by Camille Collett

I remember the day that I was diagnosed. Labelled. Legitimized. Before anyone had a name for my inability to function in normative situations (whatever those are), I was just different. *Extremely shy and withdrawn.* I was different and completely outside of the world that everyone else appeared implicitly to understand. *A good little girl—quiet and reserved.* These words described what others saw, but they did not describe the chaos of my inner world.

By the time I was old enough to understand that thinking was a process, I really believed that everyone else in the world thought the same way that I did. This meant that everyone had thousands of thoughts occurring simultaneously—like a wall of televisions all tuned to different channels blasting images and noise. The fixed volume on all the units made it difficult to differentiate one unit from another. Thinking, for me, was a process of focusing on one noise for a brief moment of absorption, without any retention, before, distracted, my thought pattern clicked onto a different television unit. As material became more detailed, my attention span diminished even further. As a consequence, I became a wealth of information that I could not organize or communicate except by impulsively blurting out facts which were unconnected and irrelevant to the events around me.

Eventually, life became too complicated to compensate for what was going on inside my head. At four, I could play piano sonatas by ear. But when I tried to learn to read music and consciously pay attention

to what both hands were doing, I became frustrated
and angry. No one would understand that the notes
dancing off the page were art in and of themselves,
engaging my curiosity. I became absorbed in a
process of meaning that I didn't understand. Overwhelmed, I retreated and lived inside of myself.
Inside I could make it calm and quiet.

After seventeen years of the qualified professionals asserting that I merely typified the shy, quiet
young woman, someone heard me. Someone listened to
my voice. The diagnosis validated the experiences
that went unseen. Attention Deficit Disorder (ADD).
Three small words became an identification number,
indelible marks on my body: a woman with a behavioural and learning disability.

ADD, or ADHD (Attention Deficit Hyperactivity
Disorder), as it is also called, results from developmental deficiencies that make it hard to inhibit,
initiate, or sustain responses to tasks or stimuli,
especially when there are few consequences. In other
words, having weak internal mechanisms for regulat-
ing behaviour, children with ADD often act impulsively and have trouble concentrating on tasks
unless their environment is highly structured.
Although the medical community cannot agree on the
actual cause of ADHD, recent research reported in
the *Globe and Mail* suggests that ADHD may be linked
to a deficit in a gene that regulates the body's use
of thyroid hormone. According to the *Globe and Mail*,
this is the first time that a "specific inborn flaw
has been linked to a common behavioural problem."
Inborn flaw. Flawed merchandise. Quality control
down. The words "common behavioural problem" are
inadequate. The words imply that all ill-mannered
and rude children are the result of a bad gene pool.
Simultaneously, words mean too much and not enough.

The signs had been there since I was born, but the
medical community was blinded by expectation. I was
a textbook case. My failure to thrive became a "milk
allergy" and my refusal to eat was "normal." My
nature came to be described as quiet and reserved
(like a good little girl) rather than as withdrawn

97

and removed. Except when people, uninvited, tried to invade my interior space, and then I would rage like a wild beast until I was left alone. Ambidextrous until I was eight, I was tested for brain dominance—not because I used both hands, but because it took me so long to decide which hand to use that I never did anything in school. The testing successfully determined that my right hand was dominant by 1%. Of course testing can only do so much and deciding which hand to use was replaced by which color crayon to use and later, in junior high school, by whether to use pen or pencil. I wanted to think but it hurt my head so I absorbed myself in books. Books became my reality and I lived inside them.

When I ventured outside the world of books and tried to talk about my frustration, I was invisible. I was white. I was blonde. I was the child of two highly educated individuals. According to the experts, I was merely the typically rebellious child of pushy parents. When I disagreed, I was told that girls don't have to do math and science. When I said I wanted to, I was told I couldn't know what I wanted because I was the child of pushy parents. When I said that the only person I was disappointing was myself, I was told that at fifteen I couldn't possibly have that kind of self-awareness.

Disability is one of those silent words that no one speaks. At least not around me. Feeling invisible, I wait for someone to speak in a language that recognizes, even if it doesn't always understand, difference. A language that I can speak as a woman with a disability. Without that language, my head is filled with speaking silence. Awkward silence. The kind of silence that follows the disclosure of difference, eyes shifting away from the body that spoke. Yet I feel uncomfortable asserting my identification with disabled women because it reduces all of us to a common denominator. I am also afraid that the community I identify with the most will refuse to recognize the disability that cannot be seen. Medication is my only visible link to that community. I am afraid of being invisible.

Some people believe that I should rejoice in my invisibility, that I should consider it a luxury that I don't have to deal with the challenges of being visually or physically disabled in an abled world. They don't understand that access to the world is something I fight for every day, because unlike the stairs that exclude the crippled, the barriers that exclude a woman with learning disabilities are unseen.

Searching for a language true to my experience, I turn to writers who challenge this kind of unquestioned cultural authority. Women writers like Audre Lorde, Toni Morrison, and Adrienne Rich have found a language for their self-awareness. Donna Williams' *Nobody Nowhere*, which describes her experience growing up with autism, was a special gift, a validation from someone who understands unseen difference on her own individual terms.

The language that I await, the language that will allow me to bridge the gap between my inner world and the world outside, is beginning to come. Being disabled is a different life experience. It is a unique perspective in a world where perception is often taken for granted.

8f

Sample Reflective Essay

Chapter 9

Expository Essays

When you write an expository essay, your purpose is to explain something. Your subject might be a short story, an historical event, a current situation, a theory. To move beyond saying what your subject is to saying what it means, you need to use methods of development such as analysis, comparison, and definition. (For a reminder of these methods, see Chapter 5, Methods of Developing Paragraphs.) The meaning you see in your subject— your interpretation of it—serves as the thesis for your essay. Regardless of the subject of your expository essay— a work of art, an idea, or whatever—the steps in the process of formulating your thesis and organizing your material are the same.

9a Writing an Expository Essay

Step 1: Exploring Methods of Development

Some essay assignments state or imply a primary method of development (*Compare legislation governing impaired driving in Ontario and Quebec*). Others simply give a list of possible subjects (*native land claims*), leaving you to choose your focus. If a primary method of development is not given or implied, make notes on what each method could contribute to your essay.

You might begin work on an expository essay on child poverty, for example, by making the following list.

Method of Development	Possible Material
Analogy	Poverty is like a chronic and debilitating disease
Process Analysis	Not applicable
Systems Analysis	How agencies dealing with the needs of poor children fit into the system of social services
Causal Analysis	What causes poverty among children
	How poverty affects children's short-term and long-term development

100

	How poverty among children affects society as a whole
Classification	Child poverty by region
	Child poverty by types of households
Comparison	Differences in the development of impoverished children and middle-class children
	Child poverty in Mexico and Canada
Definition	Meaning of poverty
Description	Typical living conditions of poor children
Evaluation	Good and bad points about programs designed to assist poor children
Narration	Stories about children who visit food banks
	A day in the life of a poor child

Step 2: Choosing a Focus and Primary Method of Development

From a list of possibilities such as that given above, you need to choose a focus for your essay. If you are writing for a newspaper or a magazine, you can let your own interests and your assumptions about the interests of your readers guide your choice of a primary method of development. Suppose you were writing on child poverty for *Châtelaine*. Your reader profile might suggest that most of its readers were middle-class women with children. To appeal to their interests, you might decide to focus on differences in the development of middle-class children and impoverished children. Your primary method of development would therefore be comparison.

When you are writing an essay for a course, on the other hand, you are likely to choose a focus that reflects the concerns, objectives, or methodology of that field of study. Sociologists, for example, study the relationships between groups and society as a whole. For a sociology course, you might focus on what causes child poverty or how child welfare agencies fit into the system of social services. For these topics, analysis would be your primary method of development.

Step 3: Gathering Material

There are many sources of material for expository essays. Brainstorming, however, will often give you enough information for expository essays based on your own experience. From working in restaurants, for example, you could write an essay explaining why staff turnovers are rapid or why some restaurants

9a

Writing an Expository Essay

fail and others succeed. Asking systematic discovery questions may enable you to gather all the information you need (see Essays Analyzing Literature, 9c; Essays Analyzing Nonfiction, 9e).

But sometimes you may have to gather information from other sources. You can conduct interviews (10a) and other types of field research for material on subjects of local interest. And of course there's always the library (see Conducting Computer-Aided Research, 12b).

However you gather material, keep your focus and method of development in mind. They will help you decide what information is relevant to your essay.

Step 4: Formulating a Thesis

Once you have gathered various bits of information, you need to ask yourself what they add up to. This process of synthesizing your material will lead you to a main idea, a thesis. A good thesis for an expository essay should **explain** some aspect of your subject: why one definition of a controversial term is better than another; how the setting in a short story contributes to the theme; what causes abusive relationships among family members. It should state an opinion about your subject and give reasons that set the limits of your discussion. A statement such as *Poverty has many effects on children* does neither. It doesn't say whether the effects are good or bad, so it offers no opinion; it doesn't name any effects, so it doesn't limit the discussion. In contrast, this thesis states an opinion and clearly defines the scope of the essay: *Poverty stunts children's physical, emotional, and intellectual development, damaging both the individual children and the society in which they live.*

Step 5: Including Other Methods of Development

You can often write your first draft using only your primary method of development. When you revise, however, you may discover that to explain the meaning of your subject clearly and fully, you need to add definitions of terms (*poverty, adequate nutrition*), comparisons (*rates of language development in middle-class children and poor children*), or other material. Incorporate these secondary methods of development, as you need to, into appropriate sections of your essay.

Step 6: Organizing Your Essay

Expository essays written for college and university courses are usually organized with the thesis up front in the introduction, topic sentences showing how each middle paragraph relates to the thesis, and a restatement and extension of the thesis in the conclusion. This method of organization offers your instructor a well-defined framework and emphasizes what he or she is most interested in—your interpretation.

If you are writing in a different situation or for a different type of reader, you may want to consider leading readers through your explanation before you state your thesis in the conclusion. This method is often an effective way of presenting unfamiliar or controversial material. (For more information on both these methods of organization, see Chapter 7, Essay Structure.)

Let's consider the choices facing the writer of the sample expository essay, "The Effects of Child Poverty." This piece, based on interviews and first-hand observation, was intended for readers of a local newspaper. Since many readers would not have any direct experience of poverty and thus might not understand its grim realities, the writer begins with facts and details that lead gradually to the thesis.

9b Sample Expository Essay

The Effects of Child Poverty

Jimmy is a two-year-old living with his mother and baby sister in government-subsidized housing. The complex is reasonably well maintained if you ignore the rusting shopping carts abandoned here and there and the mattresses soaking up rain in the disposals. Today is a good day at Jimmy's place because there is food in the fridge. A week from now the fridge will be empty and it will be ten days before the child tax credit comes through. It is now about two o'clock and Jimmy has been staring at the soaps for three hours. His mother feels she should turn off the television and take him to the playground, but he outgrew his rain boots a couple of months ago. Not that the playground offers much for him to do: two of the three swings are broken, the slide is gritty, and the sand around it is pebbled with shards of broken beer bottles. The local library has plenty

103

of books for children, but it's a kilometre away and his mother has no money for bus fare. The relief day care centre is closer and it has other children for him to play with, but his mother is reluctant to take his sister there because she has run out of baby food and does not want anyone to know.

Jimmy's situation helps to define child poverty in Canada. The problem is not just that Jimmy is missing out on the extras. His family fits the federal government's definition of poverty: more than half his mother's monthly income is spent on food, shelter, and clothing. Even so, the children are poorly clothed and fed. Because most poor children in Canada live in single-parent families headed by women, Jimmy's situation is fairly typical. How is poverty affecting Jimmy? How does poverty affect all children? How does poverty affect our society?

Let's begin with the basic physical needs for shelter, clothing, and food. Jimmy's need for shelter has been met by the subsidized housing his mother was lucky to get. The reduction in rent does not, however, give her more money to spend on food and clothing. The amount of the subsidy is just subtracted from her welfare cheque. At two, Jimmy doesn't worry about designer labels, but his mother worries about replacing the rainboots and snowsuit he's outgrown. Without appropriate clothing, Jimmy won't be able to attend a play group when he turns three. Jimmy's opportunities are thus limited by a scarcity of clothing.

Meanwhile, what happens if Jimmy doesn't get enough to eat? Like any toddler (a child between one and three), Jimmy needs 4-5 servings of grain products, 4-5 servings of vegetables and fruits, 2 servings of meat or meat alternatives, and 3 servings of milk products every day. Of course, these servings are quite small (half an apple, one third of a cup of dry cereal), but a child needs food from all the food groups every day. Unlike adults, who can cope reasonably well with periodic food shortages, a child deprived of food will be stunted both physically and intellectually. After a week of crackers and bargain macaroni dinners, Jimmy is lethargic,

uninterested in his toys, and only too willing to
park himself in front of the television. He falls
asleep when his mother tries to read to him. At two,
going on three, most children can understand complex
sentences and repeat simple ones. If they've been
read to, they can identify a picture of an elephant
or a farm. The effects of Jimmy's nutritional deficiencies show up in his inability to talk in sentences and the limitations in his vocabulary. He
can't identify a picture of a horse or pick out a
red crayon. The widening gap between what Jimmy
knows and what other children his age know means
that he's likely to do poorly in grade one, thus
setting in motion a cycle of failure, discourage-
ment, and a sense of inferiority that creates
aggression and despair in an adult.

Like any child, Jimmy has emotional needs as well
as physical needs. He needs intellectual stimula-
tion, affection, attention, and freedom from intimi-
dation. Of course, poverty itself does not
necessarily create deficiencies in meeting a child's
emotional and intellectual needs, nor does an adequate income prevent children from being neglected
and beaten. But parents with more money are more
likely to provide their offspring with music
lessons, swimming lessons, and camping trips: all
the opportunities to develop a talent and learn new
physical and social skills that Jimmy will miss because his mother can't afford them. The absence of
these recreational interests limits any child's
life, but as children like Jimmy grow up, the
effects of poverty spread far beyond the individual.

Children who are tired, cold, and hungry can't
learn much. Schools are increasingly called upon to
provide children with a place to sleep, warm clothing, and food. In some schools, teachers spend much
of their time trying to meet children's physical
needs. Moreover, many children like Jimmy succeed in
school only if they get extra instruction. But as
schools try to do more with less money, helping some
children often means depriving others. In Jimmy's
neighbourhood school, funding for a teacher's aide

*Sample
Expository
Essay*

was taken from money originally earmarked for library materials. As a result of the poverty of some children, educational opportunities for all children decline.

The broader effects of poverty are also visible in the current strains on the health care system. For example, inadequate nutrition for expectant mothers often results in low birth-weight babies. Research studies indicate that such babies not only need more hospital care at birth; they may also need more hospital care as adults. In a low birth-weight baby, organs such as the liver may not be fully functioning. The baby with the under-developed liver is more likely to need a coronary bypass as a middle-aged adult. Expensive, high-tech procedures that drive up health care costs are thus, in part, the effect of a diet of crackers and macaroni.

The costs of poverty extend far beyond welfare cheques and rent subsidies. Poverty creates a cycle of deprivation, failure, and despair. Children raised in poverty are more likely to become part of a permanent underclass of people who no longer believe they can break out of the poverty cycle. The effects of poverty, however, are not confined to the poor. Limitations in education and health care decrease the quality of life available to all citizens.

9c Essays Analyzing Literature

Purpose and Audience

When you write an essay on a piece of literature, your purpose is not to describe its content but to explain some part of its meaning. From reading the piece carefully, you develop a general sense of its major themes, such as the theme "character is fate" that runs through Thomas Hardy's novels. Then you analyze the work, or a portion of it, such as a scene of a play or the setting of a novel, by asking questions like those below. As a result of this analysis, you can refine your sense of theme and show how you arrived at your interpretation.

Since you are writing primarily for an instructor familiar with the work, you may be unsure of how much to say. You don't need to provide all the details you would for someone who had never read it, but you do need to use quotations and examples to show how you arrived at your interpretation. Instead of summarizing the plot, for example, you might explain how events bring about a character's triumph or defeat, or explain what one event reveals about a particular character. Because readers interpret works of literature differently, your interpretation will be convincing only if you support it with evidence.

Analyzing Literature

When you analyze imaginative works of literature, you concentrate on their aesthetic qualities and moral implications. When you analyze works of nonfiction, such as essays, research articles, and proposals, you may focus more on the validity of the arguments they present. You will find suggestions about how to analyze expository and persuasive nonfiction in Essays Analyzing Nonfiction (9e).

You can write a more effective essay on imaginative works by following these steps.

1. Decide on a focus and a method of development.
Most assignments in introductory literature courses give you a focus. You may be asked to explain how one or more elements, such as the setting, characterization, or title, relate to the theme of the work as a whole. The method of development for this type of literary criticism is **analysis**, the division of something into its parts in order to explain the whole more clearly. For example, you might analyze the structure and imagery of a poem to explain how they contribute to the theme.

In addition to analysis, some topics require **comparison:** *Compare the theme of initiation in stories X and Y.* Other topics will ask you to assess the strengths and weaknesses of a work: *Which film version of* Macbeth *presents a better interpretation of the thematic implications of Lady Macbeth's madness?* For this topic, in addition to analysis and comparison, you would use **evaluation** as a method to develop your ideas.

Topics like these provide specific directions about what to focus on and how to develop your ideas. If your topic is more general, such as *Discuss three poems by Margaret Atwood,* use the discovery questions below to help you find a focus.

9c

Essays
Analyzing
Literature

2. Analyze the relevant element(s) or section(s) of the work.
Use the discovery questions for imaginative literature given in the next section as a guide.

3. Formulate a thesis.
The thesis should make a point about the theme of the work and about how each element you have analyzed conveys that theme. Be sure that you have not merely restated the essay topic (for example, *This essay will analyze the use of landscape in a poem by Margaret Atwood*) or made a vague generalization (*Many poets use landscape to express a theme and mood in their poetry*). To direct your reader's attention to a specific use of landscape and thus to limit the content of the essay, you would need a thesis such as this one: *In Margaret Atwood's poem "Journey to the Interior," landscape depicts the struggle against depression.*

4. Organize your essay.
In your introduction, give the authors and titles of all the works you plan to discuss and establish the *content* of your essay. Put your thesis at the end of your introduction.

In the body of your essay keep your reader's attention focused on your subject by beginning each paragraph with a topic sentence that identifies one aspect of your subject. If you were writing an essay on colour symbolism in *The Great Gatsby*, for instance, each middle paragraph might begin with a topic sentence that stated the significance of a particular colour in the novel.

White symbolizes Daisy's empty life and the dream Gatsby associates with her.

Throughout the novel, gold symbolizes money.

Red suggests both the glittering wealth of rubies and the blood of harsh reality.

Good topic sentences focus your reader's attention on the function of an element.

NOT	This poem has five stanzas. [descriptive summary]
NOT	In the first stanza, the speaker talks about... [narrative summary]
BUT	Each stanza of the poem represents a different stage of life. [analysis]

Give reasons, details, examples, and/or quotations to support each interpretative point that you make in your middle paragraphs. Be sure to link the point and the supporting evidence clearly.

In your conclusion, restate your thesis and summarize your most important points. If appropriate, suggest a broader context into which your interpretation fits (*The distrust of conventional values that we have seen is typical of the postwar period*).

Discovery Questions: Imaginative Literature

Use these questions to guide your analysis of imaginative works.

Subject: What is this work about?

Genre: What kind of work is this (descriptive essay, revenge tragedy, dramatic monologue)? What are the characteristics of this genre?

Setting: What is the time, place, and social environment in which the work is set? (Alice Munro's *Lives of Girls and Women* is set among the working poor in rural Ontario in the late 1940s and 1950s.) What effect does the setting have on characters' lives? What values are associated with different times, places, or social environments? In drama and film, what do costumes, lighting, sets, and music contribute to the setting?

Plot: What sets the plot in motion? What are the main events? Does the plot reach a crisis (the point of greatest tension)? How are the conflicts resolved? Is there more than one plot? How are events arranged (chronologically, shifting from present to past, shifting from plot to subplots)? What is the underlying purpose that connects the events (a spiritual quest, a critique of society, a revelation of the main character's true nature)? What do we learn about the world through the plot?

Characterization: What are the characters like? Is there a broad range of characters? How would you classify them? Are the characters given depth and complexity or are they stereotypes? What techniques are used to portray them (appearance, characteristic actions, speech, opinions of others, self-revelation)? Do characters change? What do we learn about the workings of race, class, gender or other factors from the way characters live their lives?

Narrative Perspective in Fiction: Is the narrator a participant in the short story or novel, referring to himself or herself as "I"? Is this first-person narrator telling a story about his or her experiences or a story about someone else? How reliable is this narrator? What factors might impede his or her ability or desire to tell the truth? What do we learn about the nature of truth from the way the narrator tells the story?

Is the narrator a non-participant in the short story or novel, referring to the characters as *he, she or they*? Does the narrator focus on the consciousness of just one character? Is the narrator omniscient, seeing into the minds of all the characters? Does the narrator comment directly on the characters? What do we learn about the nature of truth from the way the narrator tells the story?

Style (Diction and Sentence Structure): What are the effects of language level (formal, standard, informal) and word choice? Are there any unusual or especially effective words? In poetry, what effects are achieved through the sounds of words? How does word choice contribute to the characterization, setting, and theme? What are the effects of sentence patterns? Does the writer favour long, complex sentences or short, simple ones? Are sentence fragments used to create emphasis, excitement, informality? Is parallelism used distinctively? (For more information on the effects of variations in sentence structure, see Improving Your Sentence Structure, 16e). In poetry, how are lines and stanzas used? In films and plays, what are the effects of the pacing of dialogue and action? How do these elements of language contribute to characterization, setting, and theme?

Style (Imagery and Symbolism): Does the writer use any significant figures of speech (similes, metaphors, personification)? (For more information on figurative language, see Adding Interest, 16d). Do images and symbols create patterns of meaning? How do imagery and symbolism contribute to the characterization, setting, and theme?

Theme: What is the central idea of the work?

Integrating Secondary Sources

If you wish to integrate other critics' interpretations into your essay, you will find help in Integrating Research Material (12e) and in the sample literary research paper, "*Tom Sawyer* and *Anne of Green Gables:* Two Models of Heroism" (12f). For information on how to cite your sources, see Appendix B, Documentation.

9d Sample Essay Analyzing Literature

The following sample essay illustrates the type of analysis and essay structure outlined above. In it, the writer shows how characterization conveys the theme of self-deception.

The Theme of Deception in Alice Munro's "The Office"
by Patricia McManus

The theme of deception is central to the impact of the short story "The Office," by Alice Munro. This theme is explored on three distinct levels to portray those facets of the two main characters that contribute significantly to the outcome. While the effects of deception are different in the two characters, deception at all three levels is present in both the narrator and Mr. Malley. Both lie to the world in general, to themselves, and to each other. Both use fantasy and self-deception to hide their own inadequacies.

We see the first level of deception in the story, the lies exchanged between the individual and the world around him or her, in the false images both the narrator and Mr. Malley present of themselves. For the narrator, this level of deception is indicated in the opening pages of the story by her lengthy deliberations about whether she deserves an office. To tell others that she is a writer brings "the delicate moment of exposure" and "humiliation" (263); to tell her husband that she wants an office seems "too improper a wish to be granted" (265). Self-doubt, false modesty, and guilt assail her. Society has not actually convinced her not to write, but the socialization process has given her many misgivings about it: "A woman who sits staring into space, into a country that is not her husband's or her children's, is known to be an offense against nature" (264). When asked what she will do in the office, she says she is a stenographer. We are given a more indirect image of the lies Mr. Malley tells through the description of his surroundings: the contrast between the portrait on the wall of a "prosperous, rosy, agreeable" man and Mrs. Malley, whose appearance speaks of "a life spent in close attention on a man who is by turns vigorous, crotchety, and dependent" (265). These are, in fact, the characteristics Mr. Malley turns out to have in the story.

The second level of deception Munro uses is that of lies exchanged between individuals and themselves, lies designed to provide the self-esteem neither character can provide otherwise. We see that the narrator is lying to herself at the outset of the story when she decides that an office will give her a sense of "purposefulness and importance" and "dignity and peace" (264); in fact, only she can give these feelings to herself. Mr. Malley's delusions about the chiropractor and the narrator are a more disturbing variety of self-deception. He suggests that the doctor has had sexual relations with at least one of his female patients and assumes that information about illicit sex would be of particular interest to a writer (270). Like the lies the narrator tells herself, Mr. Malley's self-deceptions are designed to supply the self-esteem he can't provide within himself. Both act out fantasies to sustain their beliefs about themselves. The writer takes an office to convince herself she is worth taking seriously; Mr. Malley fabricates a noxious fault in every other person to convince himself the shortcomings are in their personalities, not his.

But fantasies, unless they are peculiarly compatible, operate best in isolation from each other. The fantasies of the narrator and Mr. Malley are bound to collide in the third level of deception, the lies individuals tell each other. The privacy, respectability, and dignity that the narrator seeks in her office have no place in the life of a lonely failure of a man who wants to chat. And Mr. Malley's need to expand his pitifully dreary world doesn't allow for her to be indifferent to him. As a result, they trade lies with each other in order to continue their fantasies. The narrator's lies to Mr. Malley

112

are designed to placate or avoid him in the hope of regaining her privacy: "I know now that I must avoid hurting him for my own sake, not for his" (270). He, in turn, uses gifts and apologies to arouse her guilt and gain continued access to her company: "I thanked him. There was nothing else I could do, and I had the unpleasant feeling that beneath his offering of gifts and apologies he was well aware of this and in some way gratified by it" (269).

When the mutually unsatisfactory relationship between the narrator and Mr. Malley deteriorates so much that the narrator tiptoes up the stairs and locks the office door and Mr. Malley creates bizarre accusatory notes, the two characters are in a battle for the survival of their fantasies. But Mr. Malley's delusions outweigh the narrator's; he needs them more, and he has fought for their survival before: "His life was a series of calamities . . . he had been let down by people he had trusted… betrayed by the very friends to whom he had given kindness and material help" (270). A grafittied washroom definitively deprives the narrator of her office, her sanctuary from her own self-doubts. She is even deprived of her anger by Mrs. Malley's "practical and resigned" (275) participation in her departure. Instead, an "absorbing depression" (275) leaves the narrator questioning her "right to be rid of him" (275).

While there may be no doubt in the reader's mind about who has been victimized in "The Office," Munro has drawn inescapable parallels between the narrator's deceptions and Mr. Malley's. Neither has successfully come to terms with who he or she is; thus they both present a false image of themselves to the outside world. Both use fantasy to create feelings they can't provide for themselves; thus they lie to themselves. Both lie in the vain hope of getting what they want; they lie to each other. These three levels of deception in the characters' lives evolve to an outcome that is satisfactory to neither of them.

9d

*Sample
Essay
Analyzing
Literature*

Work Cited

Munro, Alice. "The Office." *Dance of the Happy Shades and Other Stories.* New York: McGraw, 1968. 59-74.

9e Essays Analyzing Nonfiction

Essays and other kinds of nonfiction, as we have seen, serve a variety of purposes, such as sharing personal experiences, presenting arguments, and providing explanations. There are also many ways of responding to nonfiction writing. You can share the feelings and reflections it evokes in you. You can agree or disagree with the views expressed (see Position Papers, 11d). Or you can analyze its rhetorical strategies.

Unlike imaginative literature, nonfiction claims to tell a truth (if not *the* truth) about the actual world. This is its main point, or thesis. To make this point convincing, the writer uses various **rhetorical strategies.** These strategies, according to Aristotle, consist of **logical appeals** (reasons and evidence), **emotional appeals** (to shared values and prejudices), and **appeals to ethos** (personal qualities of the writer, as projected in the writing; we will use the term "self-presentation").

In this section, you will find out how to write an essay analyzing a piece of nonfiction, using these three main categories.

Analyzing Nonfiction

Here are the steps to follow in preparing to write an essay analyzing a piece of nonfiction.

1. Identify the purpose and intended audience of the piece.
When was it written? Does it address an issue current at the time, if not now? Where was it published? Does the publication have a widely recognized bias (political, religious)? What do you know about the author's qualifications and/or views?

2. Outline the thesis and main points.
See Summaries (10c) for pointers.

3. Analyze the author's rhetorical strategies.
Use the list of discovery questions for nonfiction given later in this chapter.

4. Group the rhetorical strategies into strengths and weaknesses.

5. Formulate a thesis.

Decide what the most important strengths and weaknesses of the piece are and use this evaluation as the basis for your thesis.

> Although Suzuki makes strong emotional appeals to those concerned about the environment, in this piece he gives little evidence to support his argument that . . .

6. Organize your essay.

In the **introduction**, use your notes about the purpose and audience of the piece to provide a context for your thesis. Summarize the piece briefly before you begin your analysis. In each topic sentence, make a point about some aspect of the author's logic, emotional appeals, or self-presentation. Your conclusion should sum up the strengths and weaknesses of the piece.

Discovery Questions: Nonfiction

Use these questions to guide your analysis of nonfiction pieces.

Logical Appeals

These questions test the validity of the author's reasoning and evidence.

- Is it factually true? You can't, of course, verify every statement an author makes, but sometimes your knowledge of the subject or your common sense will lead you to question an assertion such as this:

  > Without the convenience of advertising, no large cities could exist.

- Does it assume the truth of a point that needs to be argued?

  > Women are more nurturing than men. Therefore...

- Does it trivialize or distort opposing points of view?

  > Those who oppose commercial developments in national parks just don't want their favourite views spoiled.

- Does it oversimplify an issue by reducing it to two extreme alternatives?

  > Either we must be willing to sink any foreign ship that enters Arctic waters without permission, or we must give up all claim to sovereignty over the North.

- Does it make sweeping generalizations that are difficult to prove or disprove?

  Throughout history humans have always yearned for adventure. *Casablanca* is the best movie ever made.

  Society forces women and men into social roles that may not fit.

- Do all the points support the thesis? Have important points been omitted?

- Are key terms defined?

- Are faulty causal connections made? Watch for these problems with causal reasoning: (1) claiming that what is true in some instances is true in all instances; (2) claiming that something happening after an event has been caused by it, when there may be no causal relation; (3) claiming a single cause or effect of something that may have multiple causes or effects. The following example illustrates all three of these problems.

  Some students who work part-time fail a course. Therefore, working part-time makes students fail courses.

- Are causes and effects actual or hypothetical? Do predicted effects seem exaggerated or unlikely?

- Are other points of view dealt with fairly? distorted? ignored?

Evidence

- Are facts and figures accurate, up to date, and taken from reliable sources? Are they used appropriately?

- Are authorities cited within their field of expertise? Do quotations support the point being made?

- Are examples actual or hypothetical? Are they sufficiently representative? Are they appropriate?

- Are comparisons made using the same basis of comparison?

  An article comparing major world cities would be suspect if it made a comparison between crime in New York and night life in London.

- Is the evidence sufficient to support the points made? Is it taken from reliable sources? Is it biased?

Emotional Appeals
These questions help you define the author's values and attitudes.

- Does the writer appeal to values he or she assumes readers to share (democracy, patriotism, family values, generosity, concern for the environment)?

- Does the writer make personal attacks on those who hold different opinions, or appeal to readers' prejudices against certain groups?

- What attitude towards the subject (anger, nostalgia, self-righteousness, concern) does the writer convey through choices in diction, sentence structure, and other stylistic devices? What use, if any, does the writer make of humour, wit, irony?

- Are emotional appeals appropriate to the purpose and audience?

Self-Presentation of the Writer
These questions help you identify the self-image the writer creates in the piece.

- What image of himself or herself does the writer project through choice of subject, methods of reasoning, and use of evidence? For example, the author of an article on RRSPs may present herself as a woman knowledgeable about economic issues, who favours conservative measures over risk-taking.

- What relationship with the reader does the writer establish through direct comments, choice of personal pronouns, or emotional appeals? For example, the author of the article on RRSPs might try to put herself on an equal footing with readers by describing her own difficulty in making financial decisions, using "I," and appealing to readers' desire for security and stability.

- How does the author's personality, as revealed in the piece, affect your response?

To illustrate how to analyze the argument presented in a work of nonfiction, we will examine a newspaper column written by Satya Das (*Edmonton Journal*, June 19, 1995: A8). Here is the article, slightly condensed.

9e

Essays
Analyzing
Nonfiction

Social spending cuts not the only path to a balanced budget

by Satya Das

9e

Essays Analyzing Nonfiction

Why are you leftists so much in favor of deficits and debt?" the caller asked. "How can you defend that?"

The call, coming after a column arguing that Alberta's deficit problem was wrongly turned into a "crisis" for Ralph Klein's political gain, gave me a jolt.

Why on Earth is debt cast as a left-right split in the political spectrum? And why is it assumed that anyone on the left favors large deficits and debt? In fact, any study of economic history shows that a large level of public debt almost always favors the affluent who have money to lend, and has harmful effects on disadvantaged people.

Where the left and right differ might be on the causes of the public debt, and on solutions. But can any thinking person seriously argue that a large and growing level of public debt is in any way acceptable?

Before the caller hung up, I tried to point out that I'm hardly a leftist. I have always found political labels to be awfully constricting. I have socialist friends who think I'm right-wing, and friends among Klein's backers who think I'm left-wing. I like to believe—and it may be a deluded belief—that I write from a common-sense perspective.

Perhaps not common sense in the mould of Ontario's new premier Mike Harris, but common enough and sensible enough in any case.

Anyway, from what passes for common sense in my world, it is clear to see that large deficits and debt offer more opportunities for the powerful to benefit at the expense of the powerless.

Take a fundamental example from the chronic budget deficits of the United States. The U.S., despite much talk of cutting spending, continues to run deficits in the order of $100 billion to $200 billion a year. What causes the deficit? Two factors. One is the desire to have the lowest rate of personal and corporate taxation among major industrial economies. The other is [the desire] to spend more money than the taxes bring in.

Any talk of raising taxes is akin to political suicide. So the alternative is spending cuts. And in this, U.S. politicians take the easy way out. They attack spending meant to help the weak and powerless. The size of the deficit becomes a reason to take the most meagre advantage away from the poor, while the need to borrow money helps those with money to lend—usually the rich...

"Yet if it wanted to, the U.S. government could balance the budget tomorrow, by cutting military spending in half. The U.S. military expenditure, in the order of $300 billion a year, sustains an armed force capable of dominating the world. Yet that's not what it's used for. Politicians say time and again that the military is to defend the U.S. and U.S. national interest abroad. Yet it is far too large and powerful for that purpose alone.

So why isn't spending cut? Because it would upset too many vested interests, too many influential and powerful lobbies. It is so much easier to pick on the powerless and defenceless. Some of that attitude spills over into Canada.

Too often, our politicians say that health care, education and social programs are too expensive. These programs are unaffordable, they say, because of large deficits and debts. That's even said in Alberta, where Premier Klein is salting away a hefty surplus.

But before people go along with the clamor for cuts, shouldn't they ask what caused the debt? And whether the debt can best be addressed by fixing the problems that are at the root of it? It takes a limited perspective indeed to argue that social programs are the cause of deficit and debt. Government overspending, such as it is, has not been limited to those areas.

The biggest source of deficit and debt, in Alberta and Canada, has been government interference in what is supposed to be a free-market economy. Rather than taxing the fruits of the free market—collecting a form of economic rent, as it were—governments have become involved, directly and indirectly, in trying to play on the turf of the private sector.

A quarter century ago, New Democrat leader Stephen Lewis spoke of the "corporate welfare bums" who were living high off taxpayers' money. Some of that history needs to be looked at, to understand debts and deficit.

Since the Second World War, Canada has had a string of federal and provincial governments that have gone out of their way to offer grants, incentives, and special benefits to companies that operate in a supposedly free-market economy. A simple change, like ending special tax incentives for business, would bring in enough revenue to virtually balance the federal budget. The budget could be balanced even without ending job-creation grants, loan guarantees, direct investments, guarantees of profitability.

Yet it is services for the needy that are held to blame for deficits. A truly progressive income tax system is no longer talked about. Taxes on the middle class are stretched to the limit, to the point where most salaried Canadians quite rightly feel that they cannot pay any more in taxes.

Yet in the past decade, tax rates for the most affluent Canadians have come down sharply. This trend seems conveniently forgotten, in the haste to cut social programs on the road to a balanced budget. Surely it's time to take a balanced view. People who want to preserve health care, education and help for the needy aren't necessarily in favor of deficits and debt. They only refuse to accept that cutting social spending is the only way to balance a budget.

Sample Analysis of Das's Article

Purpose: to persuade.

Audience: newspaper readers in Alberta.

Context: Published in *Edmonton Journal*, which has been critical of Premier Klein's budget cuts, soon after Ontario election. Das is an editorial writer for the paper.

Summary: Das argues that large government debts and deficits provide the wealthy with opportunities for making money, while hurting the disadvantaged. He cites recent U.S. deficits as an example. In the U.S., where low personal and corporate taxes and overspending have created huge annual deficits, politicians refuse to raise taxes, because to do so would be "political suicide," or to cut military spending substantially, because of "vested interests" and "powerful lobbies." Instead, politicians cut social programs. According to Das, Canada is following the U.S. example. Although Canadian politicians say that health care, education, and social programs are no longer affordable, they ignore the biggest source of deficits and debts: tax incentives and other measures designed to aid business. If federal and provincial governments ended these special incentives and raised personal taxes for wealthy Canadians, they could balance current budgets and reduce accumulated debts without cutting social spending.

Logical Appeals

Thesis and Main Points:

–treats his thesis as point to be argued, not as obviously true

–though he claims to be looking for balance, he implies that there are only two ways to balance the budget: by cutting social programs or by raising corporate and personal taxes

–tends to make broad claims rather than carefully argued case: "any study of economic history shows that... "

Relation Between Thesis and Main Points:

–points support thesis

–does not define "deficit" (annual amount by which spending exceeds revenues) and "debt" (accumulated annual deficits)

–no problems with causal reasoning, except that Das does not consider how raising corporate taxes would affect the economy as a whole

–indicates his disagreement with what "our politicians" say; recognizes that "salaried Canadians" cannot pay any more in taxes

Evidence:

–facts and figures regarding U.S. deficits and military spending, no source given (matter of public record)

–authorities: unnamed economic historians; NDP leader Stephen Lewis. Citing Lewis's reference to "corporate welfare bums" is an emotional appeal rather than a logical argument.

–example (U.S. deficits show benefits to wealthy) is appropriate, but rather unspecific

–comparison to Canada valid

–evidence probably sufficient for "common-sense" reader, but not for sceptical or hostile reader

Emotional Appeals

–appeal to values: "common sense," concern for social justice

–appeal to prejudices: against the U.S.; politicians; "corporate welfare bums"; implicit attack on Klein for "salting away a hefty surplus" (attack on policy, not personal attack)

–uses slanted language to convey sympathy for the disadvantaged, moral indignation towards politicians

Self-Presentation

–a sensible, friendly, thoughtful person who has some knowledge of economic history but doesn't speak as an expert

–establishes equal relationship with reader through anecdote about his caller, suggesting he may be "deluded" about "writing from a common-sense perspective," asking rhetorical questions

If you synthesized the strengths and weaknesses suggested by this analysis, you might come up with a thesis like this for your essay:

> *Although Das does not use a great deal of evidence to support his view that cutting social spending is not the only way to reduce government debt, his emotional appeals and self-presentation make his argument effective for the "common-sense" readers he is addressing.*

Here is the final essay analyzing Das's article.

9f

Sample Essay Analyzing Nonfiction

9f Sample Essay Analyzing Nonfiction

Canada's ongoing debate over government cutbacks is reflected in a recent *Edmonton Journal* column by editorial writer Satya Das ("Social spending cuts not the only path to a balanced budget," June 19,

1995: A8). Das does not use a great deal of evidence to support his view that raising taxes is a better means of reducing government deficits than cutting amounts spent on social programs. Nevertheless, his emotional appeals and self-presentation make his argument effective for the "common-sense" readers he is addressing.

Das argues that large government debts and deficits provide the wealthy with opportunities for making money, while hurting the disadvantaged. In the U.S., where low personal and corporate taxes and government overspending have created huge annual deficits, politicians refuse to raise taxes because to do so would be "political suicide." They also refuse to cut military spending substantially because of "vested interests" and "powerful lobbies." Instead, politicians cut social programs designed to help the disadvantaged. According to Das, Canada is following the U.S. example. Canadian politicians say that health care, education, and social programs are no longer affordable, but they ignore the biggest source of deficits and debts: tax incentives and other measures designed to aid business. If federal and provincial governments ended these special incentives and raised personal taxes for wealthy Canadians, he argues, they could balance current budgets and reduce accumulated debts without cutting social spending.

Although his chain of reasoning seems logical, Das oversimplifies the issue and gives little evidence to support his points. He presents an "either-or" position: Canadian budgets can be balanced either by cutting social programs (as governments are doing) or by raising taxes (as he recommends). He does not consider the possibility of doing both. Nor does he consider the effect of raising corporate taxes on the economy as a whole, despite the fact that consumers are the ones who will ultimately pay these taxes—through increased costs for goods and services, if not through cuts in wages or layoffs. He makes broad claims about the effects of large debts and deficits ("… any study of economic history shows that a large level of public debt almost always favors the affluent who have money to lend, and has harmful effects on disadvantaged people"), but uses only one example, that of current U.S. policy, to support his point. Even in using this example, Das makes vague references to the "vested interests" and "powerful lobbies" that prevent cuts to military spending; by implication, they represent the "affluent." But unions concerned about jobs can also function as "powerful lobbies."

The strengths of Das's column are its emotional appeals for social justice and the trust it creates between writer and reader. By presenting politicians and the affluent who profit from government policies as bullies who "pick on the powerless and defenceless," Das appeals to readers' concern for the underdog. His proposals promise to reduce the inequalities between rich and poor without raising the taxes of the middle class. His call for a "balanced view" would thus appeal to middle-class voters who are concerned about the debt and deficit but don't want their taxes raised.

Das's argument seems particularly persuasive because of the trouble he takes at the beginning of the column to establish himself as "common-sensical." By reporting his conversation with his caller, Das can position himself as neither right-wing nor left-wing, but like every other "thinking person" (and his readers are of course thinking people) who finds the current level of debt unacceptable. The many rhetorical questions further engage readers in dialogue with this responsible citizen who is concerned that his country is picking up bad habits from its neighbour.

Read from a sceptical or hostile point of view, Das's argument may seem unconvincing because it presents little detailed evidence in support of its broad claims. But by simplifying the issue of controlling government debts and deficits to one of big guys versus little guys, Das appeals to readers' sense of social justice. And because he presents himself as a responsible and likable person, readers are more easily persuaded to accept both him and his views.

*Sample
Essay
Analyzing
Nonfiction*

Chapter 10

Other Types of Expository Writing

10a Interviews

Conducting an interview, or a series of interviews, is often the best way to obtain information about local people, issues, and events. When you are writing an expository essay, interviews can provide additional information and create interest. If you were writing an essay on the Cree Circle Dance for an anthropology class, for instance, you might supplement your reading by arranging to interview participants, spectators, and Cree elders about its significance. Interviews are also interesting as self-contained pieces of writing because they allow readers to enter into another person's world.

Conducting a good interview takes planning. Here are some guidelines.

Preparing for the Interview

1. ***Choose your informant carefully.*** The most obvious choice is not always the best one. The drummer in a band, for instance, may have shrewder insights into the band's strengths and weaknesses than the lead singer. If possible, ask someone knowledgeable about your subject for names of people who would make good informants.

2. ***Make a list of questions that will give you the information you need.*** To help you both relax, start the interview with straightforward questions you already know the answer to. Limit your list to a small number of topics that will allow you to shape your material to suit your purpose. Separate key questions with less relevant ones, so that you can finish your notes on important points while your informant answers the next question. Finally, avoid asking questions that can be

answered yes or no. Instead, ask open-ended questions that invite full responses: "How do you see the band developing over the next few years?"

3. **Decide whether to take notes or to tape record the interview.** Your choice will depend on how comfortable you and your informant feel with each method and how you plan to use the material. Transcribing an interview is quite time-consuming, so if you plan to use only a few direct quotes and paraphrase the rest of the material, taking notes should be sufficient. Tape the session if you want a lengthy first-hand account of the informant's experiences, or if you plan to present your material in a question-and-answer format. Taping is also wise if misquoting your informant could cause trouble. Test the equipment ahead of time so that you and your informant won't be distracted by technical problems.

4. **When you request an interview, identify yourself and your project.** Explain why the interview is important and how you will use the information. Give the person a sense of what you already know about the subject so that he or she will know how technical to be in response to your questions.

5. **Arrange a convenient time and place for the interview and suggest how long you think the interview will take.**

Conducting the Interview

1. Express appreciation for the interview.

2. Tell the person again how you will use the information, and assure him or her that confidential information will remain confidential.

3. Refer to your list of questions as necessary, but don't stick to it so rigidly that the interview becomes boring.

4. Ask your informant to clarify, expand upon, or give examples of points. Specific details bring interviews to life.

5. If you are taking notes, don't try to write down everything your informant says. Jot down facts and opinions as you would in taking notes for a course, using key words and ideas to

10a

Interviews

125

help you remember the context (and write up your notes before you forget!). Take down a few direct quotations to capture the informant's personality and point of view. Before you end the interview, review your notes with your informant to make sure they are accurate and complete.

6. If appropriate, jot down details of the person's appearance, actions, manner of speaking, and the place so that you can include them in your piece.

Writing Up the Interview

You can present interview material in a variety of ways: in a question-and-answer format; as an edited transcript; or as an essay combining quotations, paraphrased material, background information, and a character description. You are probably most familiar with the question-and-answer format. This form, which works like a dialogue between you and your informant, is effective when you want to ask probing questions about a series of topics. The edited transcript, in contrast, allows your informant to tell a story without interruption, with you providing an introduction. Using the third method, you can select and arrange your descriptions and interview material to emphasize points you want to make.

Here are some guidelines for writing up your interview.

1. Use only the material that best suits the purpose of the piece you are writing.

2. Combine material from different parts of the interview if doing so allows you to explain a point more fully.

3. You may edit direct quotations to eliminate repetition, correct obvious mistakes, and so forth, as long as you do not distort the meaning or lose the flavour of the original.

4. If you discover that you need to check facts or fill in missing information, make a list of questions and call your informant. Try to call only once.

After the interview, write a brief letter to the person you interviewed expressing your thanks. If possible, send the person a courtesy copy of the piece in which you used the information.

10b Sample Interview

The following piece illustrates an interview written in essay form.
It gives a vivid sense of its subject, a young immigrant from India.
See if you can figure out what questions the interviewer asked.

Conveniently Canadian

by Todd Babiak

"I guess the first thing I did was look at girls.
Right off the plane."

Bobby Mehra squints his eyes and smiles, head bob-
bing to the Pearl Jam song. As he thinks of something to say, he spies on the skater kids who are
crowded around the slushie machine.

"In India we didn't have that freedom. They say
you're too young for that. Man, back there when
you're fourteen, you don't even think about them,
let alone look at them, you know, sexually. You deny
a lot there. They say it's improper. Unless you're a
poverty kid. Not to brag or anything, but my dad had
a high job, eh. We were well off in India. We gave
up a lot to come here, but I prefer the freedom. Not
only to look at girls when you're fourteen, but
other freedoms too. You know."

Bobby is seventeen. Since arriving in Canada four
years ago, he has perfected his English, lost his
Hindi accent, and forgotten how to write his native
language. Every Saturday he works in the Mac's store
his parents operate. Along with his convenience
store shirt, he wears baggy green pants and Doc
Martens with a two-inch sole. Carefully constructed
sideburns highlight his amply gelled short hair.

"Here there is so much style. Back in India, the
only magazines we ever read were comic books. What
you look like is so important here. Another difference is the studies. Studies were way harder there.
When you're young, and you're good middle class, you
don't have parties, you don't drink, you don't smoke.
You have to be twenty-one there to buy a pack of
smokes, eh. I guess I still have a bit of that in me.
Peer pressure doesn't do anything to me, I've never
taken a drink in my life. I've been everywhere, all

the bars, but I don't drink. Basically, it's just so different to be young there. You don't get depressed about girls or working or money. You just work on your studies like crazy. Now I'm used to the Canadian way. I'm lazier."

Bobby turns up the radio when a U2 song comes on, his favourite group. As customers present him with bread, sour cream, super size Cokes and French Onion Sun Chips, he comments on the heat, the melting. *I can't believe how nice it is. Hope it stays this way.*

"My parents are the coolest people I know. I had my first girlfriend a year after I came here. They were like, *This is Canada.* My dad said, *You are completely independent, whatever you do you are still my son.* It's not like that with all brown kids. I mean I can't date a my-own-race girl. Once I tried. Basically, she was Muslim and we had to keep it a total secret. Not just because I'm Hindu but if you're from India, young girls don't date. She was pretty cool but we got nailed—her dad found out. It was awful. One thing about her I didn't like is that she was mad, disgusted, when she found out I'd had white girlfriends. She only dated brown guys. I hate that shit."

He replaces the coffee filters, checks prices on sour candies and wipes counters as he talks. He likes working. After he graduates from high school this summer, he plans to study Business Administration. He wants to work for a large corporation. Or a small bank. Two of his friends come in and they discuss tonight's plans. *A movie? This girl's party?*

"There's been a little bit of racial discrimination with my parents. I mean, my dad had a really high job in India. He comes here knowing English, with so much education, and he can't get an office job. Not even a file clerk. Everywhere he went, *you don't have any Canadian experience.* My dad would never call it discrimination, but… All I know is it makes no sense.

"There is racism. This one guy in grade 8 said something racist, he called me a racist name.

Basically I beat the shit out of him right in front
of the teacher and got suspended for three days. In
grade 10 I felt it a bit with a teacher. I'd never
been late, I had good grades and I wasn't a shit in
class. I'm late one day, by around eight minutes,
and she kicked me out. My white friends were late
all the time and she always let it go. I told her I
felt like she was being racist and she got really
mad. The principal got mad at me too. Oh well, I
felt it, you know."

He tends to a bevy of customers.

"This is a good one. I just remembered it. Don't
tell my father this one, don't tell him any of it.
He just doesn't like to hear it. One night me and my
buddies were in the McDonald's drive-through. And
the girl at the speaker said they were closing. She
asked us to tell the car behind us that they were
closed. So I lean my head out the window and tell
the guy behind us—a white guy in a taxi. About 25.
The guy got out of the cab and called me a Paki.
Said something like, *You should respect me more than
that, Paki*. So we didn't order, we backed up and
chased him. But we didn't get him. Don't tell my dad
this, right. We saw him again a few weeks later,
parked at the side of the street. Basically I asked
him, eh, you know, why did you say that. So he
starts to get out of the car, and he's putting on
gloves. So some of my friends, big guys, showed up
and he took off. I still hold anger against that,
against him, against racist people. I'm young, I
just want to go out there and finish it.

"Don't get me wrong. Most of my friends are white.
Everyone is equal. When that guy said those things
to me, it was my white friends who said, *let's get
him*. If I have a friend, I don't care what colour he
is. I'm Canadian.

"I love learning about other cultures too. In the
last few months I've been trying to get this Greek
girl, eh. So I'm learning about her culture. It's
great, you know. In India, there was so much religious tension. I was young but I remember the car
bombings, the little wars. So much fighting. Even at
school, with some kids whose parents taught them to
fight Muslims or whatever. It's much better here for

*Sample
Interview*

that. It's the exact reason my parents came here.
For my future. I understand now, too, that even if I
beat up that racist guy, it wouldn't fix anything.
He'd just hate me more, he'd hate brown people more.
He'd tell his family, his parents and eventually his
kids about hating Indians. I guess that doesn't
solve anything. I'm getting older. I'm not so young
and stupid anymore, you know."

10c Summaries

A summary is a brief statement of the main points or events of a longer work, with enough detail to explain those points or events for a particular purpose and audience. A government committee, for instance, might publish a twenty-page summary of its 200-page report on the fishing industry, whereas television listings give two-sentence plot summaries of the week's movies.

Although they may be called by other names—abstracts, précis, synopses, or briefs—summaries abound in school and work-related writing. We will illustrate two types: the plot summary and the summary of an article or a chapter of a book. You will find the principles of writing plot summaries useful when you write essays analyzing literature, reviews, and reports on publications. Knowing how to summarize articles and chapters of books will help you with many other types of assignments, such as preparing abstracts, compiling annotated bibliographies, and reviewing published material.

Plot Summaries

Most plot summaries are a paragraph or two in length, depending on the amount of detail appropriate for your purpose and audience. Follow these steps.

1. In your topic sentence, state your main point about the work being summarized.

2. In the body of the paragraph, include only the events relevant to your main point and exclude most of the details. Make the causal connections among these events clear to your reader by emphasizing why an event occurred and by explaining its effects. If you are summarizing a long or complex work, you might want to set up a classification of events, such

as the events in the main plot and events in the subplot. Present events in the same order as in the original unless you need to modify this order to fit your classification.

3. End your summary with the last major event in the original. Your concluding sentence should remind your reader of the main point about the work stated in your topic sentence.

Sample Plot Summary

We will illustrate these principles with a plot summary of L. M. Montgomery's *Anne of Green Gables*, one of the novels discussed in the sample literary research paper (12f).

In *Anne of Green Gables*, L. M. Montgomery creates the story of a young orphan girl whose task is to win a secure place in the community. Anne has been sent, by mistake, to the farm of an elderly brother and sister who had wanted a boy to help with the chores. Although an imaginative, talkative, hot-tempered girl was not at all what he had in mind, Matthew Cuthbert is quickly won over. His sister's acceptance of Anne is more conditional, and since Marilla is to have charge of the child's upbringing, Anne must continually prove her willingness to change behaviour that Marilla and other adults find unacceptable. Anne loses her temper when insulted by Marilla's friend and neighbour Mrs. Rachel Lynde; scandalizes churchgoers by appearing in Sunday School with wildflowers on her bonnet; is accused of losing Marilla's brooch; refuses to attend school after being insulted by the teacher; makes her best friend, Diana, drunk on Marilla's homemade wine; unintentionally leaps into bed with Diana's imperious great-aunt; accidentally dyes her hair green; and almost brings disaster upon herself and her friends by her fanciful imagination. Gradually, however, Anne learns to curb her excesses. By the end of the novel she has made a place for herself in this small Prince Edward Island community and truly becomes Anne of Green Gables.

Summaries

Summaries of Articles or Chapters of a Book

The following instructions are for writing a self-contained summary. You would prepare a self-contained summary for an annotated bibliography or for an abstract to accompany a report or proposal. To see how you would integrate a summary into another piece of writing, see Sample Essay Analyzing Nonfiction (9f), Reviews (11h), Integrating Research Material (12e), and Reading Reports (15c).

Taking Notes

1. Write down complete bibliographical information.

Book: author(s); title; place of publication; publisher; date.

Chapter in an edited collection: author(s) and title of chapter; editor(s) and title of book; edition (if applicable); publisher, place, and date of publication; page numbers of chapter.

Article: author(s), title of article, title of publication, volume (for scholarly journals) or date (for popular magazines), page numbers. Use the format (MLA, APA, or other) appropriate to your audience (see Appendix B, Documentation).

2. Check for a list of objectives at the beginning of the work or a clearly marked summary at the beginning or end.

3. Look for visual indicators such as headings, subheadings, and boldface and italicized words to use as guideposts to the main sections and the main ideas.

4. Underline sentences containing main ideas if you are using your own book or a photocopy. Often these main ideas will be found in topic sentences located at the beginning or end of a paragraph. Try to find at least one main idea for each section of the article and state this main idea in your own words. Then locate and record subpoints and examples for each main idea. Include the page reference for each item of information.

5. Include brief quotations when the author's own words seem particularly important. Be sure to put quotation marks around any three or more consecutive words and to include the page reference.

6. Define all the key terms in your own words and include them in your summary. Look up any unfamiliar words.

7. In your own words, state the main idea of the whole article or chapter. This main idea should include both the subject of the article or chapter and the writer's central point about that

subject. Summarizing the main idea allows you to create a context for the specific points and examples.

Writing the Summary

1. Give complete bibliographical information (author, title, place of publication, publisher, date), either as a heading or in the first sentence of your summary.

2. State the writer's main idea in a sentence or two.

3. Include the main subpoints of each section of the article or chapter. Give enough details and examples to make each point clear to your reader. Show how these points connect with each other by using terms that emphasize the writer's purpose or methods of development, such as causal analysis, comparison, or classification: *This article explores two contrasting theories about the causes of breast cancer. The genetic theory holds that.... The environmental theory holds that....* If you are careful to focus on the main points and avoid merely paraphrasing every sentence (translating it into your own words), your summary will be about the right length.

4. Use your own words, but include and define key words. Put quotation marks around key terms, phrases, and excerpts, and put the page reference in parentheses following the quotation.

5. Keep the information in the same order as it appears in the original and in the same proportion. Do not exaggerate the importance of a point that you find especially interesting, or leave out a point that you find difficult to understand.

6. Use denotative (emotionally neutral) language, and focus on the article or chapter itself rather than your responses to it. Mention the writer frequently to make it clear that you are presenting his or her opinions on the subject, not your own. Do not mix your own ideas with the material you are summarizing; you may not be able to distinguish them a few days or weeks later. If you have been asked (or want) to include an evaluation of either the content or the style, put your evaluation, clearly indicated as such, in a separate paragraph.

Sample Summary of an Article

In "The Channel Surfer Blues" (*Maclean's*, August 1, 1994), Allan Fotheringham argues that because modern technology provides us with more information than we can absorb, we have become numbed to the pain of others. Fotheringham focuses on disaster stories about Haiti, the Gulf War, and Rwanda to make his point. Haiti "is about as important as Yellowknife," yet the media gave Haitian riots "huge headlines," which most Canadians ignored because they didn't even know where Haiti was. Technology became even more important in CNN's coverage of the Gulf War with the result that "nervous establishment networks" now send anchormen to every "hotspot" where they broadcast more information than viewers want or need. This overload of information, Fotheringham argues, numbs the mind and conscience. Viewers quickly became bored with the coverage of the massacres in Rwanda. "Ho hum. Somalia yesterday. Rwanda today. Let's turn to the World Cup. Where's the disaster tomorrow" (48).

10d How-to Articles

Books and articles telling how to do something fill the shelves of bookstores and the pages of newspapers and magazines. You can find advice on how to manage your money or your children, choose a doctor or a spouse, deal with anger or the plumbing. Since you probably have skills that other people would like to learn, you too can write how-to articles.

Although how-to articles cover a wide range of subjects, from the limited and concrete (how to make popcorn) to the lengthy and abstract (how to make a success of your life), the method of development is basically the same: **process analysis.** In each piece of writing, you are explaining the steps in a process or procedure (see Analysis, 5e).

Writing a How-to Article

Follow these steps.
1. Choose a process or procedure that you can explain in five to ten steps. Sharpening a pencil is too simple; building a manned spacecraft is too long and complex.

2. Decide how much explanation and what level of language are appropriate for your intended audience. If you were telling children how to make cookies, for instance, you might say, "Put the mixing bowl in the refrigerator for an hour. Then take small pieces of dough and form them into balls about half the size of your fist." For experienced cooks, you would say, "Chill the dough and form into balls."

3. Write a short introduction pointing out the benefits of learning the procedure. Include any tools or materials required and, if appropriate, where they can be obtained.

4. Describe the steps for your procedure in the order in which your reader will follow them. Number the steps or use transitional phrases that clearly identify them (*the first step... next...the third step*). Explain the purpose or reason for each step and give enough detail for the reader to carry it out.

5. Mention any problems that your reader may have in carrying out the steps and suggest how to solve them.

6. Write a short conclusion emphasizing the desirable qualities of the finished product or the benefits of learning the procedure.

10e Sample How-to Article

Here is an example of a short how-to article written for a newspaper.

How to Do Artificial Respiration
by Karlene Chorney

The hot days of summer send many of us to the water—for swimming, water-skiing, fishing, canoeing. And every year, some people drown, or nearly drown, because of freak accidents or abrupt changes in the weather. If you are heading to lakes and rivers this summer, or even the nearest swimming pool, you should know something about water safety. The most important thing to know is how to give artificial respiration. You can practise this easy-to-learn Red Cross procedure with a friend.

Artificial respiration is used to restore an unconscious person's breathing or to sustain breathing until the person can receive medical help. To start this procedure, you may need to turn the person onto his back. Then determine whether or not he is unconscious. This step is called shake and shout. Grab the person by the shoulders and shake firmly. At the same time, shout phrases that encourage him to wake up. It is important to shout in both ears in case he suffers a hearing loss in one of them. If the person does not respond, you know that he is unconscious. In order to make sure that the person's airway is clear, use the head tilt, chin lift method. Tilt the head back with one hand on the forehead and lift the chin with the other.

The next step is called *look, listen, and feel.* It will tell you whether the person is breathing. Put your ear over the person's mouth so that you are looking over her chest. Look to see if her chest is moving, listen to hear if air is being exhaled, and feel for a breath on your cheek. Make sure you look, listen, and feel for ten seconds. If the person is not breathing, go on to the next step.

Pinch his nose, seal your mouth over his, and blow two sustained breaths into his mouth. Now, let go of his nose and look, listen, and feel to see if air is going into his lungs. Check for his pulse. Then give one sustained breath. Release the nose and look, listen, and feel. Repeat this procedure, a normal breath followed by a breathing check, at five-second intervals until the person starts breathing on his own, medical help comes, or you become too exhausted to continue.

As you can see, the steps for giving mouth-to-mouth artificial respiration are easy to remember and simple to perform. You'll feel more confident in a crisis, however, if you've practised them before you set off for the swimming pool or the beach.

10e

*Sample
How-to
Article*

Chapter 11

Persuasive Essays

11a Preparing to Write a Persuasive Essay

In a **persuasive essay,** you say in a thesis what you want your readers to believe or to do and give evidence to support your position. A good persuasive essay demonstrates the author's ability to think critically about an issue, to evaluate other points of view, to see connections between general principles and particular facts, and to arrive at an independent judgment.

In deciding how to present your argument in the most effective way, you need, as always, to consider your purpose, audience, and method of organization.

Purpose and Audience

In any form of persuasive writing, your purpose is to change or reinforce your readers' opinions and, in some cases, to encourage those readers to act. How can you make your writing persuasive? Persuasion, according to Aristotle, rests on three kinds of appeals: logical appeals, emotional appeals, and appeals to *ethos* (the character of the speaker). **Logical appeals** are the reasons and evidence you present to support your position. **Emotional appeals** are the direct and indirect ways you engage readers' feelings (by referring to shared values, for instance). For the Greek *ethos* we use the term "**self-presentation**": that is, the image of yourself you create through the choices you make about content and style.

In Essays Analyzing Nonfiction (9e), we show how you can use these three kinds of appeals in analyzing another writer's work. In this section, you will put your knowledge of these three kinds of appeals to work in your own writing.

To choose an effective combination of appeals for a particular piece, you need to decide whether you are writing for a friendly audience, a hostile audience, or a neutral audience.

A friendly audience is one that shares your basic concerns but needs to be roused to action or renewed commitment. A parent speaking to community league members about building a new playground would be addressing a friendly audience, receptive to the idea but perhaps needing to be convinced that it was practical. For reviews, letters to the editor, or opinion pieces on non-controversial topics, you can usually assume you are writing for a friendly audience.

At the other extreme is the hostile audience, actively opposed to your position. An employer trying to persuade workers to accept cutbacks in wages would face a hostile audience. For a hostile audience, you need to consider emotional appeals and self-presentation as well as logical appeals. Hostile workers, for example, might be more willing to accept lower wages from an employer who argued that "we're all in this together" than from one who seemed unconcerned about their welfare. When you write essays on controversial subjects, such as abortion and euthanasia, you will need to take special care not to alienate readers hostile to your position.

Most of the essays you write for courses are directed to a neutral audience—readers who expect a carefully reasoned argument and are sceptical of emotional appeals. These readers will pay more attention to persuasive pieces that do not take extreme positions, that consider the merits of different points of view, and that present extensive evidence to support their position.

Organizing Persuasive Essays

The basic strategy for organizing a persuasive essay is to explain the issue, state your position, and give evidence to support your points. In many cases, you will also include a summary of other opinions so that you can attack or agree with them. How you arrange the parts of your essay will be determined by what your readers need to know and what you think they will find most convincing.

If you expect strong opposition, either because you are writing for an audience that you know is hostile or because you are taking an unpopular stand on a controversial issue, you may want to anticipate your readers' objections by discussing the merits and drawbacks of the counter-arguments first before presenting your thesis and the arguments that support it. By the time you reach your conclusion, your opponents may be more willing to acknowledge the validity of your position than they would have been if your thesis had appeared in your introduction. This type of organization also works well if you are writing for a friendly but perhaps complacent audience. To encourage readers to think more carefully about a position they may take for granted, you might begin with arguments upon which there is widespread agreement, and then raise the question of whether the situation is really as satisfactory as it appears. You will find an example of this strategy in the sample research essay, "Whose Turn Is It to Clean Up This Garbage?" (12g).

When you are writing for a neutral audience, it is usually best to state your position up front. Your readers will appreciate a clearly defined thesis in your introduction, topic sentences that indicate the stages of your argument, substantial paragraphs that show clear reasoning and a careful use of evidence to support your points, and a conclusion that summarizes and extends your argument.

Here you will find guidelines for four types of persuasive writing: opinion pieces, reviews, letters to the editor, and position papers. For an example of a persuasive research paper, see "Whose Turn Is It to Clean Up This Garbage?" (12g).

11b Opinion Pieces

Opinion pieces are short persuasive essays, based on your own knowledge and experience, about an issue of interest to general readers. Columnists such as Ellen Goodman, Allan Fotheringham, and Barbara Amiel write opinion pieces for newspapers and magazines. You will find an example of an opinion piece, Satya Das's column about cutting social programs, in Essays Analyzing Nonfiction (9e). As with many opinion pieces, Das uses a personal anecdote as his starting point for presenting an argument about an issue of general interest.

You will see the same pattern in the sample opinion piece below. Notice that the writer gives partial reasons for not buying a new car, leading up to a complete statement of his thesis in the final paragraph.

11b

Opinion
Pieces

11c Sample Opinion Piece

Why I Won't Buy a New Car

by Peter Banks

The third time my car broke down within a year, my friend Rebecca teased me, "Why don't you just buy a new one?" This advice was coming from someone whose parents gave her a Miata convertible for her sixteenth birthday. The carefree way she suggested I "just buy a new one" echoed through my mind for quite some time. I began to realize that in our throwaway society, many people are all too willing to "just buy a new one" regardless of any future consequences. However, an object that is more technologically advanced is not necessarily superior.

Many North Americans are deceived by the notion that acquiring the latest inventions will somehow bring them happiness. Although many new objects can bring enjoyment, they do not make the consumer any better as a person. The media prey on society's search for material happiness. Automobiles are often portrayed as the means to achieve power, success, inner peace, and popularity. They are often shown as the instant ticket to becoming a sex symbol. The one thing that advertisements seem to neglect is that these fancy machines are just that—fancy machines. The driver of a red Lamborghini would still be the same person if he or she were behind the wheel of a rusty brown station wagon. However, the media continue to portray the acquisition of material possessions as the avenue through which goals such as peace, good work, family stability, and personal happiness can be achieved. Mini-van commercials are loaded with images of loving families enjoying quality time together. Sports car advertisements attempt to associate driving that particular car with popularity and sexual attractiveness.

While consumers are racing to keep up with the latest in technology, many valuable resources are needlessly wasted. Thousands of auto wrecking yards

11c

Sample
Opinion
Piece

across North America are filled with vehicles left to rust into an ecological nightmare. Although some are eventually crushed and recycled for future use, these instances do not occur as often as they could. Many of the mechanical components left in these automobiles are still in perfect working order. However, because the majority of modern engines are composed of a tangled web of hoses and computer chips, any working parts from the older cars are completely incompatible. This makes re-using any of the older parts impossible, thereby putting to waste an entirely functional mechanism.

The needlessly complex mechanical designs of new vehicles make it impossible for individuals to take responsibility for even the most basic car maintenance. With consumers wholly dependent upon the dealership's mechanical services, the dealership is free to list exorbitant prices, to which customers must agree. When the alternator of my 1981 Honda Accord wore out, my dad and I simply rebuilt a part from an auto wrecker and replaced it ourselves. The design of the engine compartment left every component easily identifiable and accessible. The entire job took just over an hour and we spent less than eighty dollars on it. The alternator on Rebecca's Miata, however, is buried far beneath the engine block. This particular part, which is prone to wear out with accumulated mileage, is positioned so that when it does have to be replaced, the entire engine must be removed. However, a regular garage will probably not have the necessary equipment to work on this particular vehicle. When her alternator does go, Rebecca will thus have to take her car to the Mazda dealership and pay whatever price is asked.

If I did buy a new car, it probably would not break down as often as the one that I am currently driving. But it might destroy my relationship with my dad. The easiest, most enjoyable times my dad and I spend together are while we work as a team, desperately trying to repair my car. I know that "I love you" has always been a hard thing for him to come out and say. But as I think back, nothing says

11c

Sample Opinion Piece

it louder than the time we spent working in the
garage last summer. I was shocked to find him using
the old, crooked tool box that I made for him in
grade 5. I almost broke into tears when I saw that
crooked, unsymmetrical Father's Day present loaded
up with tools, while Dad's numerous other boxes,
which are much sturdier and more convenient, sat in
the basement unused. Buying a new car would end the
wonderful times my father and I spend together doing
repairs, times that I have grown to cherish.

No, I won't buy a new car. It would cost too much—
in the destruction of the environment, the waste of
precious resources, the loss of self-reliance, and
the loss of human contact.

11d Position Papers

In a **position paper,** your purpose is to present arguments
showing why you agree or disagree with something you have
read. Writing this kind of essay will help you develop your critical thinking skills, for it requires you to analyze, evaluate, and
formulate your own opinion about a significant issue.

Follow these guidelines.

1. Summarize the piece (see Summaries, 10c). You will use this
   summary in your introduction.

2. Analyze and evaluate the author's reasoning and emotional
   appeals (see Essays Analyzing Nonfiction, 9e).

3. Decide whether the author's position is based on moral, practical, logical, legal, or aesthetic criteria, or a combination of
   these perspectives (see Evaluation, 5g).

4. Decide whether you wholly agree, partially agree, or disagree
   with the author's position. If you wholly agree, make a list of
   additional points and evidence to support the position. If you
   partially agree or disagree, make a list of counter-arguments
   and evidence.

5. Decide what your own basis of evaluation is. Do the points
   you agree with reflect your moral position on the subject? Do
   you doubt the practical advantages of the author's position?

*Position
Papers*

6. Write a thesis that makes clear your response and your basis of evaluation.

7. Organize your response to include opposing arguments. One way to do this is to briefly summarize other views about your subject and indicate why you agree or disagree before you develop your thesis in more detail. You might use this method if, for example, you wanted to argue that positions X, Y, and Z were all based on self-interest rather than the common good.

Another possible approach is to take up an opposing argument point by point, examining its strengths and/or weaknesses and pointing out alternatives. You might adopt this method if, for instance, you wanted to argue against a series of proposals contained in a speech or document. These two methods are examples of an evaluative or "pro-con" structure, that is, an organization based on arguments for (*pro*) and arguments against (*con*) your position.

Evaluating an Argument

To see how you would apply these procedures, let's examine possible responses to the following excerpt from an essay by Suzanne Britt Jordan entitled "I Wants to Go to the Prose" (*Newsweek*, November 14, 1977).

In the opening paragraph, which describes her experiences as an English teacher in a community college, Jordan says that for quite a while she had "overlooked ignorance, dismissed arrogance, championed fairness, emphasized motivation, boosted egos and tolerated laziness... [and] was, in short, the classic modern educator." Here she defends a "back to the basics" approach to education.

I'm perfectly aware that I sound like an old curmudgeon and it frightens me more than it offends you. But I have accepted what educators can't seem to face. The function of schools, their first and primary obligation, is not to probe tender psyches, to feed and clothe the homeless, nor to be the papa and mama a kid never had. The job is to teach... .

Before educators lost their way and tried to diversify by getting into the business of molding human beings, a teacher was, ideally, someone who knew a certain body of information and conveyed it. Period. Remember crotchety old Miss Dinwiddie, who could recite 40 lines of the "Aeneid" at a clip? Picture Mr.

Wassleheimer, who could give a zero to a cheating student without pausing in his lecture on frog dissection. Every student knew it wasn't wise to mess around with a teacher who had the subject down cold. They were the teachers we once despised and later admired.

I want them back, those fearsome, awe-inspiring experts.... . They were hard, even at times unjust, but when they were through, we knew those multiplication tables blindfolded with both trembling hands tied behind our backs.

Before the schoolmasters and administrators change, they will have to shake off the guilt, the simpering, apologetic smiles and the Freudian theories. Which is crueller? Flunking a kid who has flunked or passing a kid who has flunked? Which teaches more about the realities of life? Which, in fact, shows more respect for the child as a human being?

If you were asked to agree or disagree with this view of education, you might work out a systematic response something like the following.

1. Summarize the main points.

The school's job is to teach. The teacher's job is to know a subject thoroughly and to convey that information to students. Students respect teachers who know their material. Students learn when the teacher inspires fear and awe. Flunking a failing student teaches him or her about the realities of life and shows respect for that person as a human being.

2. Identify the writer's basis of evaluation.

Jordan's argument is based on both moral and practical grounds. It is morally right to flunk failing students. The practical benefit of her approach is that students learn more when teachers concentrate on conveying information.

3. Evaluate the writer's arguments.

Strengths:

- Jordan appeals to an audience's belief that education is important.

Weaknesses:

- Jordan oversimplifies complex issues into either/or alternatives (e.g., teachers either know their material or they try to motivate students).
- Jordan overgeneralizes about students.
- She predicts failure to learn on the basis of that overgeneralization.
- She makes unfair emotional appeals by belittling school administrators and modern educators.
- Her argument is based on unproven assumptions about the nature of education and the role of the teacher.

4. Take a stand and formulate your arguments.

While I agree that education is important, I totally disagree with Jordan's view of how learning takes place. I don't think that the teacher knows everything and students learn by passively accepting what the teacher knows. And I don't believe students learn most effectively through fear. When I'm afraid of being ridiculed or punished for making mistakes, I don't really learn anything at all. What Jordan is advocating is conformity and rote memorization, not education.

5. Clarify your basis of evaluation.

I disagree with Jordan's stance on education on logical, practical, and moral grounds.

6. Formulate your thesis.

While Suzanne Britt Jordan makes a strong emotional appeal to those who think education is important, her argument is seriously flawed on logical, practical, and moral grounds.

7. Organize your essay to include opposing arguments.

In the sample position paper below, a response to Jordan's piece, the writer shows how the evaluative, or pro-con, structure can be used to refute an argument point by point.

11d

*Position
Papers*

11e Sample Position Paper

In an essay entitled "I Wants to Go to the Prose" (*Newsweek*, November 14, 1977), Suzanne Britt Jordan argues that the function of the school is to teach and evaluate students according to their academic progress, nothing more. Neither the school nor the teacher should be concerned with a student's emotional or social welfare, for this, Jordan says, necessitates tolerating the ignorance, arrogance, and laziness of most students. Thus the ideal teacher, according to Jordan, is the person whose thorough knowledge of a subject inspires respect, fear, and awe. This is the kind of educational setting in which students learn. While Jordan makes a strong emotional appeal to a belief in the value of education, her argument is seriously flawed on logical, practical, and moral grounds.

Although Jordan's approach to education may seem convincingly simple, it oversimplifies a complex subject (the nature of knowledge) and a complex relationship (that between teachers and students) into either/or alternatives. According to Jordan, teachers must concentrate their efforts either on conveying information or on meeting their students' emotional and social needs. Jordan's conviction that it is impossible to do both is based on an overgeneralization about students (most are ignorant, arrogant, and lazy). The prediction that these students won't learn is calculated to appeal to an audience's fear of extremely negative consequences. Given the alternatives Jordan suggests, who would want to be a "classic modern educator"?

It's worthwhile to wonder, however, about how much real learning goes on in the kind of classroom Jordan envisions. Students may be able to regurgitate information (especially if they are sufficiently afraid of the consequences of not doing so). But the concept of knowledge on which this approach to education rests is that knowledge itself is static,

11e

*Sample
Position
Paper*

predictable, compartmentalized—a fixed body of information (such as forty lines of the "Aeneid" or the anatomy of a frog) that can be poured into students. Students may be able to remember enough of this information to pass a test. What will last longer is the ability to conform to the expectations of a person in authority. This kind of education promotes conformity; it does not enable students to create their own view of reality and their own definition of themselves.

Using highly charged emotional language and personal attacks on those who oppose her position, Jordan endorses the traditional classroom hierarchy. In fact, she reinforces it with her image of students whose fear and awe of a teacher has motivated them to learn a fixed body of information (her example is that of students who have learned the multiplication tables so thoroughly that they can recite them blindfolded and with their hands tied behind their backs). By ridiculing the guilt and "simpering, apologetic smiles" of those who might hesitate to evaluate students only on such grounds, and by suggesting that this sort of classroom gives students a clearer picture of reality, Jordan seriously oversimplifies the real purpose of education and the reality that exists outside the classroom. Outside the classroom, students will need to think for themselves and define their own concepts.

To go back to teaching in the way Jordan suggests is to return to a relationship between teachers and students, and to a concept of knowledge and learning, that may impart a certain amount of factual information but that does not prepare students for the complexities of life.

11f Letters to the Editor

Most letters to the editor are intended to persuade readers that something is good or bad: the premier is doing a good job or a lousy job, park trails should or should not be paved, nurses should or should not have the right to strike. They are generally short, about 250-500 words. Paragraphs within the letter are also short because letters are usually printed in narrow columns. The following guidelines will help you make your point quickly and effectively.

1. *Focus on a particular issue of interest to a number of readers, and if possible, link that issue to a current situation.* A general plea for world peace, for example, is less likely to hold your readers' attention than an argument against selling arms to warring countries. Identify the issue in your first paragraph.

2. *Say why the issue concerns you.* Are you writing as a spokesperson for a relief organization? As a pacifist? As a citizen upholding the ideal of Canada as a peacekeeping nation?

3. *Instead of condemning people who hold other views, try to establish common ground with them.* Summarize their positions accurately and acknowledge the extent to which their point of view may be true or understandable. You might acknowledge a country's need to defend itself, for example, but point out that access to more powerful weapons increases the likelihood of bloodshed.

4. *State your own position and your reasons for holding it. Be brief but specific.*

5. *If possible, suggest a practical action that readers can take.* They can't ensure world peace; they can write a letter to an MP.

11g Sample Letter to the Editor

In this letter, the writer focuses on a local issue to raise public awareness and encourage appropriate action.

Like many Torontonians, I have often donated used clothing to Goodwill, the Salvation Army, and women's shelters in the belief that others would find useful what my family no longer needed. When I began doing volunteer work for one of these organizations, I realized that one category of clothing is desperately needed but rarely donated—underwear.

To the question "Who would want used underwear?", the answer is "Anyone who does not have any." Women and children, for example, often arrive at crisis shelters without any possessions or money. Sometimes they can collect their clothing after a few days, but often they are unable to return home. Until they can return home or go shopping, they are in desperate need of a change of clothing, including, of course, underwear.

So when you are bundling up clothing that you or your family no longer use, don't hesitate to include outgrown underwear. Or the next time you go shopping, pick up some on sale to donate. The women and children at crisis shelters, and those who use other clothing depots, will be very grateful.

L.M. Hrychuk
North York

11h Reviews

You are probably most familiar with the brief reviews of books, films, television programs, and eating places printed in newspapers and general-interest magazines, such as *Maclean's* and *Saturday Night*. These reviews are intended to give casual readers some sense of whether a new movie is worth seeing or a new restaurant worth trying.

Longer reviews—often called **review articles** or **review essays**—are designed for readers with some knowledge of the subject. Car enthusiasts, for example, might read the reviews of all the new models in *Car and Driver,* even if they are not planning to buy a car. Extended reviews in *The New York Review of Books* and similar publications might evaluate five new books on pornography in the context of the ongoing debate between individual rights and the public good. Academic journals often carry review articles on research in specific areas, such as intelligence testing. Because these reviews provide substantial background information and extensive commentary, they are useful sources of information for research papers.

We will focus on guidelines for writing brief reviews. If you wish to expand your treatment of your subject into a review essay, you can do so by consulting your library for appropriate sources of information: other reviews, other works by the same person or group, articles relevant to your subject, biographical dictionaries, newspaper files, and so forth.

Follow these guidelines when writing a brief review.

1. Include identifying information somewhere in your review. The most essential information (determined by your intended audience and type of publication) usually appears in a separate heading before your review or in your introduction. Here is what you should include:

Book review: author, title, publisher, price, type, length, hardcover or paper. As applicable: name of editor, translator, or other contributors; supplementary material provided (such as maps, illustrations, appendix, index); date of publication; edition.

CD-ROM review: title, publisher, price, system requirements.

Computer software review: product, manufacturer, price, system requirements. As applicable: other products in category, ordering information.

Film review: title, director, distributor, type, principal actors. As applicable: date of release; length; suitability rating; other contributors (music, special effects, etc.).

Live performance review (as applicable): title, name of person or group, place, date(s), type, price.

Product review: manufacturer, model, price. As applicable: availability, warranty, service record.

Record or compact disk review: title, person or group, type, label, price.

Restaurant review: name, address, type of food, business hours, price range, credit cards accepted, availability of alcoholic beverages, décor, service. As applicable: reservation requirement, dress code.

11h

Reviews

2. Try for a lively introduction, one that will catch your readers' interest and convey your general opinion of what you are reviewing.

3. Give a brief summary or description, but do not give away endings of films, plays, or novels.

4. Discuss what you liked and disliked about what you are reviewing, with specific examples. Try for a balanced view:

recognize that even the aspects you like the most may appeal only to certain people. For suggestions about what to consider, see Evaluation (5g).

5. End with a snappy summary of your overall judgment.

11i Sample Review

Here is a sample book review, written for a general-interest magazine.

Armageddon, '80s Style

by Susan Boon

Stephen King, *The Stand*, 1978. Signet pb, $2.95.

Stephen King is best known as a writer of horror novels (*Carrie*, *The Shining*, *Christine*, *Pet Sematary*). But you don't have to be a horror fan to enjoy *The Stand*, an epic story of the age-old battle between good and evil. *The Stand* depicts this conflict in the aftermath of a devastating plague which kills two thirds of the world's population.

It is June 16, 1985.

Scientists experimenting with biological warfare at a top-secret military installation in the United States accidentally contaminate the laboratory in which they have been working. Before the area can be completely sealed off, one family escapes the compound, carrying the deadly virus with them into the Texas desert.

An epidemic results, leaving only scattered groups of survivors in isolated pockets across the United States. *The Stand* documents the regrouping of these survivors as they try to reassemble their lives in post-apocalypse America. To this rather familiar story outline, King adds a novel twist—a confrontation between "The Walkin' Dude," an evil neo-Antichrist figure whose apparent destiny is to take over the world, and Mother Abigail, aged 108, a Kansas farmwoman who is the lifeblood of those who take "the stand." The scattered survivors are

11i

Sample Review

151

inexorably drawn towards one of these leaders, and the stage is set for the ensuing battle between the forces of dark and light.

The cast of characters is broad and varied. We watch spellbound as fate and chance lead characters to align themselves with good or evil: the small-town Texan who thinks adventure is opening the next can of Coors; the young unwed mother-to-be and the kinky teenage whiz-kid who is in love with her; the rock star who has lost his lust for life; the woman who has waited all her life for a man who terrifies her to the depths of her soul; the "slow" boy with the psychic powers.

Intense characterization and a complex plot weave a story in which the reader is inevitably caught up. Suspense builds as a battle looms. In hope of preventing the expected attack, four set out from their haven in Denver, Colorado, for the Enemy's stronghold in Las Vegas. Only one returns.

The central conflict in *The Stand* may seem a trifle clichéd, but the depth of this book carries it above this criticism. *The Stand* is a true saga, a story that is more than the sum of its parts. Entertaining and exciting, the book entices the reader to join in the battle. King is a master storyteller who skillfully brings his readers to the last page with a sense of having truly experienced "the stand."

11i

Sample
Review

Chapter 12

Research Papers

A research paper *is an expository or persuasive essay in which you include facts and/or opinions from other sources to support your analysis or point of view. As you will see in the sample research papers,* "Tom Sawyer *and* Anne of Green Gables: Two Models of Heroism" *(12f) and* "Whose Turn Is It to Clean Up This Garbage?" *(12g), those sources are usually published books and articles on the subject. But research material can also include interviews and other data that you gather yourself.*

A research paper should not be merely a compilation of other people's ideas. The best way to make sure it isn't is to have some idea of where you are going before you do research. You can use brainstorming or discovery questions (2a and 2c) to figure out the questions you will need to answer in your paper. Or, if you know something about your subject, you can write a draft first and then find research material to broaden or clarify your thinking.

12a Writing Research Papers

Purpose

The purpose of a research essay is to examine a subject in greater depth than would be possible on the basis of your own knowledge. In many cases, you may not have any prior knowledge to draw upon. How many of us, without using research material, could write an essay on the introduction of Buddhism into China, for example? Writing research essays is one of the best ways to extend your knowledge of a subject.

As you carry out your research, you are likely to find unanswered questions and areas of disagreement among your sources. Writing a research paper will allow you to take part in the ongoing debate about your subject.

Audience

Research papers are written by specialists for other specialists. Citations and references allow specialist readers to evaluate the sources of facts and opinions and to follow up possible lines of investigation. As a student writing a research paper, you are learning to act like a specialist in a particular field. You will therefore present your material differently than you would for a general audience. You will use a more specialized vocabulary, maintain a slightly more formal tone, and assume your readers' general familiarity with the subject. (For example, a biologist would explain what DNA is for a general audience but not for other biologists.) Nevertheless, a research paper should not sound as though it has been compiled by a committee. The best research papers are those in which the style and tone reflect something of the writer: flashes of wit, clear thinking, depth of knowledge, sudden insights, and a feeling for language.

General Guidelines

- Use the most up-to-date material available, especially for topics related to science, technology, and current issues and events.

- Don't depend too heavily upon one or two sources. If your material is too limited, you may get an inaccurate idea of the central issues about your subject. You may also find it hard to develop your own perspective.

  Six to eight references will usually give you enough material for a research paper in an introductory course. In advanced courses, you may be expected to have a more thorough knowledge of what has been written about your topic.

- To end up with six to eight usable references, you will need to start with a **working bibliography** two to three times longer (see Conducting Computer-Aided Research, 12b). This strategy will allow you to cross off material that turns out to be unavailable or irrelevant without having to do another search.

- Include articles as well as books in your working bibliography. Articles are a little harder to track down, but they are more current and less likely to be checked out when you need them.

- Take notes as you read (see Summaries, 10c). You will understand the material better when you are ready to write your research paper, and you will not lose track of where ideas and information came from. Put quotation marks around any three or more consecutive words you take directly from the source (without paraphrasing) and indicate page references for each idea, item of information, and quotation. Make sure your notes include complete bibliographical information (see Appendix B, Documentation).

- As you write each draft, put the author and page number in parentheses after each item that you take from your notes. If there is any chance of confusion (authors with the same name, more than one work by the same author), add a short form of the title or the date of publication.

- In your final draft, make sure that these parenthetical references conform to the documentation format required for your essay. For detailed guidelines on MLA and APA documentation, see Appendix B, Documentation.

12b Conducting Computer-Aided Research

Your first step in gathering research material is to compile a working bibliography: a list of ten to twenty books, articles, and similar material on your topic. The best place to begin is your library's online catalogue.

Using the online catalogue, you can search for books relevant to your topic in three main ways: by keying in the name of the authors whose works you wish to find, the titles of books you are looking for, or the general subject headings pertaining to your area of research. Subject searches are often the most useful, allowing you to locate dozens of potentially valuable items in seconds. They can also be the most frustrating and time-consuming, however, if you do not choose appropriate search terms or if you fail to limit your search sufficiently. If you need help, consult a reference librarian.

In addition to the online catalogue, many libraries now offer bibliographies, indexes, and other reference materials on CD-ROM. CD-ROM searches are a quick and efficient way of locating books; articles in newspapers, magazines, and scholarly journals; and other sources, such as encyclopedias. Some databases, such as the *MLA International Bibliography*, will give you references to works on your topic, but you will have to check the online catalogue to see whether your library has the items you want. Other databases may contain the full texts of newspapers or scholarly journals; in this case, you can skim the relevant material and print out a copy if it is useful.

A final option is to request a professional online search. Such searches, conducted by a librarian according to the search terms you provide, cover commercial databases not available on CD-ROM. Libraries generally charge a fee for this service, so you might want to avoid this option unless you can't find enough material on your topic otherwise.

If your computer is equipped with a modem, you can probably access the Internet, where you may find material on your topic via a plethora of listservs and news groups. Be cautious, however, about the authenticity and credibility of the information you get through the Internet. Electronic publications that are available in print versions are more trustworthy than bulletin board postings.

By the end of your search, you should have references to many books and articles on your topic. Choose ten to twenty that seem relevant to your focus and are accessible through your library. These references make up your working bibliography. Some items will be checked out, some won't address your topic after all, and some you won't use for other reasons; but you should end up with six to eight that you can cite in your research paper.

12c Using Research Material to Make a Point

A research paper, like other kinds of essays, must have a thesis. At earlier stages of your education, you may have collected information on a subject and presented it in an orderly fashion. A paper of this sort, however, is a report rather than an essay because it does not have a thesis. When you write a full-fledged research paper, you must organize your research material to support a point.

In writing your paper, you may be concentrating so much on organizing your material that you lose track of your thesis. Suppose, for instance, that you were writing a research paper arguing that the education faculty should take steps to improve the status of teaching as a profession. Your first draft of a paragraph recommending higher admission standards might look like the following.

Sample First Draft

Marleen C. Pugach of the University of Illinois has recommended these selection criteria for prospective Education students: 1) basic skills testing, consisting of entry-level tests in reading, mathematics, and written and oral communication; 2) a minimum grade point average; and 3) a structured interview to assess the applicant's personal qualities (161-63). At universities such as Oregon State and Northern Kentucky, students must successfully complete a two- to five-day full-responsibility teaching experience prior to being accepted into a teacher training program. The number of drop-outs increased from approximately 5% to 25% (Edgar 96).

This draft paragraph serves the writer's need to gather together information from a variety of sources. However, it does not serve the reader's need to understand the significance of this information because the point of the paragraph gets lost among the examples.

Here is the material as it appeared in the student's final draft. With the added topic sentence, sentences explaining the relevance of each example, and a summarizing sentence to connect this material to the thesis, the original paragraph has become two.

Sample Final Draft

If teaching is to be regarded as the important job that it is, pride must first be generated within the profession itself. One way to do this would be to have a more rigorous and effective set of criteria that applicants must meet before they are allowed entrance into the profession. Marleen C. Pugach of the University of Illinois has recommended a set of criteria that would function together to provide "entry-level hurdles to encourage self selection, to serve as initial points in the process of continuous judgment of student progress, and to assist faculty members in making discriminations between applicants based on multifaceted data" (161). Pugach recommends these selection criteria: 1) basic skills testing, consisting of entry-level tests in reading, mathematics, and written and oral communication; 2) a minimum grade point average; and 3) a structured interview to assess the applicant's personal qualities (161-63).

Another criterion used in universities such as Oregon State and Northern Kentucky is also helpful in selecting suitable candidates.

12c

Using Research Material to Make a Point

157

Students must successfully complete a two- to five-day full-responsibility teaching experience prior to being accepted into a teacher training program. The number of drop-outs increased from approximately 5% to 25% (Edgar 96). Clearly, such intensive selection policies would be a strong force in attracting applicants who seriously wish to pursue teaching. At the same time, these policies would deter students who now casually drift into teacher education, such as those I overhear in the undergraduate lounge. The sense of personal achievement that would come from gaining entrance to a faculty with such high entrance standards would contribute to a feeling of professionalism among candidates.

—*Carol Murray*

12d Documenting Sources

Plagiarism and Inadequate Documentation

When you use facts and opinions from outside sources, you must document where you found them. Failure to do so constitutes **plagiarism**. Plagiarism is a form of stealing: stealing someone else's words or stealing someone else's facts and ideas. And, like other forms of stealing, it is illegal.

Occasionally students, in a panic over deadlines or low marks, may be tempted to pass off as their own work a paper they have copied in whole or in part from another student or, more often, from a published source. Instructors can usually spot this kind of plagiarism easily, either because they are familiar with the original or because the writing is noticeably different from the student's other work.

Plagiarism includes more than the deliberate theft of someone else's words, however. Using facts or ideas without identifying their source is also plagiarism. Plagiarism of this sort usually arises from sloppy note-taking: the writer has failed to record the necessary information for references. Appending a list of works cited is not an adequate indication of the source of specific facts and ideas.

The consequences of both kinds of plagiarism can be severe. The student who plagiarizes may be required to rewrite the paper, may be given a failing grade on the paper or the course, or may be expelled.

You can prevent the panic that leads to deliberate plagiarism by allowing three weeks to gather material, draft, and revise your research paper. You can make sure you provide appropriate documentation of your sources by following the guidelines below.

Documenting Paraphrased Material

To show how you can paraphrase research material and identify its source appropriately, we will use source material from the sample literary research paper *"Tom Sawyer* and *Anne of Green Gables:* Two Models of Heroism" (12f). If you are not familiar with these novels by Mark Twain and L. M. Montgomery, you may want to read the sample essay first. You will also find a summary of *Anne of Green Gables* in Summaries (10c).

Imagine that you were doing research on these novels and came across the following paragraph in James L. Johnson's book *Mark Twain and the Limits of Power* (Knoxville: U. of Tennessee, 1982). In this paragraph, Johnson argues that because Tom's village is not portrayed realistically, Tom is not changed by his seemingly serious experiences:

Simply put, St. Petersburg is not a world in which children are easily turned into adults, for such a change requires that the child meet a real world and adjust himself, painfully but with more or less success, to its undesirable circumstances. Much of the idyllic quality of St. Petersburg is attributable to the fact that Twain has excluded from the novel a world in which experience produces consequent changes in character. Tom's world is one in which "adventure" replaces "experience"; his encounters with the alcoholic Muff Potter, the grave-robbing Dr. Robinson, the vengeful Injun Joe—encounters which should ordinarily produce some difference in his perception of the world—leave his character essentially untouched. (51)

You might decide that this paragraph would strongly support a point you had made in your rough draft, and so you might paraphrase Johnson's passage in your notes:

Tom is not turned into an adult by the world of St. Petersburg because he is not shown trying to adjust himself, with more or less success, to a real world. As St. Petersburg is presented as idyllic, Tom has adventures, but not experiences that would change his character. His encounters with Muff Potter, Dr. Robinson, and Injun

Joe do not change him, although encounters such as these would ordinarily affect how a person sees the world.

If you were to use this paragraph in your paper without acknowledging that the ideas were Johnson's, you would be guilty of plagiarism. Adding a citation to identify the source will protect you from a charge of plagiarism, but it may not clearly distinguish your own thinking from the work of others. If we were to add a page reference at the end of the paraphrase from Johnson, for example, a reader would not be sure whether all the ideas in the paragraph were Johnson's, or merely the last point. Using his name at the beginning of the paragraph, with the page reference at the end, would make clear that all the points come from Johnson's book:

> As James L. Johnson points out, Tom is not turned into an adult by the world of St. Petersburg... although encounters such as these would ordinarily affect how a person sees the world (51).

In most cases, you would not rely so heavily on a single critic; you would at least use your own examples to illustrate the point. Even so, this paragraph is an improvement because the reader knows whose ideas are being presented. If you are careful to identify others' facts and opinions, your reader has more confidence that what remains is your own.

12e Integrating Research Material

To see how to integrate research, we will look first at a draft paragraph on *The Adventures of Tom Sawyer* written before consulting the critics. Then we will discuss two revisions that show ways of incorporating other interpretations.

Sample Draft Paragraph: Student's Analysis

In *The Adventures of Tom Sawyer,* the adults are not presented as models of behaviour. In fact, they are often shown to be acting like children. When Tom tricks Aunt Polly at the beginning of the book, for instance, Aunt Polly has been attempting to trick him. Similarly, Tom shows off at Sunday School when Judge Thatcher visits, but the superintendent and the teachers are also described as "showing off." Even serious events in the adult world seem to parallel Tom's actions. The fight that ends with Injun Joe murdering

Dr. Robinson has many of the same elements as Tom's fight with the new boy in town. It is no wonder then that even after his harrowing escape from the cave and his recovery of the treasure, Tom returns to playing at robbers. The adult world is not portrayed as different from the world of childhood, and so there is no reason for Tom to grow up.

Sample Draft Paragraph: Adding Support from Research Material

In this revised paragraph, the material from Johnson that we noted earlier is added to summarize and expand the point that the writer made in the topic sentence.

The adults in *The Adventures of Tom Sawyer* are not presented as models of behaviour, but simply as older versions of Tom himself... [continue with examples from the original draft] It is no wonder then that even after his harrowing escape from the cave and his recovery of the treasure, Tom returns to the boyhood world of playing at robbers, for the adult world offers no incentives for growing up. James L. Johnson argues that Tom's adventures "leave his character essentially untouched" because "such a change requires that the child meet a real world and adjust himself, painfully but with more or less success, to its undesirable circumstances" (51). But St. Petersburg, as Johnson points out, is an idyllic world, not a real world that would bring about change.

Sample Draft Paragraph: Synthesis of Research + Student's Analysis

In outstanding research papers, the writer does more than cite authorities to support points: he or she synthesizes material from various sources by showing basic similarities and differences. This synthesis then provides a context for the writer's own interpretation.

In the following paragraph, the writer of the sample research paper demonstrates her grasp of the debate about Tom Sawyer's relationship to the adult world by synthesizing opposing critical views and stating her own position.

What, then, is the relation between Tom and his world? Robert Regan supports the view, originally put forward by Walter Blair, that the narrative strands of the novel "trace Tom's progress from childishness to maturity" (Regan 116). Several critics disagree. They argue that because the adults of St. Petersburg are essentially childish, there is no impetus for Tom to change (Fetterley 300; Johnson 51; Miller 73; Whitley 60).

Numerous incidents in the book support this contention... [continue with examples from the original draft].

Crediting your sources, integrating research material, and synthesizing different points of view are never easy tasks. We have used a literary topic to demonstrate these techniques because essays on literature are the first type of research paper that many students have to write. As you continue in college or university, however, you will find that these skills are increasingly important in all your courses.

12f Sample Literary Research Paper

Tom Sawyer and Anne of Green Gables:

Two Models of Heroism

by Lanette Thornton

When we think of heroic quests, we usually envision a pattern very much like that of Mark Twain's The Adventures of Tom Sawyer: the hero engages in a series of adventures through which he proves his worth and is rewarded with riches and the love of a beautiful maiden. In this version of the heroic quest, as is obvious from the way I've described it, the hero is male. L. M. Montgomery's Anne of Green Gables, I will argue, presents a female version of the making of the hero. In the mythic pattern of separation, initiation, and reintegration into the society, Tom's tests of courage and his rewards are largely external, and neither he nor his world is transformed by them. Anne's tests, on the other hand, are largely internal, and her rewards depend upon her ability to transform both herself and her world.

Tom's separation from his community lies in his flouting of convention. Although one critic has argued that finally "Tom sacrifices freedom to gain community" (Towers 520), the first episode of the book seems to bear out John Whitley's contention that Tom "is never in any danger of expulsion from the community" (64). In this episode, which sets up our expectations for the rest of the novel, Tom escapes punishment for sneaking jam by outwitting his Aunt Polly. Her response—"a gentle laugh" (8)—immediately establishes her as an indulgent parental figure who likes Tom's mischievousness:

> He 'pears to know just how long he can torment me before I get my dander up, and he knows if he can make out to put me off for a minute, or make me laugh, it's all down again, and I can't hit him a lick. I ain't doing my duty by that boy, and that's the Lord's truth, goodness knows…. Every time I let him off my conscience does hurt me so; and every time I hit him my old heart 'most breaks. (8)

Furthermore, the "model boy" of the village—Tom's half brother Sid—is presented as dull and self-righteous, always willing to get Tom into trouble by tattling. Whenever we as readers, like Aunt Polly, are ready to condemn Tom's lying, his thoughtlessness, his prankish behaviour, Twain reminds us, usually through Aunt Polly, that Tom is good at heart. And we, like his aunt and the community gathered for his mock funeral (Miller 71-72), forgive him.

Although Leslie Willis dismisses *Anne of Green Gables* as sentimental because Anne "suffers no real hardships" except over her initial reception and Matthew's death at the end of the novel (250), Anne does not have the security in her world that Tom has in his. Tom is at home in St. Petersburg, under the care of a doting, if at times punitive, aunt. But the orphaned Anne has already lost a series of homes. When she reaches Green Gables, she learns that Matthew and Marilla had wanted a boy to help with the farm, not a girl at all. Furthermore, although Marilla soon discovers that Anne is "smart and obedient, willing to work and quick to learn" (57), the girl is also a talkative, imaginative, hot-tempered redhead. Anne, like Tom, is presented as essentially good. But unlike Tom, if Anne is to

12f

Sample Literary Research Paper

have the home she so desperately wants, she must learn to control her behaviour.

This control, moreover, must come from her desire to please others rather than from a fear of punishment. When Anne's temper flares up over Mrs. Rachel Lynde's disparaging comments about her looks, for example, Marilla admits that her neighbour "is too outspoken. But," she adds, "that is no excuse for such behaviour on your part. She was a stranger and an elderly person and my visitor—all three very good reasons why you should have been respectful to her" (72). Although at first Anne refuses to apologize to Mrs. Lynde—the punishment Marilla lights upon—Anne eventually does so to please Matthew. As Matthew had immediately recognized, Anne is "one of the sort you can do anything with if you only get her to love you" (52). The threat of expulsion is always present, however, for as Muriel Whitaker points out, Marilla's favourite punishment when Anne has misbehaved is isolation, banishment, ostracism (53).

If Anne's heroic task is to learn the self-control that will make her pleasing to others, Tom's is to translate his imaginary heroism into real heroism. If Tom were a "model boy" like his half brother Sid, he would not fight, play truant from school, sneak out at night, "hook" provisions, and so on. But without these boyish pranks, he would not have the courage and resourcefulness he needs to become a hero. Thus the ingenuity, self-sufficiency, and leadership Tom demonstrates when he, Joe, and Huck run away to Jackson's Island to become pirates are the same qualities he needs to find a way out when he and Becky become lost in the cave. Similarly, Tom's desire to act on his book-knowledge of buried treasure and the ways of robbers leads him and Huck to discover the whereabouts of Injun Joe and his treasure. As a result of these exploits, Tom becomes rich, by his standards, and wins the approval of Becky's father, the imposing Judge Thatcher. As Lyall Powers puts it, "the heroic game becomes impressively the Heroic reality" (321).

Anne's quest, on the other hand, leads her to heroic sacrifice: she gives up her hard-won scholarship to university to stay on the farm and care for Marilla. She is able to make this loving choice because she has learned to consider the rights and welfare of others without sacrificing her own individuality. As she tells Marilla on several occasions, Anne never does "the same naughty thing twice" (102). When her scrapes are her own fault—as in losing her temper with Mrs. Lynde, meddling with Marilla's brooch, and hitting Gilbert Blythe with her slate—Anne takes her punishment and mends her ways. But when her scrapes are not entirely her own fault—as when Diana gets drunk on mulberry wine or Anne puts liniment in the cake instead of vanilla—Anne also learns valuable lessons, for the willing-ness of Marilla and other adults to admit their own failings makes possible the sense of love and secu-rity that turn this initially hostile world into the home Anne so intensely desires. When her romantic views are "sabotaged by 'life' in incident after incident," Anne learns to distinguish romance from reality (Ross 46-48).

In the process of learning from her experiences, Anne is both transformed and transforms others (Whitaker 55). She overcomes Matthew's fear of females; awakens Marilla's undeveloped sense of humour; humbles the judgmental Mrs. Barry; sweetens the temper of Diana's crochety Aunt Josephine. By the end of the novel, even Mrs. Rachel Lynde, who is initially presented as the norm of the village, has become less rigid (Rubio 29). Anne is thus presented as a child who can exert some control over her envi-ronment by furnishing the "psychological, emotional, and imaginative dimensions which are lacking" in the adults' own lives (Rubio 35). In the process, as Whitaker points out, Anne has come to conform "pretty closely to the adult view of propriety" (52). By the time she reaches seventeen, Anne has become what Marilla wanted: "All I want is that you should behave like other little girls and not make yourself ridiculous" (89). But she has done so because this is what she too wants. Her essential nature, like her imagination, has been tempered by her trials, but not destroyed. This match between desire and fulfillment is possible because the world of Green Gables, like Anne herself, is essentially good. Integration into the community is thus itself the goal of Anne's heroic quest and her reward, earned through experience.

In contrast, neither Tom nor his world is transformed by his adventures. Although Robert Regan supports the view, originally put forward by Walter Blair, that the novel "trace(s) Tom's progress from childishness to maturity" (Regan 116), several critics disagree. They argue that because the adults of St. Petersburg are essentially childish, there is no impetus for Tom to change (Fetterley 300; Johnson 51; Miller 73; Whitley 60). Numerous incidents in the book support this contention. Thus Tom's trickery is echoed by Aunt Polly's attempt to catch him out, and Tom's showing off when Judge Thatcher visits the Sunday School by the antics of the staff:

> Mr. Walters [the Sunday School superintendent] fell to *showing off* with all sorts of official bustlings and activities… . The librarian *showed off*, running hither and thither with his arms full of books…. The young lady teachers *showed off*—bending sweetly over pupils that were lately being boxed…. The young gentleman teachers *showed off* with small scoldings and other little displays of authority…(33) [emphasis mine].

Similarly, the fight that ends in the murder of Dr. Robinson is an adult version of Tom's fight, at the beginning of the book, with the new boy in town.

It is no wonder then that even after his harrowing escape from the cave and his recovery of the treasure, Tom returns to playing at robbers. The adult world is not portrayed as different from the world of childhood, and so there is no reason for Tom to grow up. In this respect, the worlds of Tom Sawyer and Anne of Green Gables are not similar, as Mary Rubio suggests (30), but radically different. If, as one critic suggests, Tom is not required "to sacrifice his boy's freedom in return for his success" (Regan 121), the reason may be that Twain "protects

12f

Sample Literary Research Paper

166

Tom from any experience that might seriously impair his 'unrestricted domination': boredom, humiliation, the serious threat of death, lasting or serious disappointment, growing up . . ." (Johnson 59). Tom's initiation thus consists of a series of adventures, not experiences that would lead to maturity (Johnson 51), and his rewards are correspondingly external.

I suggested earlier that these novels can be seen as presenting male and female models of heroism, Twain's novel celebrating individual exploits that lead to external rewards and Montgomery's celebrating a reciprocal process of internal change that leads to transformation of self and society. Robert Keith Miller points out that Twain saw himself as rebelling against the stereotype of the Model Boy portrayed in nineteenth-century children's books and creating instead a portrait of (in Walter Blair's words) "what a normal boy should be" (67). Montgomery's goal seems somewhat different. As we have seen, Anne's first task is to convince Matthew and Marilla that she is worth keeping even though she is not a boy. Anne's rivalry with Gilbert throughout the novel establishes their equality, in keeping with Montgomery's view of there being little difference between men and women (Burns 44–45). If we are tempted to read Anne's story as stereotypically that of the female who triumphs through selfsacrifice, we must remember that Gilbert is also forced to relinquish his chance for a university education because of his responsibility for his family.

This observation leads us to the possibility that the difference between the models of heroism portrayed in the two novels is not merely one of gender but also one of nationality. Tom's story, Lyall Powers argues, reflects the American dream and the American paradox: "The ideal hero is the stout individualist, the non-conforming natural man, American Rousseau, who yet lives snugly in suburbia as a regular fellow" (323). Does Anne then reflect the Canadian dream of social harmony with the recognition of the price we pay in individual sacrifice?

12f

*Sample
Literary
Research
Paper*

Works Cited

Burns, Jane. "Anne and Emily: L. M. Montgomery's Children." *Room of One's Own* 3.3: 37-47.

Fetterley, Judith. "The Sanctioned Rebel." *Studies in the Novel* 3.3 (1971): 293-304.

Johnson, James L. *Mark Twain and the Limits of Power: Emerson's God in Ruins.* Knoxville: U of Tennessee P, 1982.

Miller, Robert Keith. *Mark Twain.* New York: Ungar, 1983.

Montgomery, L. M. *Anne of Green Gables.* Toronto: McGraw, 1968.

Powers, Lyall. "The Sweet Success of Twain's Tom." *Dalhousie Review* 53.2 (1973): 310-24.

Regan, Robert. *Unpromising Heroes: Mark Twain and His Characters.* Berkeley: U of California P, 1966.

Ross, Catherine S. "Calling Back the Ghost of the Old-Time Heroine: Duncan, Montgomery, Atwood, Laurence, and Munro." *Studies in Canadian Literature* 4.1 (1979): 43-58.

Rubio, Mary. "Satire, Realism, and Imagination in *Anne of Green Gables.*" *L. M. Montgomery: An Assessment.* Ed. John R. Sorfleet. Guelph: Canadian Children's P, 1976. 27-36.

Towers, Tom H. "I Never Thought We Might Want to Come Back: Strategies of Transcendence in *Tom Sawyer.*" *Modern Fiction Studies* 21.4 (1975-76): 509-20.

Twain, Mark. *The Adventures of Tom Sawyer.* London: Penguin, 1986.

Whitaker, Muriel, "'Queer Children': L. M. Montgomery's Heroines." *L. M. Montgomery: An Assessment.* Ed. John R. Sorfleet. Guelph: Canadian Children's P, 1976. 50-59.

Whitley, John S. "Kids' Stuff: Mark Twain's Boys." *Mark Twain: A Sumptuous Variety.* Ed. Robert Giddings. London: Vision, 1985. 57-76.

Willis, Leslie. "The Bogus Ugly Duckling: Anne Shirley Unmasked." *Dalhousie Review* 56.2 (1976): 247-51.

12f

Sample Literary Research Paper

12g Sample Non-Literary Research Paper

When you write on a non-literary topic, your research includes finding facts as well as opinions about your subject. You must clearly indicate the source of these facts as well as the source of opinions from experts in the field, whether you use direct quotations or put the information into your own words. The following research paper shows how to give in-text citations and bibliographical references using the American Psychological Association (APA) format. For guidelines on APA format, see Appendix B, Documentation.

Sample Title Page

Whose Turn Is It to Clean Up This Garbage?

Tom De Boeck
Communications 309 XI
November 23, 1995
Professor K. Stewart

A man carrying a large, bulging garbage bag over his shoulder is heading from the front door of his suburban house towards the end of the driveway. He doesn't make it. Sensing that the bag is about to burst, he spins around in an effort to keep it intact, but is too late. He stares down angrily at the ugly pile of debris now strewn about his feet. He notices the used-up deodorant stick and disposable razors; the empty shampoo and detergent bottles; his son's broken tractor; the frozen dinner containers and empty juice cans; and the seemingly countless soiled diapers, each rolled neatly into a ball. Feeling suddenly as if some intensely personal material has been exposed to the probing eyes of his neighbours, the man hurries off for a new bag, fills it up, and deposits it beside three identical bags along the edge of the road. He walks quickly back to the house, relieved to be rid of the mess.

"Taking out the garbage" is a ritual performed once or twice a week in millions of households throughout Canada, the United States, and much of the developed world. Consumers thus rid themselves of a recurring nuisance whose apparent source is an evil conglomeration of advertiser, retailer, producer, and packager, ruthlessly driven to make money. Indeed, few Canadian consumers would accept any responsibility for the looming ecological and political crisis in waste disposal; surely governments and industry should be blamed!

Is the buying public correct in shifting the blame from itself onto big business and big government, and if not, should it know better? In part, consumers cannot be faulted for believing their role in waste production to be a minor one, since quite often their knowledge of the pertinent issues does not extend much beyond their own front yards. But even those who know about the difficulty in locating new garbage dump sites, or about the fact that Canadians produce three to four pounds of garbage per person per day (Canadian Flexible Packaging Institute)—even these people may perceive themselves to be helpless to do anything about the problem. Could they be wrong? Could it be that manufacturers produce what consumers want, and if consumers want convenience, fancy packaging, and disposability, then manufacturers must see that they get it, or risk going out of business? Are consumers the real culprits?

The waste produced by consumers derives, for the most part, from packaging material. What is a package? In a report prepared for the Department of the Environment, Flockton (1973) defines a package in the following manner: "A package contains or holds merchandise, protects it, unitizes it, and communicates a message about it. These packaging services also imply that the package makes a product easier to handle and ship, display and sell" (p. 4). Flockton goes on to say that packaging developed primarily as a response to urbanization, which led to centralized food production and processing. Packaging provided a means for maintaining food for longer periods, and eventually was instrumental in the rise of the self-service store.

How does packaging waste rate in terms of overall refuse production? It is estimated that packaging materials alone account for over half the volume of household, commercial, and municipal waste produced in Canada (Flockton, 1973). Pavan (1981), citing figures for the European Economic Community, states that packaging accounts for 20 to 30% of the weight, and 50% of the volume of total urban refuse in the EEC. In Canada, over half of all consumer packaging is used for food and beverages, while such items as paper, textiles and apparel, hardware, and petroleum products make up less than 12% combined of total packaging output (Flockton, 1973). In short, packaging material would appear to be by far the dominant form of household and municipal waste, thus potentially casting the consumer in the role of culprit in this form of environmental pollution.

What specific attitudes, behaviours, or characteristics of consumers cause them to contribute, unwittingly or not, to the problem of garbage pollution? One important tendency is the pursuit of convenience.

Sample Non-Literary Research Paper

As Flockton (1973) puts it, "The exploitation of man's (or woman's) inherent laziness through packaged convenience is likely to be the single biggest contributor to the overall solid waste accumulation during the next decade" (p. 66). Flockton also notes that as leisure time increases, so does the unwillingness of people to devote time "to such mundane tasks as preparing food, cooking, and washing up" (p. 66). Hugh Connolly (1972) describes some of this convenience packaging, citing "such achievements as the flip-top box, the pull-ring can, the push-button aerosol, the spray-on bandage, etc." (p. 1).

In addition to contributing enormously to household waste, convenience packaging is very expensive. In his book *Packaging as a Marketing Tool*, Stanley Sacharow (1982) reminds us, however, that "Consumers do not resent packages because they think they have to pay for them" (p. 111). Aerosol cans, for example, in addition to being a well-known environmental hazard (chlorofluorocarbons in the propellant destroy the ozone layer), actually cost more than their contents, but sold (and sell) well nevertheless (Flockton, 1973). Consumers are not easily swayed to move from convenient packaging to environmentally responsible packaging either. Joseph Murtha (1972) cites the example of an industry award-winning poly-pouch design for frozen orange juice being totally rejected by consumers in test markets in spite of its functionality, because the design required the buyer to add water to the concentrate. Obviously, frozen juices have finally gained acceptance in the marketplace, but it took several years to overcome consumers' aversion to doing a little extra work.

Unfortunately, shoppers also have a weakness for flashy but often wasteful package designs. Murtha (1972) uses gift packaging of liquor as a case in point: "40% of the liquor sold in the U.S. is sold during the holiday season... and every year it becomes more of a challenge to use more composite materials, to use more aluminum, to use more ribbons, even to put plastic symbols attached to the outside carton. Just in this area alone there could be a tremendous savings in packaging materials and a saving in solid wastes" (p. 41). Sacharow (1982) feels that in an abundant society like ours, "even those with low incomes want psychological satisfactions. . . . straw-covered wine bottles, more expensive than plain glass bottles, give the feeling of real care and naturalness" (p. 111). Consumer fussiness is further illustrated by the fact that, whereas in 1950, a product had a life expectancy of 15 to 20 years, in the 1980s it is less than 3 years (Sacharow, 1982). Each new product means a new package—one that is often more sophisticated and more wasteful in order to capture shoppers' attention in a way the old product was unable to do. Consumer preference for style over function just exacerbates the solid waste disposal problem.

An especially distressing aspect of consumer laziness is the resistance to using returnable containers in favour of disposable ones. Michel de Grave (1981), speaking at a waste management conference in Europe, describes why it is in consumers' best interests to end the use of non-refillable containers:

> The wasteful society with the production of disposable objects has many consequences for consumers. They have to pay for packaging, which can account for 15 to 30 per cent of the retail price and they pay again as taxpayers for the packaging to be cleared away. Then again they have to put up with pollution in the form of litter or collected refuse. Most important of all, they live in a society that sacrifices the future to the present and to a quick profit for some (p. 78).

Merely telling consumers that a container is returnable is not enough. Legislation, frequently grounded in Litter Acts, has had to impose five and ten cent refunds on containers in order to force purchasers to return empties to a depot to recoup the added purchase cost. Success so far has been

12g

Sample Non-Literary Research Paper

mixed at best. Beer bottles achieve a better than 90% return rate (Flockton, 1973), but beer cans probably far less. In the important soft drink sector, consumers have chosen the disposable metal can over the refillable bottle, virtually wiping out the latter in this segment of the market. Taking out the garbage is apparently easier than taking empties to the corner store.

Consumers are spoiled children, ducking their heads when accusing fingers get pointed, blaming others for their naughty acts, but always first in line when shiny new toys are to be had. Spoiled children who fail to play by the rules eventually don't play at all. For consumers, the rules mean recognition of the shameless manner in which they want to be coddled and amused by the goods they buy. The rules also state that cleaning up the environment is a team effort, requiring some sacrifice of leisure and convenience for the sake of ecological survival. Unlike the spoiled child, however, the consumer who is told that he or she can no longer run around in the playground may not get a reprieve.

The news has been filled recently with stories of garbage ships being unable to find a place to dump their cargo, of battles over new garbage dump locations, and of concern over "leaking" garbage dumps polluting the environment or even causing explosions through methane gas ignition. It requires little detective work to figure out who the biggest culprit in all of this is. It is the consumer—you and I. Even animals know better than to foul their own living space. Let's hope we learn, too—before it's too late.

References

12g

Sample Non-Literary Research Paper

Canadian Flexible Packaging Institute. (n.d.). *Flexible packaging and our environment*. Toronto: Author.

Connolly, H. (1972). Packaging and solid waste management. In G. Sachsel (Ed.), *Design of consumer containers for re-use or disposal* (pp. 1-15). Washington: USEPA.

de Grave, M. (1981). Packaging. In J. Woolfe (Ed.),

Waste management (pp. 75-82). Dordrecht, Holland: D. Reidel.

Flockton, P. R. (1973). *Packaging and solid waste.* Ottawa: Dept. of the Environment.

Murtha, J. M. (1972). Packaging and environmental protection. In G. Sachsel (Ed.), *Design of consumer containers for re-use or disposal* (pp. 30-48). Washington: USEPA.

Pavan, L. (1981). Fence sitting by industry is wasteful in the long run. In J. Woolfe (Ed.), *Waste management* (pp. 53-63). Dordrecht, Holland: D. Reidel.

Sacharow, S. (1982). *The package as a marketing tool.* Radnor, PA: Chilton.

12g

Sample
Non-Literary
Research
Paper

Writing an Essay—an overview with a sample essay included

http://josnet.jostens.com/kb/essay.html

University of Victoria—Excellent Essay Writer's Guide

http://webserver.maclab.comp.uvic.ca/writersguide/ es saysTOC.html

Ryerson Polytechnic University—The Writing Centre Guide #3: Writing a University Essay

http://gopher.ryerson.ca:70/0/.services/.write/.essay

The Purdue Online Writing Laboratory research paper guidelines

http://owl.trc.purdue.edu/files/Research-Papers.html

Part 4

WRITING BUSINESS LETTERS, RÉSUMÉS, AND REPORTS

CHECKLIST

Business Writing

	OK	NEEDS WORK

General

1. Is your purpose clear? □ □

2. Does the content meet your readers' needs? (Is there too much or too little information?) □ □

3. Is the tone effective? □ □

4. Is the information accurate and complete? □ □

5. Are the explanations and details adequate to your purpose? □ □

6. Is the sentence structure appropriate to your purpose? □ □

7. Is the word choice effective? □ □

8. Are the transitions between statements clear? □ □

9. Is the format of the document correct? □ □

Business Letters

1. Is the problem or request clearly stated? □ □

2. Have you avoided outmoded expressions? □ □

3. Is the closing appropriate? □ □

Résumés

1. Have you limited your résumé to a maximum of two pages? ☐ ☐

2. Have you chosen a style of résumé (chronological, functional, or combination) that suits your purpose and audience? ☐ ☐

3. Have you included your name, address, and telephone number? ☐ ☐

4. Have you included letters of reference and/or a list of three references? Have you asked each of your references for permission to use his or her name? ☐ ☐

Business Reports

1. Are the parts organized effectively? ☐ ☐

2. Is the degree of formality appropriate? ☐ ☐

3. Have you maintained an appropriate degree of objectivity? ☐ ☐

4. Have you included the necessary preliminary and end matter (for formal reports)? ☐ ☐

Chapter 13

Business Letters

13a General Guidelines for Business Writing

Audience and Purpose

Both business letters and reports often involve writing to someone you do not know personally. For this reason, you will need to make educated guesses about what your reader—a college registrar, a grant committee, a student loans officer—needs to know. It's worthwhile to ask yourself these questions before you begin:

- What is my position in relation to this reader—taxpayer? employee? client?

- What tone, style, and format are appropriate for this relationship?

- How much background information does this reader need?

- What do I want my reader to do in response to this letter or report?

Although business writing deals with factual information, you need to do more than just state the facts. You need to provide an **interpretation** of the facts to make it easier for your reader to understand their significance. By connecting the fact that food preparation staff are inexperienced with the fact that the deep fat fryer is in an awkward location, you can help your reader to see how an employee burned herself. Sometimes this interpretation will help you to clarify an explanation; often it will help you to be persuasive.

Most of the time, business writing involves a combination of exposition and persuasion. If you are writing a report on accidents in a restaurant, you need to explain why the accidents have occurred, but your main purpose is to persuade your reader to adopt your recommendations for solving this problem. If you are writing a job application letter, you need to explain your qualifications, but your main purpose is to convince your reader to interview you. In both writing situations, your explanations should serve your overall persuasive purpose.

If you are unsure about the purpose or audience of your letter or report, consult Chapter 1, Identifying Your Purpose and Audience.

Completeness, Accuracy, Precision

- *Check your letter or report for completeness.* Include all the background information (*who, what, when, where, why, how*) your reader needs to understand the context of your subject and all the factual information and analysis required to support your conclusions and/or recommendations.

- *Be sure that your information is accurate and precise.* Telling your insurance agent that T*he car skidded twenty metres* is more precise than saying *The car skidded a short distance,* but neither statement is accurate if the car actually skidded forty metres.

- *Make your writing clear, businesslike, and friendly.* You can use contractions (*can't, I'd, we'll*) in most business writing except formal reports, but avoid slang. Also avoid outmoded expressions, such as *with regard to your inquiry,* and contemporary bureaucratese, such as *prioritize our objectives* (set our goals) and *implement procedures* (take action).

- *Keep your sentences and paragraphs fairly short, but avoid stringing together a series of very short sentences (which can sound monotonous or aggressive) or a series of one-sentence paragraphs (which can make it difficult for a reader to see connections among your ideas).* Put main points in short sentences. Use longer sentences to fill in details. Varying the length of your sentences will give your writing a more conversational tone.

13b Business Letters

Like other kinds of writing, business letters have their own conventions that raise certain expectations in a reader. By adhering to these conventions, you create a favourable first impression—one suggesting that you know what you are doing and should be taken seriously. Even if your handwriting is perfectly legible, type all business letters.

Here is the standard format for business letters. Every business letter should have the first six components.

1. Your address and the date.

Place this information in the upper right or left corner, single-spaced. If you are using letterhead stationery that includes the address, type the date below it. Do not include your name with your address.

> 123 Juniper Drive
> Thompson, MB   R7N 2K8
> April 26, 19XX [or 19XX 04 26]

2. Your correspondent's name and address.

Place this information on the left margin, single-spaced. It should include everything you would type on the envelope.

3. The salutation (Dear . . .), followed by a colon.

If you do not know the name of the person to whom you are writing, use the title of the individual or department (*Dear Editor or Attention: Customer Relations Department*) or the name of the organization (*Dear Eaton's*).

4. The body of the letter.

Your business letter will normally consist of at least two short paragraphs. Business letters are seldom more than one page. If you need a second sheet, place the page number at the top. Never use the back of a page.

5. The complimentary closing.

Use *Yours truly* for more formal letters and *Yours sincerely* or *Sincerely* for less formal letters. Capitalize the first word of the closing. Place a comma at the end.

6. Your signature.

Type your name below the signature.

7. Enclosures.

Draw your reader's attention to any enclosures, such as a brochure or a cheque, by typing either *Enclosure* or *Enc.* beside the left margin after the signature. Indicate more than one enclosure like this: *Enc. 2*. Name an especially important enclosure in this way: *Enc.: contract.*

8. Copies forwarded.

Use the notation *c* or *copy*, followed by either a colon or a period, to indicate that copies of the letter are being sent to other people:

    c: Mrs. Elizabeth Nelson
    copy: Dr. F. D. Schmidt

13c Sample Business Letter (General)

In the following business letter, you will see the eight components labelled.

```
Centre for Applied Language Studies
Carleton University                   1
Ottawa, ON K18 6B6


October 30, 1995


Dr. Samuel Lieberman
English Department
Mount Saint Vincent University        2
Halifax, NS B3M 2J6


Dear Dr. Lieberman:    3

Thank you for responding so fully and promptly to
our questionnaire on computer-assisted learning
programs for second-language English students. Your
detailed critique of several popular software pack-
ages was especially useful.

    Please find enclosed our latest issue of      4
Carleton Papers in Applied Language Studies. We
would be especially interested in your response to
self-assessment as a guide to placing second lan-
guage students.

    I am looking forward to talking with you again at
our summer retreat in July. Don't forget to bring
your fishing tackle.

Sincerely,     5

ⒶBlack         6

Alison Black

Enc. Carleton Papers   7
c: R. B. McKim, Editor, Carleton Papers      8
```

13d Letters of Request

Like most people, you will occasionally need to write a **letter of request** asking someone to do something for you. For example, you might want to write to your provincial bureau of vital statistics for a copy of your birth certificate or to a former teacher for a letter of recommendation.

An effective letter of request usually contains these three parts:

1. An explanation of why you are asking for help.

2. An explanation of what you want.

3. An expression of appreciation for the help you hope to receive.

Sometimes you can combine all three parts in a single sentence, as in this request for a university calendar:

> I am planning to attend the University of Regina in the fall and would appreciate your sending a calendar of Arts courses to Mary Wong, 543 Queen Street, Guelph, Ontario, N1G 2W2.

If you are requesting a letter of recommendation, on the other hand, you need to provide a more complete explanation, as in the sample letter (13f) on page 185.

13e Letters of Complaint

Letters of complaint and letters of request have much in common. Quite often, in fact, a letter of complaint is also a letter of request. You want to complain about something done badly or not done at all, but you also want something done about it. Therefore, unless your sole purpose in writing a letter of complaint is to express your frustration, it's best to maintain a courteous, friendly tone throughout.

The letter of complaint typically has three parts:

1. A clear explanation of the problem.

2. A clear statement of what you want done about it.

3. An expression of appreciation for the help you hope to receive.

You can see these three parts in the sample letter of complaint below (13g).

13f Sample Letter of Request

#304, 10256103 Avenue
Edmonton, Alberta T5P 2K7

July 10, 1996

Ms. Susan Stephenson, Chairperson
English Department
Capilano College
2055 Purcell Way
North Vancouver, BC V7S 3H5

Dear Ms. Stephenson:

I was a student in your Contemporary Literature class in the fall of 1995. I am applying for a position as a general assignments reporter for the *Smith Lake Weekly* and would greatly appreciate a letter of recommendation from you.

The advertisement for this job states that a person with good writing skills and a background in English would be preferred. Perhaps you could mention the mark I received in your course (A) and the editorial work I did on the class magazine.

Please call me at 732-4710 if you need any more information, and to let me know if it is convenient for you to write this letter of recommendation. You would send the letter directly to the editor: Mr. Frank Burgess, Editor, *Smith Lake Weekly*, 106 Main Street, Smith Lake, BC, V0T 0L0.

Sincerely,

Jim Robinson

Jim Robinson

37 Aldergrove Lane
Kingston, ON K9P 5P7

June 30, 1996

Mr. Daniel Kaniganti, Claims Adjuster
ABC General Insurance Services Ltd.
800 College Drive
Kingston, ON K7K 5L8

Dear Mr. Kaniganti:

On March 6, 1996 I was involved in a car accident in which my 1985 Audi Fox station wagon was hit by a driver who ran a red light at the intersection of King Street and College Drive. The other driver was charged with failing to stop for a red light. My car was damaged beyond repair. I was pleased with the prompt service I received from your company and with the settlement reached on the value of my car.

One problem, however, remains outstanding. During the week of March 7-14, I rented a car from Avis on the verbal understanding I had received from your office that Prairie Mutual Insurance Company, with whom the other driver was insured, would cover my car rental costs. I therefore submitted receipts from Avis to ABC General Insurance Services on the understanding that they would be forwarded to Prairie Mutual for reimbursement. It is now almost four months later and I have not received any money.

As the accident was clearly not my fault, it seems only fair that I should be compensated for the week it took your adjuster to settle my claim. I would not have rented a car had I not received assurance from you that this expense of $210 would be covered. I would greatly appreciate your contacting Mrs. Lynne Black of Prairie Mutual and checking into this matter for me.

If you need more information, please telephone me at 897-5431 (home) or 865-7320 (work).

Sincerely,

Caterine Peterson

Caterine Peterson
Policy Number 7660963

13h Letters of Application

The letter of application accompanies your résumé when you apply for a job. Your aim in both pieces of writing is to create enough interest to secure an interview.

In your letter, you create interest principally by showing how your qualifications meet the requirements for the position. To achieve this purpose, you need a clear sense both of what your qualifications are and of what the job demands. Before you write your application letter, then, you need to do two things: prepare your résumé (see Chapter 14) and find out as much as you can about the position. Examine the job ad carefully and note any particular skills and abilities the job demands, such as a driver's licence or experience with a particular computer program. Talk with anyone you know who has had a similar job or worked for the same employer. Then make a matching list of job requirements and your qualifications so that you can anticipate questions and provide answers.

You also create interest by the way you present yourself. Your letter should convey those aspects of your personality that are most appropriate for the job you are applying for—your enthusiasm, initiative, personal warmth, experience in the field. But don't get carried away; this is a business letter. Choose your words carefully so that you don't sound too gushy, too pushy, or overly casual. And since spelling mistakes and grammatical errors make a very bad impression, proofread carefully.

Parts of the Job Application Letter

Job application letters usually have three parts:

1. An introductory paragraph stating the position you are applying for and indicating where you found out about the job. If possible, establish a connection with the employer by naming the person who suggested you apply. Express enthusiasm for the aims of the organization you want to join.

2. A summary of your skills, knowledge, and personal characteristics that are most relevant to the specific requirements for this position. This may take more than one paragraph. (See the sample letter of application, 13i.)

3. A closing paragraph referring to your résumé and indicating that you are available for an interview at the employer's convenience.

13i Sample Letter of Application

The sample letter was written in response to the following job advertisement. (See 14c for the applicant's résumé.)

Opportunity for experienced, enthusiastic waiter/waitress in well-established, busy operation. Olsen's Bar and Grill, downtown location.

```
#352 Henday Hall
Lister Residence
87th Avenue and 116th Street
Edmonton, AB T6G 2H6

March 10, 1996

Mr. Ron Olsen
Olsen's Bar and Grill
10210 Jasper Avenue
Edmonton, AB T5P 3Y3

Dear Mr. Olsen:
```

I am applying for the waitress job advertised in the *Edmonton Journal* on March 9, 1996. I have experience as a food server, bus person, hostess, and cashier and I would like to work in your restaurant.

For the past three summers, I have worked as a server and hostess at Smitty's Family Restaurant. Our restaurant in Edson was known as one of the three busiest Smitty's in the province. Because this restaurant was so busy, I learned to work well under pressure and to deal with stressful situations.

In addition to serving food and clearing tables, my duties included mixing and serving drinks, a skill that would be a valuable asset in the position you are offering. I have also had some experience working the cash register and handling cash. My duties as a hostess required me to be friendly and polite to customers. I have been told that I am a hard worker who gets along well with others and is pleasant to work with.

Thank you for taking the time to read my résumé. I hope you will consider me for this position. I would be happy to come in for an interview at your convenience.

Sincerely,

Christie Homeniuk

Christie Homeniuk

Enc.: *Résumé*

Chapter 14

Résumés

A résumé is a one- or two-page summary of your educational background and work experience. The first step in preparing a résumé is to think carefully about your potential employer so that you can present your qualifications in the most favourable light. For this reason, it's a good idea to tailor your résumé to the specific job you are applying for, rather than to rely on an all-purpose résumé. If you are using a computer, keep a standard résumé on disk and modify it to suit the job you are applying for. Note, for example, the differences in the two résumés written by a university education student: one to apply for a summer job in a restaurant, one to apply for a teaching job.

Résumés are often filed separately from letters of application, so make sure that your résumé includes your name, address, and telephone number. If possible, drop off your résumé in person; it will mean more to the person who has met you.

14a What Goes into a Résumé

1. Personal information

Put your name, address, and telephone number at the top of the page. If your address and telephone number are temporary, give a permanent address and number where you can be reached.

2. Job target

This statement is optional. Include a brief description of your career goal if you think it will clarify why you are applying for a specific position. State the skills and abilities you would like to use.

To broaden my administrative responsibilities in the health care field where my nursing background and effectiveness in dealing with people would be assets.

189

3. Work experience and educational background

These are the most important parts of the résumé. The way you present this information depends on the kind of résumé you are writing (see below), but your main purpose is to demonstrate that you can do the job you are applying for. Emphasize your achievements and the range of your responsibilities rather than merely giving your job title. Include the names of the institution(s) you have attended and the degrees or certificates you have received. If you haven't gone beyond high school, include the name of the school you attended and the type of diploma you received. You might also indicate that you have met the entrance requirements for college or university. If you are a college or university student, you can omit information about your high school education. List any work-related workshops, training sessions, and non-credit courses you have completed because they indicate enthusiasm for your field.

4. Interests, activities, recognition, and awards

This personal information is optional in a résumé. You can include sports, hobbies, and awards to indicate that you have diverse skills and interests (some of which might be relevant to the job) and qualities, such as courage or perseverance, that an employer would value. This information should be current, so don't include everything you have ever been interested in.

5. References

List the names of people willing to provide references (three is the usual number). Be sure to ask referees' permission before you give their names. Choose people who can provide the best information about you for the job, usually former employers and teachers. Include the person's full name, position, address (if not local), and telephone number. Make clear what your referee's relation to you is (a former teacher, a former employer, a current employer).

It's a good idea to include one or two letters of recommendation with your résumé, if possible. Although they will be addressed to a general reader rather than to a specific employer, these letters are useful (especially when you are one of many applicants for a position) because they provide readily accessible validation of what you have said about yourself in your letter and résumé. For this reason, you might request a letter of reference when you leave a job or if you have done particularly well in a job-related course.

The major drawback to these general letters of recommendation is that they lack confidentiality. For this reason, you should include the name of at least one reference whose letter of recommendation you have not attached to your résumé.

There are three common types of résumés: the **chronological résumé**, the **functional résumé**, and the **combination résumé**. Each has advantages and disadvantages.

14b The Chronological Résumé

This style of résumé presents your educational background and work experience in a chronological sequence from most recent to least recent. It is easy to read and prepare, and because of its simplicity, it is especially useful if you are just entering the work force. On the other hand, if you haven't worked for some time, if you've changed jobs frequently, or if you have remained in the same job without promotion for a long period, it may not be a good choice because it quickly reveals these potential weaknesses. A chronological résumé also makes it more difficult to highlight your achievements.

14c Sample Chronological Résumés

The following résumé was prepared by a fourth-year university student looking for a summer job.

Christie D. Homeniuk
#352 Henday Hall
Lister Residence
87th Avenue and 116th Street
Edmonton, AB T6G 2H6
Telephone: (403) 432-8975

Work Experience: 1992-Present (summers only):
Worked at Smitty's Family
Restaurant in Edson, Alberta as a
server and occasional hostess.
Duties included taking orders,
serving food, mixing alcoholic
beverages, cleaning and setting
tables, greeting and seating customers, working the cash register
and handling cash. Can work well
under pressure and am friendly and
courteous with the public.

Education: Currently in fourth year of secondary education degree program at
the University of Alberta.

Interests: Swimming, attending live theatre
performances, hiking.

References: Mrs. Rose Adria, Manager
Smitty's Family Restaurant
2216 Bear Street
Edson, AB T8G P7Y
(403) 723-3479

Mr. Don Cheung, Assistant Manager
Smitty's Family Restaurant
2216 Bear Street
Edson, AB T8G P7Y
(403) 723-3479

Dr. Jeanne Leblanc
Department of Romance Languages
University of Alberta
(403) 456-9754

This next résumé was written by the same fourth-year education student looking for a teaching job.

```
Christie D. Homeniuk
#352 Henday Hall
Lister Residence
87th Avenue and 116th Street
Edmonton, AB T6G 2H6
Telephone: (403) 432-8975
```

Job Target:	To teach language arts and French courses to junior high students.
Education:	1996: Bachelor of Education/Bachelor of English Combined Degree, University of Alberta. Options in multimedia presentation, the teaching of literature and writing skills, as well as an extensive background in English literature. Three years of university French language and literature courses.
Work Experience:	1994-1995: Gave presentations to students on essay writing skills while employed as a Peer Educator.
1993-1996:	Tutored in English literature, writing skills, and French language skills.
1992-Present (summers):	Worked as a server at Smitty's Family Restaurant in Edson, Alberta.
Interests:	Travelled in France for three weeks in a tour for high school students. Swimming, attending plays, hiking.
References:	Dr. Peter Despines, Professor English Department University of Alberta (403) 456-9814
	Dr. Jeanne Leblanc, Professor Department of Romance Languages University of Alberta (403) 456-9754
	Mrs. Rose Adria, Manager Smitty's Family Restaurant 2216 Bear Street Edson, AB T8G P7Y (403) 723-3479

14d The Functional Résumé

Headings for this type of résumé focus on specific skills and accomplishments relevant to the position you are applying for, rather than a chronological listing of education and work experience. This format is particularly useful for people who haven't worked for some time or whose work experience has come chiefly through volunteer activities. It can disguise an erratic work record and enable you to emphasize your strengths. The major disadvantage of the functional résumé is that some employers distrust it and may think you are trying to hide something.

14e

*Sample
Functional
Résumé*

14e Sample Functional Résumé

A social worker changing jobs might prepare a résumé like this one.

```
WILLIAM FORREST
1235 Elm Street
Halifax, NS B3M 3J6
TELEPHONE: (902) 663-7854


JOB TARGET          Personnel manager in a major retail
                    firm where problem-solving, commu-
                    nication, and administrative skills
                    would be assets.

EMPLOYMENT          Worked with a caseload of 150 fami-
HIGHLIGHTS          lies for five years. Counselled and
                    provided practical assistance to
                    parents and children. Had the repu-
                    tation of offering skilled assis-
                    tance to families in economic and
                    emotional crisis.

COMMUNICATION       Set up and provided editorial
SKILLS              assistance for a newsletter giving
                    information to people on welfare.
                    This newsletter now provides vital
                    information to 10 000 people in the
                    Halifax area. Wrote reports on all
                    clients and wrote proposals for
                    projects requiring special funding
```

from the provincial government. A proposal for a project to provide special services to runaway teenagers was successful in securing an annual grant of $30 000. Regarded as an interesting and informative speaker on family problems, organizational dynamics, and liaisons with government agencies.

ADMINISTRATIVE SKILLS
For three years supervised and assisted recent social work graduates in their first year of employment. Set up and directed a special project to assist runaway teenagers. This project now employs three full-time counsellors and has provided assistance to over 100 young people and their families. The present director continues to maintain contact for ideas, advice, and support.

Had the reputation of being able to select the right person for a particular job and provide assistance to improve the efficiency and effectiveness of all employees.

EDUCATION
Bachelor of Social Work (University of Calgary, 1985)

Bachelor of Arts (major in sociology and English, Mount St. Vincent, 1979)

Participated in workshops and seminars in group dynamics, crisis intervention, and effective management skills.

ACTIVITIES
President Toastmasters Club, 1980, 92-94; member 1986-present

Treasurer, Mount Pleasant Community League, 1984-85

RECOGNITION AND AWARDS
Volunteer Service Award, Westside United Church, 1991

REFERENCES	Dionne Harris, Director
	Youth Emergency Shelter
	1310 Glengarry Avenue
	Halifax, NS B5J 2P4
	(902) 685-4221
	Jean-Paul Sartre, Editor
	No Exit
	Box 1341, Postal Station B
	Halifax, NS B2N 1J7
	(902) 673-0000
	Alastair MacLeod, Supervisor
	Families in Transition
	123 Boat Harbour Drive
	Halifax, NS B2R 3P6
	(902) 633-2957

14f The Combination Résumé

As its name suggests, this résumé combines the features of the chronological résumé and the functional résumé. As in the functional résumé, you use skills and accomplishments as the major headings, but within these headings, you list the relevant information in a chronological sequence. The major advantage of the combination résumé is that it enables you to present a more complete picture of yourself. The major disadvantage is that it must be carefully organized so that it is neither boring nor confusing.

14g Sample Combination Résumé

This résumé was prepared by a person returning to the work force.

196

MURIEL LE BLANC
445 Twenty-Fifth Street
Winnipeg, MB R3T 2N2
TELEPHONE: (204) 335-6529

OBJECTIVE	To use my knowledge of the community and my communication skills to assume administrative responsibilities in the Portage and Main Recreation Centre for Senior Citizens.
CAPABILITIES	Able to assist people with different needs and interests to make decisions through consensus. Able to think creatively and build on others' ideas. Can plan, develop, and follow a project through to completion. Able to work effectively with others by emphasizing strengths and minimizing weaknesses.
ACHIEVEMENTS	Initiated and helped to manage a community-based relief day care centre, now in its tenth year of operation.

ACHIEVEMENTS

Initiated and helped to manage a community-based relief day care centre, now in its tenth year of operation.

President of the River Flats Community League, 1982-84. Responsible for coordinating volunteer activities for a new building, and negotiating the financing, and overseeing construction. The community league is now out of debt and making a modest profit every year. It provides a wide variety of recreational services, including tennis, skating, squash, and fitness classes to over 500 families each year.

Active member of the parents' music support group (Central Junior High) for five years. Coordinated volunteer support for band camps and chaperoned a group of fifty students performing in London, England.

Have been a returning officer in
municipal, provincial, and federal
elections, 1988-present.

EDUCATION   Bachelor of Arts (major in fine
                 arts), University of Manitoba, 1974.

                 Completed extension courses offered
                 by the University of Manitoba on
                 retirement planning, alcoholism and
                 the elderly, and recreation for
                 seniors.

PERSONAL   Skilled at budgeting, purchasing,
                 and household management. Experienced
                 in recreational and holiday planning.
                 Special interest in opportunities for
                 the retired person. An enthusiastic
                 hiker, bowler, and bridge player.

REFERENCES   Available upon request.

Chapter 15

Reports

The term **report** can refer to many kinds of communication, from an informal discussion over the telephone to a lengthy, formal document with a title page, table of contents, and bibliography. In most work situations, you will be given detailed guidelines for the content and the form of the reports you are expected to write. You can then adapt the more general information in this text to your particular task.

In this section, the problem-solving report, the reading report, and the progress report provide examples of short, informal reports, which, as you will see, are often written as memos. The proposal illustrates the characteristics of the lengthy, formal report.

Audience and Purpose

All reports are based on factual information, which is collected, analyzed, and then presented in an organized form. This information will be more credible and useful to your reader if you don't let your interests and biases (such as personal involvement with any of the participants) slant your presentation of the facts.

The degree of objectivity required depends, however, on the kind of report and the needs of your reader. If you are reporting a burglary, you should be as objective as possible. In a reading report, on the other hand, you would be expected to include your opinions on the suitability of the book for a particular audience and purpose. In any report, be sure to distinguish clearly between the facts you present and your interpretation of their significance.

15a Problem-Solving Reports

As its name suggests, a **problem-solving report** is appropriate when you want to analyze a problem and suggest ways to solve it. A dance student, for example, might write a report on the reasons for injuries to first-year students. A restaurant manager might write a report on the effects of staff reductions on the quality of service.

The more specifically you define the problem you want to solve, the more useful your report is likely to be. Try to narrow a general subject, such as security problems, to something more precise, such as *a 30% increase in locker room thefts in the last six months.*

A problem-solving report usually has three sections:

1. Background

Fill in enough information to give your reader a good sense of the context and the importance of the problem. How often does the problem occur? When and where does it occur? How many people are affected? What are the costs in money, efficiency, safety, prestige, morale?

2. Analysis

You should develop this section of your report through causal analysis. Make a list of all the factors contributing to the problem. Be sure to include both immediate causes (inadequate supervision contributes to theft by employees) and more remote causes (employees are dissatisfied with their wages and benefits and therefore some feel entitled to steal).

You can organize this analysis as a list of independent causes or as a chain of interdependent causes (low wages cause employee dissatisfaction; this dissatisfaction causes resentment against the employer; this resentment causes employees to steal). Depending on the complexity of the problem you are analyzing, you may want to combine both methods of developing a causal analysis. (For more information, see Causal Analysis, 5e.) Connect your analysis directly with the information in the background section so that your reader can see how your analysis explains the causes of the problem.

3. Recommendations and implementation

Suggest solutions to the problem you have analyzed. Your recommendations should follow logically from the analysis section. If you are suggesting a number of possible solutions, indicate which one is best and explain why. If appropriate, describe how the recommendations could be implemented.

15b Sample Problem-Solving Report

Date: May 28, 1996

TO: Susan Finkel, Willow Creek Museum Director

FROM: Tim Johnson, Summer Employee

SUBJECT: Unsafe Conditions at the Museum

Over the past month, I have noticed some problems
with the museum facility that should be corrected
before they injure our patrons. As you know, our
resident badger has enlarged his home under the
wooden sidewalk leading to the museum's entrance. A
six-foot section of this sidewalk is ready to collapse. The shaky plank in the third step of the
stairs into the museum has collapsed. Yesterday, I
watched an elderly patron lose her footing on this
step and reach for the handrail. Unfortunately, the
handrail is shaky too, with the result that she
barely managed to keep her balance. We need to correct these problems immediately to protect the
safety of our patrons and ourselves from possible
lawsuits.

We also need to do more routine maintenance to
prevent problems like these from recurring.
Structural damage to the museum, especially the
leaking roof, has reached the point that it threat-
ens our collections.

One reason we have not been able to repair the
museum is that our municipal grant is hardly sufficient to cover our operating costs. A second reason
is that the museum itself, like any older building,
needs a good deal of routine maintenance, which we
have neglected for the past ten years. If we don't
fix the sidewalk and the front steps, only our most
athletic patrons will be able to get into the
museum. If we don't fix the roof, the collections
themselves will be damaged by the elements.

We could apply for a grant increase, but even if we
get it (and that's by no means assured given the
council's preoccupation with water treatment problems), an increase in next year's grant will not
solve our immediate problems. I therefore suggest
the following solutions:

1. Reassign the duties of summer staff workers. At
   present, Ashley cares for the collections and I
   conduct the tours. Ashley is now sufficiently

```
familiar with the collections to conduct most of
the tours herself, an opportunity she says she
would welcome. I could spend the hours freed from
tour guiding on fixing the most pressing prob-
lems, an opportunity that I would welcome as a
source of more variety in my job. We could use
the $50.00 in petty cash to cover the costs of
repairing the front steps and railing.

2. Ask museum patrons for donations and volunteer
   assistance. Patrons who see that we are trying to
   maintain the facility are more likely to con-
   tribute to our efforts. A donations jar and a
   volunteer sign-up sheet listing specific jobs
   will alert patrons to the problems and encourage
   their support.
```

15c Product Reports/Reading Reports

It might seem odd to put a report on a book in the same category as a report on a new brand of microwave ovens, but the main purpose of both documents is to assess the strengths and weaknesses of a product for a particular purpose and audience. Like reviews, these reports help readers to make choices based on the evaluation you provide. The audience for product reports and reading reports, however, is not the general audience you address when you write reviews; it is a single person or small group with a specific need. For more information on evaluation, see Evaluation, (5g). For more information on reviews, see Reviews (11h).

We'll focus on the reading report, but you could adapt this format to report on any product, such as a new photocopier.

The purpose of any reading report is to help your reader decide whether the publication fulfills a specific need. You might, for instance, write a report on a new magazine to support your recommendation that the school library should purchase it.

Or you might survey several children's books on divorce so that the director of a day care centre could choose the most suitable one to read to the children. The more accurately you anticipate your reader's needs, the more useful your report will be.

Most reading reports consist of four parts:

1. Bibliography
Provide information about the publication and suggest where it can be obtained.

2. Summary

Include a description of the publication's most notable features. For more on summaries, see Summaries (10c).

3. Content and style analysis

Analyze the content and style of the publication with respect to its suitability for the intended readers. Be sure to include its practical suitability (cost, length) as well as its aesthetic and moral worth.

4. Evaluation and recommendations

Assess the strengths and weaknesses of the publication for the intended purpose and audience. Make recommendations for its use.

15d Sample Reading Report

You can see these features in this sample reading report. It was prepared for instructors who were considering using Yves Thériault's novel *Agaguk* for a developmental reading class in a community college. As you read this report, note its features and decide whether it meets the needs of the developmental reading instructors for whom it was intended.

```
DATE:      February 3, 1995

TO:        Developmental Reading Instructors

FROM:      Sandra MacGregor

SUBJECT:   Suitability of Agaguk for College Reading
           Students


Agaguk by Yves Thériault, translated from the
French by Miriam Chapin (Toronto: McGraw-Hill
Ryerson, 1963), tells the story of two Inuit
teenagers who leave their village to begin a new
life on the tundra. The novel is intended for the
general reader who is attracted to a fast-paced and
fairly easy-to-read tale of action and adventure.
Agaguk has more than action to offer a more
advanced reader, but its short chapters (usually
3-4 pages) and relatively brief length (229 pages)
make it accessible to a college student in a develop-
mental reading class. An instructor considering this
novel should, however, pay close attention to the
```

---

suitability of its content for a particular group
of students.

Agaguk will interest students who want to know
more about native culture, but it should be noted
(as Thériault points out in his foreword) that the
novel is not intended as a portrayal of contemporary Inuit life. Instead, it shows Inuit life as it
was in the early 1940s, twenty years before the
novel was written. It thus depicts a society and a
way of life just beginning to disintegrate as a
result of the intrusion of white culture in the
North.

The tightly structured plot and the various levels of conflict arouse the interest of most readers. *Agaguk* is, indeed, a novel filled with
conflict. In Part One, these conflicts with the
environment, the white traders, the police, the
villagers, and between the two main characters,
Agaguk and Iriook, have no serious consequences and
the values of traditional Inuit life remain intact.
In Part Two, however, Agaguk begins to experience
defeat as conflicts, both external and internal,
overwhelm him. His misfortunes force his young
wife, Iriook, to assume a more dominant role in
their relationship, a situation that enables
Thériault to portray the gradual erosion of traditional Inuit values. The tension between them
builds as Agaguk struggles with his gratitude to
Iriook and his fear of her new power. Finally,
Agaguk realizes that Iriook's love means more to
him than his own power. He thus achieves a new
maturity and independence as he separates himself
from the oppression of his own tradition and overcomes his fears.

Although *Agaguk* is short and quite easy to read,
its adult content may be disturbing to younger
readers. The graphic depictions of sex and violence
throughout the novel add to its thematic complexity, but they may offend some students. It is also
important to note the ambivalence of Thériault's
attitudes towards the Inuit. He suggests, for
instance, that moral evolution for the Inuit means
leaving behind much of their traditional culture.
In a chapter aptly titled "The Butchers," which
describes the murder and mutilation of a police officer, Thériault seems clearly to be saying that
the imposition of white law is necessary because

the Inuit are so morally primitive. On the other
hand, Thériault portrays individual Inuit quite
sympathetically and shows their exploitation by the
white traders.

With these cautions, *Agaguk* is a novel that works
well in a developmental reading class for college
students. In the six classes in which I have taught
the novel, students have found it interesting and
emotionally engaging. It is simple and short enough
to be enjoyable for less advanced readers while
offering more advanced readers a great deal to
ponder.

15e Proposals

Proposals are the detailed plans that researchers, community
groups, agencies, and businesses submit to government depart-
ments or other organizations when they request money to carry
out specific projects or bid to provide a service or product.
Medical researchers, for example, might submit a grant proposal
to develop new procedures for diagnosing lung cancer. Or several companies might submit competing bids to provide sports
equipment for a school district. We will focus on proposals requesting money.

Many of us find ourselves requesting money, whether it's applying for student loans or seeking funds for student and community groups. The proposals you write for these purposes may
vary in length and complexity. You may write a letter to the parents of a community softball team proposing a bottle drive to
collect money for new uniforms, for example. Or you may be
given a form to fill out and some fairly specific questions to answer, as in applications for student loans. You may even be expected to prepare a lengthy, formal document, especially if you
are requesting a substantial amount of money.

Whatever the form of your proposal, you are more likely to receive support if you can convince your readers that

- your project is worthwhile
- you are capable of carrying it out
- it is cost-effective
- it will further your readers' interests or enhance the reputation of the funding agency.

205

Format for Formal Reports

Our sample proposal is the lengthy, formal kind and thus illustrates most of the characteristics of the formal report. You can therefore follow the format described below to write a formal report on any subject.

Preliminary Matter

- **Transmittal letter or memorandum**

This introductory communication allows you to comment on matters such as why the report was requested, the main problem it addresses, and/or why a particular action is important. It is often very brief, saying not much more than *Here is the report you requested on....*

- **Title page**

Centre the title of the report (not underlined or enclosed in quotation marks) on the page. Be sure the title clearly identifies the subject of the report. In the lower left-hand corner and on separate lines, put the name of the person or the organization for whom the report was written, your name, and the date.

- **Table of contents**

The contents should be an outline of the major sections of the report. Put the heading *Contents* (not underlined or enclosed in quotation marks) at the top of the page.

- **List of figures**

Figures include all charts, maps, graphs, or other illustrations. If your report includes more than three figures, list them separately after your table of contents.

- **Summary or abstract**

This is a one- or two-paragraph summary of all the essential points of the report. Emphasize the report's purpose.

A good summary for a proposal includes the following:

- the names of the person(s) and the organization submitting the proposal, and a brief statement about their qualifications for undertaking the project

- the problem the project will solve

- why a solution to this problem is important
- the specific objectives of the project
- how the project will be carried out
- the total costs involved and the specific amount requested (if applicable).

The Body of the Report

The essential divisions are an **introduction**, a **body**, and a **conclusion**. Subheadings in the body will help your reader to see the main divisions more clearly. Notice the headings you might use in the body of a proposal.

• *Introduction*

In a proposal, the purpose of your introduction is to lead readers naturally and logically to the statement of the problem that your project will solve. If you belong to an organization, begin by stating its qualifications for funding. Include the organization's purposes and goals, a brief description of the people it serves, and its most important activities and programs. Statistics providing evidence of success will reinforce your credibility.

You will be more persuasive if you present a specific problem of manageable proportions. Instead of trying to end world hunger, you might try to feed the hungry children at a local school. Explain the rationale for the project in terms of how the clients' needs are served. Focus, for example, on the needs of children who are too hungry to learn rather than on the benefits to the Home and School Association of providing them with lunches.

• *Project Objectives and Methods*

When you state your objectives, you say **what** you want to accomplish. When you state your methods, you explain **how** you will reach these goals.

Your objectives should focus on what you will achieve, not what you will do. *We would like to give every grade 3 student a nourishing lunch* is a less convincing goal than *By providing lunch we will increase the number of children successfully completing grade 3*. Be sure that your objectives cover all the problems you have identified. Include the beginning and end dates for the project.

When you explain your methods, be specific about the sequence of activities you plan to undertake, who will be responsible for their completion, and whom they will serve. Sometimes a chart will provide your reader with a useful summary of your activities.

• *Evaluation*

Clearly indicate what standards you will use to assess the effectiveness of your project. Give the credentials of the evaluators. You can include samples of questionnaires and explain how the evaluation data will be collected. Explain how you will change your methods if the evaluation indicates weaknesses.

• *Future funding*

You may want to include this section if you are requesting funding for a project. An agency granting funds may be dismayed by the prospect of a proposal that seems like a bottomless pit. If you can show how your project will continue without future funding, and if you can provide letters of commitment for future funds from other sources, your proposal will be stronger.

• *Budget*

Itemize all the expenses involved in your proposal. These will include both direct costs (everything you pay for, from salaries to postage) and indirect costs (goods and services provided at no cost that you would otherwise have to pay for, such as volunteers' time and donated equipment). Itemize all the projected income as well: the amount you are requesting, the amount you've received from other sources, and the value of donated time and equipment. The total budget should be sufficient to cover all the activities described in the proposal.

End Matter

• *Appendix.* Include information in the appendix or appendices that is related to your report but not of central interest to your readers. Detailed technical information and reviews of related research belong here.

• *Bibliography.* List the references you used in the order in which they appear in the report.

15f Sample Proposal

This sample proposal has all the components of a full-scale request for money. Note the emphasis on the importance of the problem and the careful attention to detail necessary to make the proposers credible and their request for money persuasive.

A REQUEST FOR INNOVATIVE PROJECTS FUND SUPPORT

PROJECT TITLE: Self-Help Group for the Unemployed

PROJECT DIRECTOR: Elizabeth Rogers
                  Chair, Northwood Coalition of
                  Unemployed Workers
                  Member, Social Responsibility
                  Committee
                  Northwood Unitarian Society
                  Wilmox, NB

SUMMARY

Five members of the Northwood Coalition of
Unemployed Workers propose to establish a self-help
group to provide emotional support and practical
advice to people experiencing the hardships of unemployment. Although unemployment creates serious
practical and emotional problems for both the unemployed person and his or her family, these problems
are not given much importance in our society. Self-
help groups have proved especially effective in
providing assistance to people whose problems are
given low status by society.

As a result of the closure of our local sawmill
and the reduction in rail service, unemployment has
increased 15 percent over the past eighteen months.
Our self-help group would create a supportive environment and provide practical information for unemployed people. Our plans include bringing in guest
speakers to provide expert advice on such topics as
nutrition, budgeting, and stress management.
Members will be encouraged to assess their own
needs and share their experiences.

The Northwood Unitarian Society has agreed to
provide us with a meeting room, child-care facilities during meetings, and three hours a week of
clerical assistance free of charge. We require
$4800 to cover publicity, child-care assistance,
clerical supplies, and honoraria for guest speakers. The self-help project will run twelve months
beginning January 1, 1996 and ending December 1,
1997.

INTRODUCTION

The Northwood Coalition of Unemployed Workers provides clerical assistance to people attempting to find work. The emotional and practical problems of actually being unemployed, however, fall outside the scope of the Coalition's activities. The isolation and stress created by unemployment undermine the health of the whole family, often creating conditions that make it more difficult for a person to find a job.

Over the past six months we have noticed an increasing number of requests for the sort of assistance that a self-help group can provide. Because many of these requests come from family members of the unemployed person, it is especially important to create a self-help group that includes their needs. Our own survey of the Northwood Coalition indicates that forty members are interested in a self-help group. Half of these are single parents who require the supervised child care we will provide during the meetings.

The five members of the Coalition requesting these funds have a wide range of practical experience and administrative skills necessary to run an effective self-help group. Two are active members of self-help groups for other organizations and two have been presidents of volunteer groups. We realize that ours would be the first self-help group to receive support from the Innovative Projects Fund, but we are confident that our purposes and activities fall within the scope of other projects sponsored by the Fund, such as the successful recreation program for seniors at the Melrose Nursing Home and the day care centre for Alzheimer's victims.

PROJECT OBJECTIVES AND METHODS

We have two main objectives:

1. To create an environment that provides emotional support for all members and their families.

2. To provide knowledgeable advice and practical assistance to unemployed persons, enabling them to cope more effectively with the experience of being out of work.

Our activities will include the following:

1. Weekly meetings at the Northwood Unitarian Church from January 1, 1996 to December 31, 1997.

2. A guest speaker once a month.

3. A newsletter, prepared by members, listing relevant community resources and providing practical tips on coping with all aspects of unemployment.

The planning group will arrange for publicity, hire a child-care worker, arrange for guest speakers, and assume responsibility for the use of the meeting room.

EVALUATION

The success of the self-help group for the unemployed will be judged by the following:

1. The number of people attending the meetings.

2. The response of members during the meetings and to the questionnaires, which will be distributed every two months.

3. The effectiveness of the publicity in attracting new members.

The executive of the self-help group called Unsung Heroes have agreed to meet with our planning committee to provide suggestions and feedback on our questionnaires and meetings. We will modify the proposed activities of the group in response to this feedback and our own questionnaires.

FUTURE FUNDING

Enclosed with this proposal is a letter from the Social Responsibility Committee of the Northwood Unitarian Church promising continued use of their facilities and continued clerical assistance for 1998. We anticipate lower publicity costs when the self-help group has been established for one year.

BUDGET

Publicity	$1000.00
Hospitality	$500.00
Honoraria for Guest Speakers	$2000.00
Clerical Supplies	$300.00
Child-Care Costs	$1000.00
Meeting room and child-care facilities (donated by the Northwood Unitarian Society)	$1000.00
Clerical assistance—3 hours a week	

```
(donated by the Northwood Unitarian
Society)                              $2500.00
Planning, organizing, and evaluating
self-help group activities (time donated
by the project planning committee)    $1500.00
Evaluation assistance from Unsung Heroes
(time donated by executive—see enclosed
letter of commitment)                  $500.00
Report for the Innovative Projects Fund:
February, 1998                         $500.00
(time donated by the project planning
committee)


TOTAL PROJECT COSTS                 $10 800.00
AMOUNT DONATED                       $6000.00
AMOUNT REQUESTED                     $4800.00
```

15g Project Reports

You would write a project report, sometimes called an interim report, when you need to report on your progress in carrying out a project. Project reports usually have these five parts:

1. Introduction
Identify the project, the participants, the time frame, and the purpose.

2. Background
Provide background information and summarize the work already completed.

3. Work-in-progress
Give a detailed description of work now being done and any problems that may affect the completion of the project.

4. Future plans
Provide a brief description of plans for the future.

5. Recommendations
Add these, if appropriate, to your report.

You can see all these features of project reports in the following sample.

15h Sample Project Report

DATE: April 10, 1996

TO: Alice Daniels, Pool Supervisor

FROM: Susan Goldberg, Lifeguard

SUBJECT: Reducing Collisions in the Distance
            Swimming Lanes

As you know, for the past two months the lifeguards and staff at the Eastglen Swimming Pool have been trying to prevent congestion and collisions in the two lanes reserved for distance swimming during the noon hour. Here is an update on the effectiveness of our new policies.

First we changed the designation of these lanes. Originally, the wall lane was designated for fast swimmers. Unfortunately, slower swimmers preferred this lane because they could rest momentarily by hanging on to the wall. Now that the second lane is designated for fast swimmers, there are fewer collisions between slow and fast swimmers.

We are currently working on reducing congestion in both lanes. This congestion has two sources: the intrusion of non-length swimmers and the number of patrons trying to swim lengths in the same lane. Because most intruders were retrieving balls, we have kept most of them out of these lanes by prohibiting games during the noon hour. Problems caused by too many swimmers (often as many as ten) in these lanes persist. Since these patrons swim at different speeds, it is difficult for more than four swimmers to share a lane without collisions.

To solve this problem of overcrowding, we need to limit the number of distance swimmers. We propose providing the pool cashier with cards to be given to patrons who want to swim lengths. Only eight of these cards would be in use simultaneously. Length swimmers would give their card to the lifeguard when they enter the pool. When they leave, they would return the card to the cashier.

Changing the designation of the lanes and prohibiting games during the noon hour have helped to reduce collisions in the lengths-swimming lanes. The problem of too many swimmers in these lanes remains and causes frustration for patrons. I therefore recommend that we try issuing cards for lengths swimmers for a test period of two months to see if this strategy helps to solve the problem.

15i Memorandums

Memorandums, or memos, are the usual form of communication between members of the same organization. Memos may be sent on hard copy, via interoffice mail, or more and more frequently, they may be transmitted from one computer to others, via electronic mail (e-mail). Follow the guidelines for letter writing to organize the content of your memorandum. The format conventions are illustrated below.

15j Sample Memorandum

```
DATE:      July 23, 1995

TO:        Susan Schnell, Franchise Manager [name
           and title of the person to whom the memo-
           randum is sent]

FROM:      Luigi Amodio [name of the writer]

SUBJECT:   Bunk Bed Safety [precise statement of the
           main focus]
```

Last week I received a letter from the Consumers' Advocates of Sarnia reporting complaints about the safety of children's bunk beds. These complaints included concerns about ladders that became detached from the bed frames and bunks that were not securely bolted together.

The most serious problems, however, occurred when sleeping children were caught between the guard rail and the mattress. The enclosed safety guidelines from Consumers' Advocates clearly show how a child can suffocate.

Please use these guidelines to check your stock and warn all sales personnel of the dangers posed by the models listed in the second enclosure. Sales staff should alert prospective buyers of the risks bunk beds may pose to children under six years of age.

Enc. 1.: safety guidelines

Enc. 2.: list of bunk bed models

Luigi Amodio

Luigi Amodio

Punctuation Guide—from NASA's *A Handbook for Technical Writers and Editors*

http://sti.larc.nasa.gov/html/Chapt3/Chapt3-TOC.html

Capitalization Guide—from NASA's *A Handbook for Technical Writers and Editors*

http://sti.larc.nasa.gov/html/Chapt3/Chapt3-TOC.html

Online Careers Resources—a collection of sources of information about résumé writing, interview skills, success in the workplace, rights in the workplace, and Canadian career and job search centres

http://www.etc.bc.ca/provdocs/careers/subskills.html

The Rensselaer Writing Centre offers a variety of online handouts including information on résumé and cover letters.

http://www.rpi.edu/dept/llc/writecenter/web/ handouts.html

Business and Technical Writing Links from the Purdue OWL

http://owl.trc.purdue.edu/resources.html#business

The Riley Guide: Employment Opportunities and Job Resources on the Internet

http://www.jobtrak.com/jobguide/

Part 5

WRITING WITH STYLE

Chapter 16

Improving Your Style

What Is Style?

Style is the result of all the conscious and unconscious choices you make as you write, including choices about the words you use, the kinds of sentences you construct, the length and structure of your paragraphs. So you already have a style—in fact, you likely have many styles you shift among as you write for different purposes and audiences.

But perhaps you would like your writing to be more vivid or more concise, or to flow more smoothly. If so, you will find numerous suggestions below.

16a *Improving Your Word Choice*

Some writers use informal language in writing that requires more formal diction. Others adopt a formal vocabulary so completely that their writing becomes stilted. Still others coast along, using words that are safe but dull. Paying attention to the words you use will help you remedy these problems.

Understanding **levels of language** will help you choose words appropriate for your purpose and audience. Consider these words meaning *poor*:

Formal	Standard	Informal

impecunious, destitute, poverty-stricken, poor, hard up, broke, busted.

These words illustrate what we mean by levels of language, with "big words" such as *impecunious* and *destitute* at the formal end of the scale; colloquial and slang terms such as *hard up* and *busted* at the informal end; and the standard vocabulary of public writing and speaking in the middle (*poverty-stricken, poor*). Most of the words you use in writing for college or university should come from a standard vocabulary. You will find suggestions below about when and how to use formal and informal language.

16b Choosing Appropriate Language: Formal Writing

When you are writing academic essays, reports, and business letters, keep these suggestions about word choice in mind.

1. Aim for a serious, knowledgeable, and businesslike tone but avoid sounding stuffy or pompous.

Choose *some* key words from the slightly formal range (*poverty-stricken* or *destitute*, but not *impecunious*), but in general prefer standard words to more formal terms (*need* rather than *necessity*, and *uses* rather than *utilizes*).

2. Use specialized terms only when necessary.

Part of what you learn when you study psychology, sociology, and other academic disciplines is the language that specialists in the field use in talking and writing to other specialists. In an essay discussing Freud's theory of the unconscious, for example, you would use Freud's terms *id*, *ego*, and *superego*. There are no other words that would precisely convey the meaning of these concepts.

But when a specialized vocabulary is used inappropriately, it is called *jargon*. Jargon obscures meaning rather than making meaning more precise. When jargon combines with an unnecessarily formal vocabulary, writing can become almost unintelligible, as in the examples below.

NOT
As the precepts of individual psychology are ultimately reflected in social psychology, the psychic impairment experienced by the student as part of the educational process will be augmented within the context of the social environment.

BUT
Since students carry their perceptions of themselves into the larger social world, any damage to their self-esteem will become more severe when they leave school.

NOT
Management will access the input of all interested parties, prioritize their responses, and introduce modifications to the terms of the proposal accordingly.

219

The manager will ask all interested parties for their reactions to the proposal, review their responses, and make changes accordingly.

3. Avoid slang and colloquial expressions.

many rather than *a lot of*
an acquaintance rather than *a guy I know*

4. Avoid clichés.

Clichés serve a useful purpose in spoken language, but in formal writing they may suggest that the writer is treating the subject superficially, as in this example:

> Undoubtedly, there is pressure for change from within South Africa, including pressure from Afrikaaners. This is a small number, but at least it is a number, and every little bit helps.

5. Use contractions sparingly.

Some readers object to contractions in formal writing; others don't. If you use an occasional contraction to keep from sounding too stiff, make sure you use the apostrophe correctly (see Apostrophes, 21h).

6. Use I and you sparingly.

Don't distract your readers from your subject by constant references to yourself: *I think, I feel, I believe, it seems to me that.* When it is appropriate to use *I*, use it rather than substituting *one* or *this writer.*

NOT	It seems to me that this anthology is unsuitable for the high school curriculum.
NOT	In the opinion of this writer, this anthology is unsuitable for the high school curriculum.
BUT	This anthology is unsuitable for the high school curriculum.
OR	Although other reviewers consider this anthology suitable for the high school curriculum, I disagree.

Similarly, avoid using *you* in formal writing to mean *people in general.*

16b

*Choosing
Appropriate
Language:
Formal
Writing*

NOT	The university's marking system can be frustrating when all of your professors have their own scale within the scale.
BUT	The university's marking system can be frustrating when professors have their own scale within the scale.

Exercise 16.1

Comment briefly on the effect of jargon and big words in the following paragraph, taken from a research paper on the back-to-basics movement in education. Then rewrite the paragraph in simpler, more concrete language.

16b

Choosing Appropriate Language: Formal Writing

> The teacher I interviewed perceived her role as a socializing agent with a humanistic approach. She added that although students lacked skills to handle grade five curriculum, her priority was to allow student-directed activities in a safe environment free of negative labelling. Correcting exams and clerical tasks presented a strain on her role. She felt psychology was the most beneficial course she had taken at university: she taught many children experiencing stress from broken families or families who did not share time.

Exercise 16.2

Find a paragraph of your own expository writing in which jargon and big words obscure your meaning or fail to convey your attitude towards your subject. Rewrite your paragraph to make the diction more effective.

Exercise 16.3

Underline inappropriate word choices in the following paragraph (adapted from a research paper on impaired driving). Then rewrite the paragraph so that the diction is more appropriate for the subject and audience.

> Kathy Stechert's research on drunk driving (1984) has suggested some prevention techniques that you should consider when entertaining guests in your home: serve lots of food; provide non-alcoholic beverages; don't pressure guests to drink; water down drinks when guys are consuming too much alcohol. Don't let guests leave the house if they've had too much to drive safely; ask them to wait until they've sobered up or to stay overnight. If they make a fuss and insist on leaving, drive them home. It is really amazing that many people don't think about what could happen after guests leave the party. It doesn't take a genius to see that these measures would help reduce drunk driving.

Exercise 16.4

Find a paragraph of your own expository writing that you can improve by maintaining a more formal level of diction.

16c Choosing Appropriate Language: Informal Writing

For personal and persuasive writing intended for a general audience:

1. Try for the friendly, engaged tone of one person talking to another.

That means choosing most of your words from the standard to slightly informal range (*poor, hard up*). Choose short, common words over longer synonyms.

possess=own, have	automobile=car
retain=keep	residence=house
purchase=buy	difficulties=troubles

2. Use more formal words to create suggestive images, humour or satire, and subtle shades of meaning.

the undulations of the wheat
the writer was lionized in London, lampooned in L.A.
serpentine streets

3. Choose concrete nouns *over* abstract nouns *and* specific nouns *over* general nouns.

Abstract nouns name qualities (*friendship, heroism*) or concepts (*the state, conservatism*). **Concrete nouns** name things we can perceive through our senses (*your friend, the brain*). **General nouns** apply to a class of things (*adolescents, buildings*) rather than to a single, specific thing (*the teenager who works at The Bay, the CN Tower*). Abstract and general nouns keep your reader at a distance.

4 Use first- and second-person pronouns (**I, you**)*, where appropriate, to establish a personal relationship with your reader.*

5. Use occasional contractions, colloquial expressions, or slang terms, if appropriate to your subject and audience.

6. Choose active verbs *over* state-of-being verbs *and* verbs in the passive voice.

By changing **state-of-being**, or **linking**, verbs (*is, seems, exists, has, contains, feels*) to active verbs, you can often make a vague, general statement into a precise, vivid image.

NOT	She *has* short brown hair. Her face is round.
BUT	Her short brown hair *cups* her round face.
NOT	I *felt* angry.
BUT	I *throbbed* with anger.
OR	I *stalked* out of the room.

Verbs in the **passive voice** may take the energy out of your writing:

| NOT | The winning goal was scored by me. |
| BUT | I scored the winning goal. |

To see how changing the diction can improve a piece of writing, compare the following versions of a paragraph on the perils of sailing. In the first, the formal language makes the danger seem remote.

Sample Draft Paragraph

Of course there are those who endure the elements as necessitated to earn a living. Traditionally they are the men of the sea. Sailors maintain many fears in terms of the elements. For instance, atmospheric electricity playing around the mast might cause a fire. To the sailor's peril, ice can cover the rigging, leaving the ship topheavy and in danger of "turtling." Thrashing waves and Titanic swells can consume both craft and crew.

In the revised paragraph, the simpler language, active verbs, and concrete nouns create a vivid image of a ship in danger.

Sample Revised Paragraph

Sailors have traditionally earned their living by enduring the dangers of the elements. Sailors fear the blue haze of St. Elmo's fire encircling the mast, and its acrid smell of burning. They fear the surge that rises twelve metres above the mizzen and the waves that slam the hull from every direction. The wind, as it sings through the stays, charts a new course without aid of a compass, without earthly reason. But at no time is a sailor's job so perilous as when the wind chill plunges the mercury to minus thirty-five and droplets of mist condense on the supercooled rigging. Then layer upon layer of ice forms. When an ice-laden ship gets top-heavy, no amount of praying will keep it afloat. The captain's call goes out: "The gyros are toppling."

—Chris Paterson

Exercise 16.5

16d

Adding Interest

Underline word choices in the following paragraph that you find ineffective for a personal essay. Then rewrite the paragraph using more vivid language.

Chuck is, simply put, a mean person. One would not say that he is a sadist, exactly. He is not of the character to pull the wings off flies, albeit he does on occasion step on ant hills. No, Chuck is not precisely demented. He merely loves practical jokes—mean-spirited practical jokes. He seems to thrive on them. One time a small, plastic-wrapped packet of cloves was left by Chuck on the desk of a fellow student named Ramona. Attached to the packet with tape was a note that read, "Cloves make an effective breath freshener." Ramona was, with justification, mortified and offended. On other occasions sample bottles of deodorant and acne medication have been left on classmates' desks. One could say that these tactics work to undermine a person's self-confidence. Chuck also has an inconsiderate mouth. In the recent past, on the day we were being photographed for the yearbook, Jerry Johnson wore a new suit. Hiding behind his most sincere smile, Chuck told Jerry, "Jer, my man, that suit really suits you, ha, ha. I donated one just like it to the Sally Ann last week." I used to laugh at Chuck's peccadilloes, until this morning. As we were walking out of math class, the teacher directly behind us, that insensitive Chuck enunciated clearly, "Ken, I wish you would not say those things about Mr. Mueller. I think he is a fine teacher." I am planning how to asphyxiate Chuck in his sleep. The deed will definitely be done with malice aforethought.

Exercise 16.6

Find a paragraph in one of your personal essays where the diction seems flat and colourless. Rewrite the paragraph according to the suggestions above.

16d Adding Interest

Enliven your writing by using quotations and other kinds of allusions, dialogue, and figurative language.

Quotations

Use familiar quotations—proverbs, lines from songs, advertising slogans, sayings of famous people, well-known bits of poetry and prose—to make an emotional appeal and to create a sense of shared experience. You don't need to give complete bibliographical information for quotations used in passing, but do put them in quotation marks and identify the source.

> When you are backpacking through Europe, your money will start to dwindle and you will feel moments of fear and desperation. As *The Hitchhiker's Guide to the Galaxy* so wisely advises, "Don't panic."
>
> —*Lori Yanish*

16d

Adding Interest

Allusions

An allusion is a casual reference to a figure, event, or document from history, literature, mythology, popular culture, or religion. Allusions help to establish your authority as a writer by indicating the breadth of your knowledge or experience. They may also have a strong emotional impact because they evoke shared experiences.

> Like Caesar, he came, he saw, he restored order where confusion reigned. —*Chris Carleton*
>
> Her hopes, like Miss Havisham's wedding cake, had been eaten away. —*Chris Carleton*
>
> I suspected life at Stephanie's house might be just like life at Dick and Jane's. —*Suzanne Cook*

Dialogue

Use dialogue for dramatic effect. Direct speech allows you to show what happened rather than merely to tell the story. It also gives variety to your writing by introducing other voices.

> My parents were glued to a small black and white television in room #107. I wandered into the room and tugged on my mother's skirt until she lifted me into her lap. "Look, it's Neil Armstrong," she said as she directed my gaze at the small screen. "He's about to walk on the moon."
>
> —*Mario Trono*

Figurative Language

Figures of speech create vivid mental images for your readers. Use them to sharpen your descriptions and to convey your attitude towards your subject. Try your hand at the five types illustrated below: simile, metaphor, personification, hyperbole, and irony. Avoid clichés (*dead as a doornail*) and mixed metaphors (*flooded with an iron resolve*).

A clock, hanging like a sign of doom over my head, showed the lateness of the hour (simile). —*Terri Dana*

We are nothing but a jar full of flour beetles, continually eating and reproducing (metaphor). —*Cheryl Lewis*

The unruly maple holds fast to her golden gown (personification). —*Lillian Darling*

Those demonic savages, those cruel, sadistic, verminous beings, those bus drivers, have persisted in their heinous acts (hyperbole). —*Amanda Thompson*

Mr. Simpson would pretend to drive into Miss Merril's little BMW just to terrify her in a neighbourly way (irony). —*Alex Cheung*

Exercise 16.7

Rewrite a paragraph from one of your personal essays so that it includes two or more of the devices discussed in this section.

16e Improving Your Sentence Structure

Keep your sentence structure consistent with your purpose and audience. To create a conversational tone in personal essays and other informal types of writing, use occasional sentence fragments (see Fragments, 17d) and avoid sentence patterns that require formal punctuation such as semicolons and colons. For more formal writing, avoid using sentence fragments or informal punctuation such as dashes and exclamation marks.

Reading your work out loud, to yourself or to a classmate, will help you determine whether your writing "flows." If in places the rhythm of your sentences seems jerky, monotonous, or at odds with the effect you want you create, try these suggestions.

1. Vary your sentence patterns.

2. Vary your sentence length.

Sentence Patterns

Most of your sentences are likely to follow Pattern 1 below, Subject + Verb + Modifier. But if all your sentences fall into this pattern, your writing is likely to become monotonous. You can use other sentence patterns to create emphasis, to mimic the process of thinking, or to engage your readers more directly.

Pattern 1. The Loose Sentence: Subject + Verb + Modifier

Karen never won, no matter how hard she tried.

This sentence illustrates the most common sentence pattern in English, and the one most easily understood by readers: subject + verb + modifier. Since the most emphatic position in the sentence is normally at the end, this sentence would lead naturally into a discussion of how hard Karen tried.

Pattern 2. The Periodic Sentence: Modifier + Subject + Verb

No matter how hard she tried, Karen never won.

Because we have to wait for the subject and verb, this sentence pattern creates interest and suspense. It also throws heavy emphasis upon Karen's inability to win, and thus would prepare readers for a discussion of the reasons for her lack of success or for examples of her failures.

Pattern 3. The Embedded Sentence: Subject + Modifier + Verb

Karen, no matter how hard she tried, never won.

Here subject and verb are separated by a lengthy modifier. Because this sentence pattern slows the reader down, it effectively imitates the process of thinking through a problem or situation. The modifier also shifts the emphasis to the beginning of the sentence. As readers, we might therefore expect to explore less obvious aspects of Karen's personality or background that would account for her lack of success.

227

Pattern 4. Sentences Employing Parallelism

There are two ways to use parallelism in sentences.

• Join two or more closely related clauses with a coordinate conjunction or semicolon. (This pattern is also called a **balanced construction.**)

You can allow your anxieties to rob you of sleep and satisfaction, or you can plan your time wisely and then enjoy your free time thoroughly.

—Wendy Amy

• Arrange a series of words, phrases, or clauses in order of increasing importance.

Friends listen to you babble, tell you honest opinions when you prefer lies but need the truth, tell you *I told you so* at annoying times, defend your reputation from others, and generally mother, father, grandparent, and sibling (brother or sister) you.

—Amanda Thompson

Pattern 5. Rhetorical Questions

How many times have you waited in the rain or snow for a bus that is ten minutes late? How many times has a surly bus driver snapped an answer to your innocent question? How many times have you stood for half an hour in a bus crammed with people?

—Cheryl Lewis

Pattern 6. Uncommon Constructions

• Use paired conjunctions (*both/and, neither/nor, not only/ but also*) to link ideas.

Neither fear of failure nor desire for glory drove her to practise that trumpet hour after hour.

• Use a noun clause as the subject.

That he would win the election was certain.

Sentence Length

To create rhythm and emphasize important points, use a combination of short sentences (ten words or fewer), long sentences (thirty words or more), and medium-length sentences.

- Short sentences are effective for rendering abrupt actions, giving directions, stating main points, and creating emphasis.

ABRUPT ACTIONS | She stopped.

DIRECTIONS | First stop the bleeding.

MAIN POINTS | One cause of high unemployment is government policy. (*Essay topic sentence*)

Safety violations have increased 10% over last year. (*Report topic sentence*)

EMPHASIS | He loved no one.

The war was over.

16e

Improving Your Sentence Structure

- Long sentences are effective for expressing continuous action, giving a series of details or examples, and creating a sense of closure.

CONTINUOUS ACTION | After discovering Jack's country address, Algernon assumes his friend's secret identity and poses as wicked Ernest Worthing for his meeting with Cecily, Jack's sheltered young ward; but when they meet for the first time, the worldly, cynical Algernon is momentarily confounded by the sophisticated wit of "little" Cecily.

DETAILS | According to the criteria for student loans, students are considered to be financially independent only if they have no parent, guardian, or sponsor; are married or a single parent; have been out of secondary school for four years; or have been in the labour force for twenty-four months.

CLOSURE | In the final analysis, the losers are not merely those who have been jailed for insider trading, nor the firms whose reputations have been sullied, nor the stockholders who have lost money; the losers are all those who have lost confidence in the integrity of the stock market.

Exercise 16.8

The following paragraph on how actors learn a scene has been reduced to a series of short sentences. Rewrite the paragraph using a variety of sentence lengths and sentence patterns to make it more interesting.

Preparing a scene of a play is time-consuming. It may not appear time-consuming. First the actor reads the scene. The actor becomes familiar with it. Then he or she reads the entire play. The play gives the actor an idea of the events that lead up to the scene. It also gives the actor insights into the characters. The actor then asks questions about the character. The actor asks what the character looks like. The actor asks questions about the character's family. The actor asks what happened in the past. The actor asks these questions until he or she can picture the character. Then the actor goes back to the script. The actor reads each line. The actor is looking for hidden meanings. The actor figures out what is not being said. The actor thinks about what the character wants. The actor thinks about what the character does. The two things may be in conflict. Next the actor plays the scene. He or she does what the script indicates. He or she thinks about what the character really wants. For example, the character may look happy. Inside the character may want to cry. Finally the actor knows the character inside out. Then the actor can memorize the scene.

Exercise 16.9

Find a paragraph of your own that you can improve by varying sentence length and sentence patterns. Rewrite it.

Exercise 16.10

The following paragraph sounds choppy because it is written almost entirely in short, simple sentences. Rewrite the paragraph to improve the rhythm, using several of the techniques discussed above.

Being your own boss has its down side. I learned the hard way. One summer I decided to go into business for myself. I was tired of my usual part-time jobs. I was tired of the long hours and low pay at the fast-food restaurants and laundries I'd worked at in the past. I decided to strike out on my own. I started up the Domestic Bliss Home and Pet Care Service. It was a house-sitting service for clients away on vacation. I contracted to water plants, take in mail and newspapers, and feed pets. This last responsibility soon proved the most challenging. One of my charges was Baby. Baby was lonely. She was affectionate. She was untrained. She was a twenty-five kilogram Golden Retriever who leapt into my arms with joy every time I stepped into her house. Another of my charges was the Queen of Sheba. She was an overstuffed Persian cat with surgical steel claws capable of slicing through even the thickest denim. Another of my charges was Jabberwocky, the parrot, who had apparently committed to memory *A Complete Dictionary of the Vulgar Tongue*. I spent a month cleaning up accidents and cleaning up litter boxes. I longed to be back in uniform behind a counter serving up chicken and fries. I completed the contracts with my current customers. I said farewell to all my furry and feathered friends. I closed the door on Domestic Bliss.

Exercise 16.11

Read aloud a paragraph from one of your personal essays. Mark places where you could improve the rhythm by changing your sentence patterns. Then rewrite the paragraph.

16f Providing Continuity

As you move from sentence to sentence and paragraph to paragraph, you constantly present your readers with a mixture of known information (terms and ideas you have already introduced) and new information. You can emphasize the continuity between known and new information by using these stylistic devices.

1. Repeat key words or phrases.
Repeating a key word lets your readers know you are still talking about the same subject. If you introduce synonyms, readers may think you are offering new information. For example, in this short paragraph, the many synonyms for *bear* and *hunting partner* distract attention from the main subject, the father.

> Dad was fearless. Once when he and a hunting partner were tracking deer in the foothills, they surprised a wounded bear in a thicket. When the maimed animal knocked his friend down, Dad struck the brute with an empty rifle, distracting the angry monster long enough for his companion to get up and shoot the beast.

The paragraph reads much more smoothly when fewer terms are introduced:

> Dad was fearless. Once when he and a hunting partner were tracking deer in the foothills, they surprised a wounded bear in a thicket. When the bear knocked George down, Dad struck it with an empty rifle, distracting it long enough for George to get up and shoot it.

2. Use personal pronouns to refer to subjects you have previously named.

Pronouns (*he, she, it, they*), like repeated terms, signal known information; in the example above, the pronoun *it* refers to the bear.

3. Put the idea you plan to discuss next at the end of the sentence.

Link sentences by repeating the last word(s) of one sentence at the beginning of the next or by using a synonym and a demonstrative pronoun (*this, that, these, those*).

> British suffragettes challenged the existing system first through marches on Parliament, then through **civil disobedience**. When **civil disobedience** failed, they turned to property damage.

> British suffragettes challenged the existing system first through marches on Parliament, then through **civil disobedience**. When **these measures** failed, they turned to property damage.

4. Use sentence structure to indicate logical relationships.

To show that two or more sentences contain equivalent points (as when you are giving a list of reasons, examples, or actions), use **parallel sentence structure**.

FIRST SENTENCE	Slander may involve. . . .
SECOND SENTENCE	It can also be. . . .
THIRD SENTENCE	It is quite often. . . .

When you move from a general point to a specific detail, or vice versa, signal the shift by changing your sentence structure.

GENERAL POINT	To be blunt, slander is an ugly, malicious lie about someone. [The sentence begins with an introductory modifier.]
SPECIFIC EXAMPLE	It may involve… [The sentence begins with a subject and verb—change in sentence structure.]

5. Use transitional words and phrases.

The transitions in the list below can help your readers to understand how you have organized your material, making it easier for them to move from one point to the next in your writing. (The terms listed before each semicolon are less formal; those listed after the semicolon are more formal.)

NARRATION	first, next, then, last, as soon as, early the following morning, later that day; in the beginning, in the end
DESCRIPTION	nearer, farther, on the right, on the left, at the top, at the bottom, to the east, beside, between, above; adjacent to
CLASSIFICATION	one group, another kind, a third type; one subcategory, moreover, furthermore
EXAMPLE	for example, for instance; to illustrate, a case in point
PROCESS ANALYSIS	first step, second step, next stage, final stage
SYSTEMS ANALYSIS	one component, another part, the most important element
CAUSAL ANALYSIS	one reason, a final reason, the most important effect, although, because, despite, however; therefore, nevertheless, consequently, as a result, thus, if...then, provided that
DEFINITION	one meaning, another meaning, the most relevant meaning; primary meaning, secondary meaning
COMPARISON	and also, but too; in comparison, in contrast, similarly, just as...so too, not only...but also, neither...nor
EVALUATION	a practical advantage, a logical inconsistency, another legal aspect, from a moral perspective, an aesthetic weakness

16g Sample Paragraphs

If you compare the following paragraphs, you will see how these devices for achieving continuity can dramatically increase the flow of your writing. The material is from a personal essay on the writer's experiences with judo.

Sample Draft Paragraph

Bullies always have their little rituals. They go through a talking phase with a new kid who might be tough. If they aren't sure, they leave subtle threats and go away. After this little talk they hammer an opponent who reveals a weakness. They try to make friends with the "mark" who appears too formidable. I was skinny and scared, and so bullies always beat me up.

Sample Revised Paragraph

When bullies encounter a "mark" who might be tough, they go through little rituals. First they talk to him. If this talk reveals a weakness in their opponent, they hammer him. If they still aren't sure, they leave subtle threats and go away. If he appears too formidable, they make friendship gestures. But when the new kid is skinny and scared, like me, there is no ritual. It's all fists.

—Dan Martin

Exercise 16.12

Visualize a landscape containing the following list of elements. Then write a paragraph describing the landscape. Make sure you indicate the spatial relationships as you have visualized them.

white house	storage	blue sky
four silos	fence	snow
windbreak of poplars	hill	clouds
three giant spruce trees	road	horses
narrow river	shed	barn

Exercise 16.13

Improve the following narrative paragraph by adding transitions and revising sentences to show how the events are related in time.

I generally pride myself on my attention to detail, but on one occasion a careless error worked to my advantage. My friends Doug and Janice and I decided to attend a Christmas concert at which Karen Kain and Frank Augustyn were guest performers. Doug picked up five tickets from the box office and dropped off three for me and my Aunt Beth and Uncle Jack, whom I was treating to a special night out. Doug and Janice agreed to meet the three of us at the theatre. My aunt and uncle and I waited in the lobby. At five minutes to curtain, Doug and Janice still had not arrived. I carefully checked the seat numbers on the tickets. I suggested to Aunt Beth and Uncle Jack that we go in. Never having been to this theatre before, I asked an usher for assistance. He checked the tickets. He showed us to three excellent seats on the main floor. We were thrilled at our perfect view of the fine performances by Kain and Augustyn. However, throughout the concert the two seats beside us remained empty. I was puzzled by my friends' absence, but not concerned. We arrived home. Doug and Janice phoned to ask why I hadn't been at the theatre. I assured them that I had indeed been there. Pulling out the ticket stubs, I read the seat assignments out loud. I saw the one word I had not seen before—BALCONY. I should have been in those modestly priced seats, for which I had paid, not among the privileged on the main floor. I apologized to Doug and Janice. I confessed how embarrassed I was at my carelessness. However, I couldn't really regret a mistake that had given Aunt Beth, Uncle Jack, and me such pleasure for such a reasonable price.

Exercise 16.14

Improve the following analysis paragraph by adding transitions and revising sentences to show the causal relationship between ideas.

There are a number of reasons for the rise in customer complaints against our department store. We have not been living up to our promises. We have a sale. Usually several items advertised in our flyers remain on back order. Often the selection of available items is very poor. Customers complain that the store is poorly laid out. Aisles are blocked by overflowing display tables and unpacked boxes. Trying to get from one department to another becomes an exercise in frustration. Finding particular merchandise is difficult. Customers have to wrestle with clothes jammed onto racks or struggle with linens stuffed into shelves. The store is chronically understaffed. Service is slow and at times nonexistent. Customers are annoyed at having to wait too long for assistance and at standing in crowded lines at sales counters. We must solve these problems as quickly as possible.

Exercise 16.15

Revise the following paragraph to eliminate excessive transitions.

In his essay "Politics and the English Language," George Orwell argues that modern English is in decline. He notes that speakers and writers tend to use vague, pretentious language that conceals rather than reveals meaning. For example, he deplores, for instance, political euphemisms such as *pacification*, for bombing enemy villages, and *elimination of unreliable elements*, for imprisoning or shooting one's enemy. He also condemns as well the use of long-winded phrases where simple, concrete terms would do. Although there is an element of despair in the essay, Orwell does, despite this fact, offer hope that the process can be stopped and furthermore suggests ways of simplifying and clarifying our speech and writing. Unfortunately, however, although Orwell issued his warning over forty years ago, the abuses have not stopped. Indeed, jargon and doublespeak are, in fact, even more pervasive today. We do not put our garbage into dumps. Instead, our refuse ends up in landfill sites or environmental waste management facilities. We do not talk to people—we interface or dialogue with them. Personnel with the United States Defence Department requisition manually powered, fastener-driving impact devices rather than hammers. And, in addition, Revenue Canada mails out income tax returns in envelopes containing "a minimum of 50% post-consumer recovered material," otherwise known as recycled paper. It is clear that Orwell's concerns are still timely and that those who respect English must fight to defend it against such abuses.

16h Being Concise

In good writing, every word counts. Pruning the deadwood—words, phrases, and sentences that are not essential to your purpose—clarifies your meaning and makes your writing easier to read.

To make sure that every word counts, many writers set a goal of cutting their writing by 10%. If you tend to be wordy, you may want to set your goal higher. Here are four practical suggestions.

1. Eliminate unnecessary repetition of words and ideas.

Often whole sentences merely repeat a previous point.

REPETITIOUS PHRASE   Formerly women's clothes were much more restrictive in the past.

REVISED	Women's clothes were much more restrictive in the past.
REPETITIOUS SENTENCES	Macbeth seems shaken by the witches' announcement that he will become king. He is uneasy when they tell him he is destined to gain the throne.
REVISED	Macbeth seems shaken by the witches' announcement that he will become king.

2. Reduce phrases, clauses, and sentences.

Reduce phrases to single words (*in a short time = shortly; a lot of = many or much; at this point in time = now*).

Reduce clauses beginning with *that, which,* or *who* to words or phrases.

NOT	the person who owns the store
BUT	the store owner
NOT	at the position that I was assigned
BUT	at my position
NOT	*School Violence*, which is another study of this problem
BUT	*School Violence*, another study of this problem
NOT	The magazine is designed for women who are from 25 to 50 years of age.
BUT	The magazine is designed for women aged 25 to 50.

3. Rewrite wordy constructions.

NOT	It is a fact that the car has been stolen.
BUT	The car has been stolen.
NOT	What this means is that profits are down.
BUT	This means that profits are down.

4. Eliminate unnecessary modifiers.

WORDY	The small, sporty-looking red car just left us in the dust.
BETTER	The red sportscar left us in the dust.

To see how being concise can make your meaning clearer, consider these two versions of a paragraph from an essay on the importance of options in the school curriculum.

16i Sample Paragraphs: Conciseness

Sample Draft Paragraph

There are a lot of other courses that are very important to children growing up in the nineties. Courses such as home economics, industrial education, accounting, computer courses, and typing help children function better in the outside world—whether in the job market or in the home. These courses enable the children to be able to learn about a wide variety of things. Students today learn about health and nutrition, they learn about first aid, how to look after a home (boys as well as girls), they learn how to look after a vehicle, and even how to budget themselves and to do their own taxes. [106 words]

Sample Revised Paragraph

Many other courses are also important to today's adolescents. Courses such as home economics, industrial education, accounting, computer science, and typing help them function better in the home as well as in the job market. These courses enable students to learn about health and nutrition, first aid, and home maintenance. Students also learn how to look after a vehicle, how to budget, and how to do their own taxes. [69 words]

Exercise 16.16

Underline unnecessary words, phrases, and sentences. Then rewrite the paragraph in 110 words or fewer. Do not leave out any ideas.

Some bright, successful people suffer from the Impostor Phenomenon. What this means is that they are unable to recognize their intelligence and the success they have achieved. These people fear that they cannot maintain their success in spite of all the evidence of their accomplishments. If these feelings of being an impostor persist in the person, the person might never be able to relax and feel comfortable with himself. The feelings may stop these people from reaching their potential goal. The people who are suffering from the Impostor Phenomenon need to get rid of the guilty feelings. First they need to acknowledge their problem. They also have to realize they are not alone. There are many people who suffer from the Impostor Phenomenon. They don't have to be perfect. For some people, all they need is just a brief discussion to know what they are doing to themselves. For others it's not that simple; they very much need counselling to help them sort things out. [165 words]

Exercise 16.17

Take a paragraph of your own writing and cut it by at least 10%.

16i

*Sample
Paragraphs:
Conciseness*

CHECKLIST

Proofreading

	OK	NEEDS WORK

1. Sentence Structure

Have you eliminated:
- comma faults? ☐ ☐
- fused sentences? ☐ ☐
- fragments? ☐ ☐
- faulty parallelism? ☐ ☐
- faulty subordination? ☐ ☐
- mixed constructions? ☐ ☐

2. Modifiers

Have you eliminated:
- misplaced modifiers? ☐ ☐
- split infinitives? ☐ ☐
- dangling modifiers? ☐ ☐

3. Verbs

Have you eliminated errors in:
- principal parts of verbs? ☐ ☐
- verb tense? ☐ ☐
- use of the passive voice? ☐ ☐
- subject-verb agreement? ☐ ☐

4. Pronouns

Have you eliminated errors in:
- pronoun agreement? ☐ ☐
- pronoun case? ☐ ☐
- possessive pronoun use? ☐ ☐
- pronoun reference? ☐ ☐
- pronouns of address? ☐ ☐

5. Punctuation

Have you eliminated errors in the use of:

- commas?   □   □
- semicolons?   □   □
- colons?   □   □
- dashes?   □   □
- parentheses?   □   □
- quotation marks?   □   □
- italics and underlining? □   □
- hyphens?   □   □
- apostrophes?   □   □

6. Mechanics

Have you eliminated errors in:

- abbreviations?   □   □
- capitalization?   □   □
- numbers?   □   □
- spelling?   □   □

Chapter 17

Proofreading: Sentence Structure

The guidelines given in the last chapter will help to smooth the rough edges in your writing. Once you are satisfied with the way your work sounds, you need to proofread it. This chapter and those that follow cover most of the common errors you should be aware of as you make your final corrections.

17a

17a What Is Proofreading?

Proofreading involves looking for errors in sentence structure, grammar, spelling, and punctuation. Don't skip this last step, even if you are pressed for time or simply tired of a piece of writing. Awkward, wordy sentences and slips in grammar or spelling can bring an A paper down to a B, or a D paper down to an F. Spelling errors in a job application letter can mean that you are not asked for an interview. Wordy writing in a report might mean that your carefully thought-out recommendations are ignored. You will assure your reader of your credibility and competence if you take the time to give your writing a final polish.

Proofreading Strategies

To locate the rough spots in your writing, try these strategies:

- Leave your paper for at least a day. You will then be able to see what you actually wrote more clearly.

- Read your paper aloud either to yourself or to a friend. Revise awkward or unclear sentences.

- Read your paper backwards, sentence by sentence. This strategy is especially good for highlighting sentence fragments and spelling errors.

- Recheck the format of your letter, report, or essay using one of the checklists provided in earlier chapters.

Every time you complete a piece of writing, use the proof-reading checklist in this book to make a list of the types of errors you and other readers have noted in your work. After a while, you will get to know the kinds of errors you are most likely to make, and can create your own personal checklist of common errors to avoid in future projects.

17b Comma Fault

When you're proofreading for errors in sentence structure, be especially careful to watch for **comma faults**. This error, sometimes called a *comma splice*, occurs when two main clauses are joined by only a comma.

COMMA FAULT   The wind whipped up dead leaves in the yard, violent drops of rain beat against the ground.

Recognizing Comma Faults

1. Figure out whether your sentence contains two or more clauses.

You can do this if you understand the difference between a clause and a phrase. A **clause** is a group of words with a subject and a verb.

    she waved at the helicopter
    when *she waved* at the helicopter

A **phrase** is a group of words without a subject and a verb.

    after waving at the helicopter
    to wave at the helicopter
    in the sky overhead

Exercise 17.1

Underline the clause(s) in each of the following sentences:

1. To pass your driver's test, you will need to improve your parallel parking.

2. The car screeched to a stop, with the driver leaning on the horn.

3. Entering the final period with a two-goal advantage, the Flames began to falter.

4. On the left shoulder of the road, Paula noticed the signal: one stone placed on top of the other.

5. After staring vacantly into space for a full fifteen minutes, Martin pulled himself together and tackled the first question.

2. Figure out whether the clauses are main clauses or subordinate clauses.

A **main clause** can stand alone as an independent sentence:

Marta stared in disbelief.

A **subordinate clause** cannot stand alone.

While Marta stared in disbelief

Adverbial subordinate clauses begin with subordinate conjunctions (*after, during, while, when, if, unless, until, because, although*).

Comma Fault

Exercise 17.2

Underline the main clause(s) in each of the following sentences:

1. Startled by a scratching sound on the window, Lockwood awoke from a fitful sleep.

2. He could hear something crying and moaning, but he was afraid to leave his bed.

3. When he finally looked through the window, he saw the ghost-like form of a little girl.

4. The window rattled as the ghost scratched on it; Lockwood was terrified.

5. Determined to make the noise stop, Lockwood shattered the glass.

3. If the sentence contains two main clauses, are they joined by only a comma?

If so, the sentence contains a comma fault.

Be especially careful to avoid comma faults when the sentence has a main clause followed by a subordinate clause and another main clause.

COMMA FAULT   Tim completed a four-year degree in nursing, when he graduated, however, there were no jobs.

REVISED | Tim completed a four-year degree in nursing; when he graduated, however, there were no jobs.

Correcting Comma Faults

There are six ways to correct a comma fault.

1. Use a period to separate the two clauses.

COMMA FAULT | An enormous wave hit the boat, all those on deck were swept overboard.

REVISED | An enormous wave hit the boat. All those on deck were swept overboard.

2. Use a semicolon to join the two clauses if they contain closely related ideas.

COMMA FAULT | Fish stocks have declined in the last ten years, fishing licences are now difficult to obtain.

REVISED | Fish stocks have declined in the last ten years; fishing licences are now difficult to obtain.

3. Use a colon to join the two clauses if the second clause explains, expands, or emphasizes the first.

COMMA FAULT | After six months of treatment, Louisa was feeling much better, she now eagerly anticipated returning to school.

REVISED | After six months of treatment, Louisa was feeling much better: she now eagerly anticipated returning to school.

4. Use a semicolon and a conjunctive adverb, such as *moreover*, *however*, *therefore*, *thus*, or *then* to join the two clauses.

COMMA FAULT | Sean drifted out of high school without a diploma, he now has the job of his dreams.

REVISED | Sean drifted out of high school without a diploma; however, he now has the job of his dreams.

17b

Comma Fault

5. Use a comma and coordinate conjunction (*and, but, or, nor, yet, so, for*) to join the two clauses.

COMMA FAULT   Peering through the darkness, they could see the lights of the settlement, they struggled onward.

REVISED   Peering through the darkness, they could see the lights of the settlement, so they struggled onward.

6. Change one of the main clauses into a subordinate clause. Put a comma after the subordinate clause if it comes first in the sentence.

COMMA FAULT   You need more rest, you will get sick.

REVISED   If you don't get more rest, you will get sick.

Exercise 17.3

Revise the following sentences to eliminate all comma faults. Try a number of revision methods.

1. Visiting the SPCA can be a distressing experience, there are so many unwanted pets in need of a home.

2. Frank promised to wait for me, when I arrived, however, he had already gone.

3. As we watched, the light-air balloon drifted towards the house, we were concerned that it might not clear the large tree in the front yard.

4. Corinne pushed the door open, she boldly entered the deserted house.

5. That joke is corny and outdated, I still laugh every time I hear it.

Exercise 17.4

The following passage is from an essay comparing two science fiction horror movies, *Dr. Jekyll and Mr. Hyde*, made in the 1930s, and *The Fly*, made in the 1980s. Revise it to eliminate all comma faults.

Technology is presented as much less powerful in *Dr. Jekyll and Mr. Hyde* than in *The Fly*. Dr. Jekyll remains recognizably human as Mr. Hyde, Seth Brundle becomes completely non-human by the end of *The Fly*. Of course, Dr. Jekyll remains human-looking partly because special effects were more limited in the 1930s. Thus there are only minor changes in his appearance when he becomes Mr. Hyde, his hair is longer, his eyes are brighter and darker, and his jaw is larger to accommodate his bigger teeth. The focus in this movie is less on the power of science than on the evil part of Dr. Jekyll's nature when it is acted out by Mr. Hyde. Science is much more threatening in *The Fly*, it has the power to change not only a man's appearance but his species as well. In fact, the focus in *The Fly* is almost entirely on the horrifying changes taking place in Seth Brundle's appearance. By the end of the film, he is spitting teeth into a sink and accidentally tearing off parts of his face, his inner organs are now mostly outside his skeleton. This, the film is telling us, is what happens to scientists who do not know how to control the technology they have created. They can turn the machine on, they cannot predict what it will do or stop it once it has started.

17c Fused Sentences

A **fused sentence**, sometimes called a *run-on sentence*, occurs when two main clauses are written as one with no punctuation between them. The length of the sentence will not tell you whether or not it is fused. A sentence can be quite long without being run-on.

CORRECT   Wendy stopped and glared angrily at the
                    mischievous children as another snowball
                    flew by her head.

On the other hand, some fused sentences are quite short.

FUSED   Open the window I need some fresh air.

You can correct this error by using one of the following techniques:

1. Separate the two clauses with a period.

   Open the window. I need some fresh air.

2. Use a semicolon to join the two clauses.

   Open the window; I need some fresh air.

3. Use a comma and a coordinate conjunction to join the two clauses.

Open the window, for I need some fresh air.

4. Change one of the main clauses into a subordinate clause.

Open the window because I need some fresh air.

Exercise 17.5

Revise the following to eliminate all fused sentences.

1. Damion maintained a regular exercise schedule and a sensible diet he was therefore able to lose ten pounds.

2. Max was sorry to miss the show he had waited all week to see it.

3. The chairlift ride to the top of the hill terrified Rena even worse was the prospect of having to ski down the hill.

4. Hearing the alarm, Linda stood up, left the room, and closed the door behind her she then walked quickly but calmly to the nearest exit.

5. Stop talking you will not hear crucial instructions.

Exercise 17.6

The following paragraph is the conclusion to an essay comparing two science fiction horror movies, *Dr. Jekyll and Mr. Hyde*, made in the 1930s, and *The Fly*, made in the 1980s. Revise it to eliminate all fused sentences.

The contrasting endings of the two films reveal very clearly the difference fifty years have made in people's attitudes towards scientific technology. In the earlier film, Mr. Hyde becomes Dr. Jekyll again as soon as the potion wears off in the later film Seth Brundle can do nothing to stop his transformation into a fly once the computer has locked him into its program. In *Dr. Jekyll and Mr. Hyde*, the focus is more on the character and intentions of the scientist than on the technology he employs the implication in this film is that we have nothing to fear from science as long as it is in the hands of the right people. In *The Fly*, on the other hand, the technology is so powerful that the character and intentions of the people who use it are much less important. In this film, scientists create machines with minds of their own these machines are indifferent to the wishes and best interests of their creators. In the 1930s scientists could control their creations they were responsible for them. In the 1980s no one could be sure what would happen when high-tech machinery was set into motion.

17d Fragments

A **fragment** is an incomplete sentence. In some contexts, such as informal personal letters, press releases, and advertising, a fragment is a good way to catch your reader's attention.

A wonderful occasion for all of us.

The best buy ever!

The end of the line for him.

A small step, but an important one.

If the rest of your sentences are grammatically complete, a fragment will stand out effectively for emphasis. On the other hand, if you mix unintentional fragments with intentional fragments, you'll confuse your reader and lose your intended emphasis.

Remember, too, that fragments will make your writing seem less formal. Unless you wish your work to appear somewhat casual, avoid fragments in reports, business letters, and essays. When you are proofreading for sentence fragments, watch for the following errors.

• *Phrases or subordinate clauses punctuated as complete sentences*

Sometimes the fragment belongs with the complete sentence that comes before or after it in the passage.

FRAGMENT   Bill could balance a glass of water on his head. Without spilling a drop. [*The second construction is a prepositional phrase and, like all phrases, lacks a subject and a verb.*]

COMPLETE SENTENCE   Bill could balance a glass of water on his head without spilling a drop. [*The phrase has been joined to the sentence before it.*]

FRAGMENT   Because there had been two major rent increases in the last two years. Maureen decided to look for a new apartment. [*The first construction is a subordinate clause, not a complete sentence.*]

249

COMPLETE SENTENCE   Because there had been two major rent increases in the last two years, Maureen decided to look for a new apartment. [*The subordinate clause has been joined to the following sentence. There is a comma between the clauses because the subordinate clause is first.*]

• **Sentences with missing verbs**

If you remember that every verb ending with *ing* must have an auxiliary in order to be a complete verb, you'll be less likely to write this kind of fragment.

17d

FRAGMENT   The child frantically searching for her mother.

Fragments

COMPLETE SENTENCE   The child was frantically searching for her mother.

Be especially careful with *being*, which is a participle, not a verb. Avoid the phrase *the reason being*. Use *because* instead.

FRAGMENT   The reason for her sore back being that she had fallen.

COMPLETE SENTENCE   Her back was sore because she had fallen.

Exercise 17.7

Revise the following constructions to make them complete sentences.

1. The old man wearing tattered, dirty clothes and carrying a large shopping bag filled with bottles and odds and ends of junk.

2. At present, those people who hold boarding passes for rows fourteen through twenty-five.

3. Unable to pay his rent, for Ramon had spent his last dollar at the race track.

4. Having filled the tank, checked the tires, and replaced the defective headlight. Maria was ready to leave for Jasper.

5. Pi, the symbol designating the ratio of the circumference of a circle to its diameter.

Exercise 17.8

Revise the following constructions to make them complete sentences. If the sentence is correct, write *C*.

1. Please go to the store and buy me a newspaper.
2. The child riding joyfully back and forth on the sidewalk, testing out her new bike.
3. The reason for the current disruption in production being a shortage of trained staff.
4. Unable to understand either the problem or the explanation and giving up in temporary despair.
5. After staying up half the night to finish an assignment. Debbie was dismayed to discover that the professor had cancelled the class.
6. Although interest rates have been steady for six months.
7. A movie with an extraordinarily sensitive portrayal of family relationships.
8. Wanting to lose weight, but he rebelled against the restrictions of any diet.
9. After ten games without making a point, she scored the winning goal in overtime.
10. Always intimidated by the possibility of rejection, but she gathered up her courage and called him.

Exercise 17.9

Restore the following paragraph to its original form by eliminating all inappropriate **sentence fragments**.

There Lan stood, waving the children off to school. She always looked the same in the morning; nothing about her ever changed. Blond hair falling out of its rollers. Her face was covered with face cream. Leaving only her swollen blue eyes showing. Morning was definitely the worst part of the day for her. A partly smoked cigarette in the corner of her mouth giving her a tough look. As the wind blew against her, Lan pulled her old housecoat tightly across her body. She wasn't fat; however, she needed to lose some weight. A few pounds anyway. Lan shut the door and turned to walk across the floor. Her slippers making a scratchy sound. Lan had always dragged her feet when she walked. "Another day," she growled. Then she sat down at the kitchen table, reached for the newspaper, and crossed her unshaven legs in a lady-like manner. She looked down at her rough, chapped hands. With the nail polish a month old and chipping terribly. "Oh, well, there's no hurry," she thought to herself. "There isn't much to do today anyway."

—Joyena Luck

17e Faulty Parallelism

The principle of **parallelism** is that similar ideas should be expressed in grammatically similar ways.

Her New Year's resolutions were to **quit smoking**, **lose weight**, and **exercise regularly**.

Faulty parallelism occurs when ideas of equal value are not expressed in the same grammatical form.

Avoiding Faulty Parallelism

• *Use the same part of speech for each item in a series of words.*

NOT	The family has wealth, reputation, and **is powerful**.
BUT	The family has wealth, reputation, and **power**.

• *Use the same construction for each phrase or clause in a series.*

Do not mix phrases and clauses, or even different kinds of phrases.

NOT	Maurice decided to complete his second year at college, look for a job, and **then he and Eva would get married**.
BUT	Maurice decided to complete his second year at college, look for a job, and **then marry Eva**.

• *Include both elements in a comparison.*

NOT	My paper is as long as **Bill**.
BUT	My paper is as long as **Bill's**.

252

NOT	The more I work on this assignment, **I don't seem to accomplish much**.
BUT	The more I work on this assignment, **the less I seem to accomplish**.

- *Make sure correlative conjunctions join grammatically similar sentence elements.*

The correlative conjunctions are *either... or, neither... nor, not only... but also, whether... or, both... and.*

NOT	Not only did the horse lose, **but the right leg of the jockey was broken**.
BUT	Not only did the horse lose, but **the jockey broke her right leg**.

17e

Faulty Parallelism

Exercise 17.10

Make elements in the following sentences parallel. Put *C* beside a correct sentence.

1. Library patrons are not permitted to bring in food or beverages or smoke.

2. Magdalena's bedroom is bigger than her sister.

3. The less exercise I get, I don't feel good.

4. His favourite television shows are old movies, political documentaries, and he likes the cartoons that are shown on Saturday mornings.

5. Susanne was sentenced for both impaired driving and she resisted arrest.

6. Not only did Lawrence not show up for work but he also failed to inform anyone of his intended absence.

7. I have neither the time nor do I want to clean the oven this afternoon.

8. A number of words have been coined by famous writers, including John Milton, who invented the word *pandemonium*, and Lewis Carroll's *chortle*.

9. Margaret can either join the company pension plan or opt out and invest in a private retirement savings plan.

10. The further Mario gets behind in his work, he feels discouraged.

Exercise 17.11

The errors in parallel sentence structure introduced into this passage make it wordy and confusing. Revise where necessary to make sentence elements parallel.

When I first entered university two years ago, I began to realize how important the human convention of keeping track of time is to day-to-day living. I found myself asking questions such as, "Will I be able to get that essay done on time?", "Is it possible for me to learn to organize my time better?", "Will I have time to answer all the questions on the exam?", "I wonder if I'll ever have some time to myself." I realized fairly quickly that it was almost impossible to function at university without a watch.

I have had many watches enter my life only to die shortly thereafter. The causes of their deaths have been many. Some of them drowned a week after I got them because I forgot to take them off when I showered. Two of them were fatally wounded in violent collisions: the first one against the corner of a table and I smashed the second between the *N* and *OP* volumes of *The Encyclopaedia Britannica*. Old age killed many more. "Old age" for these watches was, on the average, two months because every one of them was one of those new digital types that are disposable and that are so cheaply mass-produced that they can be sold (at a profit) for the "low, low price of $3.99."

—*Sandy Block*

17f Faulty Subordination

Faulty subordination occurs when you fail to differentiate less important ideas from more important ideas.

Avoiding Faulty Subordination

- *Check that you have attached the subordinate conjunction to the appropriate clause.*

Some common subordinate conjunctions are *before, after, during, while, when, if, unless, until, because, although.* You can signal the connections among your ideas more accurately by putting the less important idea in the subordinate clause and by beginning the subordinate clause with the appropriate conjunction.

NOT   He wanted to make a good impression, **because** he dressed carefully for the interview.

BUT	**Because** he wanted to make a good impression, he dressed carefully for the interview.

• *Use the most precise subordinate conjunction.*

Pay particular attention to your use of *since* and *as. Since* can mean *because,* but it can also mean *from the time that.* In some sentences, *since* is confusing. In such cases, it is best to rephrase the sentence.

CONFUSING	Since Sandy broke her leg, she hasn't been playing basketball.
CLEAR	Sandy hasn't played basketball since she broke her leg.
CLEAR	Because Sandy broke her leg, she hasn't been playing basketball.

As is another troublesome conjunction. Sometimes *as* means because, but it's clearer to use *as* to mean *during the time that.*

CLEAR	**As** the rain poured down, we made our way to the deserted cabin.
CONFUSING	**As** she cycles to work, she never gets stuck in traffic.
CLEAR	**Because** she cycles to work, she never gets stuck in traffic.

Note: Don't be afraid to begin a sentence with *because.* Just make sure to include a main clause in the sentence.

• *Limit the number of subordinate clauses in a single sentence.*

Piling subordinate clauses on top of each other can make it difficult to judge how ideas are related. Revise sentences with too many subordinate clauses by rephrasing the sentence or by reducing some of the clauses to phrases or single words.

NOT	**Because the committee could not reach a decision**, the project was stalled **because no one knew what to do next**.

17f

Faulty Subordination

BUT	The **committee's failure to reach a decision** stalled the project because no one knew what to do next.
NOT	The party **that wins the election, which will be held on November 10**, will set economic policies **that will affect the country** for the next ten years.
BUT	The party **that wins the November 10 election** will set the **country's** economic policies for the next ten years.

Exercise 17.12

17f

Faulty Subordination

Revise the following sentences to correct faulty or excessive subordination.

1. This is a paper that is a useful resource for the research paper that you are writing on the influence that the mass media have on public opinion.

2. Mr. Gertler has been out of work for fifteen months although he is not discouraged.

3. Since we have come to appreciate the high quality of your work over the past year, we are awarding you the contract.

4. When she had fed the baby and put him to bed, she went out to a movie when she had washed the dishes.

5. Because Katia did not make her payment before the due date, so she had to pay interest on the full amount of the bill.

6. The speaker who has been invited is Dr. Margaret Choy, who will discuss the social systems of primates that are non-human.

7. As Devon wasn't paying attention, he drove right through a stop sign.

8. Susan hated math in high school even though she majored in statistics at university.

9. In 1923 Frederick Banting was a Canadian doctor who won the Nobel Prize for medicine because he made a major contribution to the discovery of insulin, which is a therapy for diabetes mellitus.

10. Although he didn't have much money, he wanted to buy his wife a piano for Christmas although he might not be able to cover the rent.

17g Mixed Constructions

Mixed constructions get their name because they mix incompatible grammatical units and thus produce sentences that will seem awkward to your reader. Mixed constructions result from the writer thinking of two similar sentences and then using parts of each in a single sentence. For example, let's say you have these two perfectly reasonable sentences in mind:

> Because June has three small children, she is exhausted.
>
> June's three small children are the reason she is exhausted.

If you are not paying attention, you might change your mind as you are writing and produce a mixed construction something like this:

MIXED   June has three small children is the reason she is exhausted.

You can recognize awkward constructions like this by reading your work aloud to yourself or to a classmate. Here are some tips to help you avoid three common types of mixed constructions.

1. Avoid **is when** *and* **is because** *constructions.*

MIXED   **An example** of her snobbery **is when** she criticizes her neighbours for their ungrammatical speech.

REVISED   An example of her snobbery is **her criticism** [*noun*] of her neighbour's ungrammatical speech.

REVISED   She **reveals** her snobbery when she criticizes her neighbours' ungrammatical speech. [*linking verb replaced*]

MIXED   **The reason** the brakes failed **is because** the brake fluid was accidentally removed.

REVISED   The reason the brakes failed is **that the brake fluid was accidentally removed**. [*noun clause*]

REVISED   The brakes **failed** because the brake fluid was accidentally removed. [*linking verb replaced*]

257

Occasionally the subordinate clause appears before the verb:

MIXED
Because he was always late [*subordinate clause*] **was** [*verb*] **the reason** he was fired.

REVISED
His lateness [*noun*] was the reason he was fired.

REVISED
Because he was always late, he **was fired**. [*linking verb replaced*]

2. Make sure you have a subject in the main clause.

Remember that a prepositional phrase is never the subject of a sentence.

17g

*Mixed
Constructions*

MIXED
In the article "Anorexia and the Adolescent" [*prepositional phrase*] explains Lilian Donaldson's views on the connection between self-starvation and the adolescent's need for control.

REVISED
In the article "Anorexia and the Adolescent," Lilian Donaldson [*subject*] explains the connection between self-starvation and the adolescent's need for control.

REVISED
The article "Anorexia and the Adolescent" [*subject*] explains Lilian Donaldson's view on the connection between self-starvation and the adolescent's need for control.

3. Don't confuse questions with statements.

MIXED
She wondered how long will it be until I see him again?

REVISED
She wondered how long it would be until she saw him again.

REVISED
She wondered, "How long will it be until I see him again?"

Exercise 17.13

Revise the following sentences to eliminate mixed constructions.

1. Without a suitable organ donor means that the heart patient has only a few months to live.

2. An example of Elizabeth's independence is when she refuses to marry Mr. Collins.

3. The reason my report is late is because I lost the graphs and had to redo them.

4. I asked, could the post office keep my mail until I return from Sweden?

5. On the inside of the cover shows Paul wearing an Ontario Provincial Police shoulder flash.

6. Whenever he is faced with talking to a large group is when he breaks out in a nervous rash.

7. The children wondered would their grandmother ever leave China?

8. By going to bed when you have the flu means you will get well sooner.

9. In *Sunshine Sketches of a Little Town* portrays the laughable faults of the residents of a small Ontario town.

10. Because of the long hours she spent practising was the reason Elizabeth Manley became a champion skater.

Mixed Constructions

Chapter 18

Proofreading: Modifiers

18a Key Terms to Know

Adjectives modify nouns and pronouns.

> The quick brown fox jumped over the lazy dog. [Quick *and* brown *modify* fox; lazy *modifies* dog.]

Adverbs modify verbs, adjectives, and other adverbs.

> The cat stretched lazily in the sun. [Lazily *modifies the verb* stretched.]

> Dr. Lucas' lecture on the shortage of clean water in Ghana was extremely interesting. [Extremely *modifies the adjective* interesting.]

> The car went by too quickly for me to see who was in it. [Too *modifies the adverb* quickly.]

18b Comparative Forms of Adjectives and Adverbs

Adjectives and adverbs have degrees of comparison (*pretty, prettier, prettiest; interesting, more interesting, most interesting*). If you are not sure of the comparative form of a particular adjective or adverb (should it be *clearer* or *more clear*?), consult your dictionary.

Avoid using double comparisons, such as *more happier* or *most fastest*. Some adjectives (such as *unique, perfect, empty*) express absolute concepts. One piece of pottery cannot be *more unique* than the rest, one math test cannot be the *most perfect* in the class, one glass cannot be *more empty* than another.

18b

*Comparative
Forms of
Adjectives
and Adverbs*

18c   Troublesome Adjectives and Adverbs

- **Well** is usually an adverb.

NOT   Declan **ran good** in the last race.

BUT   Declan **ran well** in the last race.

- **Well** in reference to health is an adjective.

  Jane hasn't been **well** since her bout of mononucleosis.

- **Good** is an adjective.

  I haven't seen a **good** movie for ages.

  His health is **good** now because he has his allergies under control.

- **Bad** and **real** are adjectives.

  This is a **bad** photograph of me.

  The huge boulder looks **real**, but it is actually made of papier-mâché.

- **Badly** and **really** are adverbs.

NOT   The roof was damaged **bad** in the hail-
               storm.

BUT   The roof was **badly** damaged in the hail-
               storm.

NOT   Ben is **real** eager to begin his new job on
               Monday.

BUT   Ben is **really** eager to begin his new job
               on Monday.

- **Less** and **fewer** are used differently. **Less** (the comparative
  of *little*) is an adjective used with items that cannot be considered as separate objects: *less* food, *less* kindness, *less* snow.
  Fewer (the comparative of *few*) is an adjective used with
  things that can be counted individually: *fewer* students, *fewer*
  courses, *fewer* responsibilities.

NOT   I have **less** errands to run tomorrow than
               I had anticipated.

BUT   I have **fewer** errands to run tomorrow
               than I had anticipated.

Exercise 18.1

Revise the following sentences so that adjectives and adverbs are used correctly.

1. I wouldn't bother Allison right now; she's in a real bad mood.
2. Malcolm is a fine pianist, but Louise is the most technically accomplished of the two.
3. Less guests came than were expected.
4. Pina sings good enough to deserve at least an audition with the band.
5. Brent is speaking so soft that I can't hear what he is saying.

Exercise 18.2

Revise the following sentences so that adjectives and adverbs are used correctly. If the sentence is correct, write *C*.

1. Even though Elan did good in the interview, he didn't get the job.
2. Now that she has become a chartered accountant, Sharna earns more money but finds that she has less opportunities to spend it.
3. The dog tried real hard to catch his own tail, but he could never get quite close enough.
4. Your cold seems more worse than when I saw you last.
5. I did bad on my first driver's test, but I passed it the second time, mostly because I was less tense.
6. The club members collected less money from the paper drive than they had expected.
7. Kareem is the most tallest player on the team.
8. Both Francis and Brad are capable of doing the job, but Francis is the best worker.
9. The bride's gown, designed exclusively for her, is a very unique and beautiful creation.
10. This year I am planting fewer zucchini plants and more tomatoes.

18d Misplaced Modifiers

A **misplaced modifier**, as its name suggests, is in the wrong place. The resulting sentence is confusing and sometimes unintentionally amusing.

> Mr. Kowalski saw a horse by the side of the road on his way home from work.

Since Mr. Kowalski is more likely to be on his way home from work than the horse is, the prepositional phrase *on his way home from work* should be placed closer to *Mr. Kowalski* in the sentence.

> On his way home from work, Mr. Kowalski saw a horse by the side of the road.

Words such as *only, hardly, barely, nearly,* and *almost* are especially troublesome because they can be easily misplaced.

18e

Split Infinitives

NOT
: After a few lessons, James could **almost swim** the entire length of the pool.

BUT
: After a few lessons, James could swim **almost the entire length** of the pool.

NOT
: **I only want** a minute of your time.

BUT
: I want **only a minute** of your time.

Note: Do not use *hardly* and *barely* with *not.*

NOT
: **I can't hardly** hear you.

BUT
: **I can hardly** hear you.

NOT
: **She couldn't barely** hear the faint sound coming from the basket on the front steps.

BUT
: She **could barely** hear the faint sound coming from the basket on the front steps.

18e Split Infinitives

An **infinitive** is *to* + a verb: *to think, to walk, to breathe.* A **split infinitive** occurs when a modifier (usually an adverb) is misplaced between *to* and the verb (*to quickly run*). It is best to avoid splitting an infinitive, especially when the resulting construction is awkward. You can correct a split infinitive by rephrasing the sentence.

SPLIT INFINITIVE   Marjorie needed time to **mentally prepare** or the exam.

REVISED   Marjorie needed time to **prepare mentally** for the exam.

Sometimes, however, a split infinitive sounds less awkward than when the modifier is relocated in the sentence.

The diners asked the man at the next table **to please stop** smoking his cigar. [Putting *please* anywhere else in the sentence would be clumsy.]

Exercise 18.3

18e

Split Infinitives

Revise the following sentences to avoid split infinitives and to place modifiers as close as possible to what they modify.

1. Tangled in the ball of string, I laughed when I saw the kitten.

2. Maria has nearly seen every James Stewart movie ever made.

3. The exercise instructor advised Helen to slowly warm up before beginning the cardiovascular exercises.

4. Standing just outside the net, the puck whizzed past the goalie.

5. We had an excellent view of both the American and Horseshoe Falls standing at the top of the observation tower.

Exercise 18.4

Revise the following sentences to avoid split infinitives and to place modifiers as close as possible to what they modify. If the sentence is correct, write *C*.

1. There is a monument to those soldiers who died in foreign wars in the park.

2. I only have two dollars, not enough to get into the movie.

3. We waited for the first newspaper reviews of the play to be published at the restaurant.

4. When we visited Kealekekua Bay, we saw the monument honouring the eighteenth-century British navigator James Cook, who was killed by islanders last year.

5. The candidate tripped almost on the first word of her speech.

6. Be sure to carefully read all the instructions.

7. Doug pushed his way through the crowd of shoppers in the mall carrying a large bag of groceries.

8. Stopping in mid-stride, Elynor realized that someone was following her in the dark, deserted parkade.

9. The dental hygienist demonstrated the correct method of brushing one's teeth using a plaster model and a toothbrush.

10. Then the fire broke out, the people were told to calmly but quickly leave the building.

18f Dangling Modifiers

An introductory phrase normally modifies the closest noun in the sentence. When it does not, it is called a **dangling modifier**.

DANGLING   **Driving down the mountain**, three bears were seen.

Recognizing Dangling Modifiers

1. Does the sentence begin with a participial phrase or an infinitive?

Participial phrases are formed with the present or past participle of a verb.

hanging on the wall

stricken with AIDS

Infinitive phrases are formed with an infinitive (*to* + verb).

to drive defensively

to bake the perfect cake

to listen carefully

2. Does this participial or infinitive phrase logically modify the closest noun or pronoun in the sentence?

NOT	Sitting on the beach under the boiling sun, **a swim** was inviting.
BUT	Sitting on the beach under the boiling sun, **we** looked forward to a swim.
NOT	To swim a mile, **endurance** must be built up gradually.
BUT	To swim a mile, **you** must build up your endurance gradually.

3. Is the verb in the main clause in the passive voice?

Verbs have two voices: active and passive. When the verb is in the active voice, the subject of the sentence performs the action: *Amin signed the documents.* When the verb is in the passive voice, the subject of the sentence is acted on by the verb: *The documents were signed by Amin.*

Be careful with passive constructions. Introductory phrases are more likely to dangle when the verb in the main clause is in the passive voice.

NOT	After hours of frustrating discussion, an agreement on the verdict was finally reached by the jury.
BUT	After hours of frustrating discussion, the jury finally agreed on a verdict.

Exercise 18.5

Identify the verbs in the following sentences as **A** (active) or **P** (passive).

1. The patient was given an insulin injection at 11:45 p.m.

2. Bears were sighted on the western ridge by two alarmed campers.

3. Amidst the antics of the other swimmers, Mario was floating happily on his air mattress.

4. The garage roof finally collapsed under the weight of two feet of wet snow.

18f

Dangling Modifiers

5. The agreement for an immediate ceasefire was ignored by both sides.

Correcting Dangling Modifiers

When an introductory phrase dangles, you can revise the sentence in one of two ways. You can either expand the phrase to a subordinate clause or revise the main clause so that the introductory phrase logically modifies its subject.

NOT   Intending to finish the report by the end of the day, my plan was to work through lunch and coffee breaks.

BUT   Because I intended to finish the report by the end of the day, my plan was to work through lunch and coffee breaks.

OR   Intending to finish the report by the end of the day, I planned to work through lunch and coffee breaks.

18f

Dangling Modifiers

You could correct the dangling modifier in the next sentence by changing the prepositional phrase to a clause, with the subject clearly stated.

NOT   After being honoured by sports writers and fellow athletes, the retired hockey star's name was inscribed in the Hall of Fame.

BUT   After the retired hockey star was honoured by sports writers and fellow athletes, his name was inscribed in the Hall of Fame.

Sometimes it is necessary to revise a sentence extensively to eliminate the dangling modifier.

NOT   Upon learning about the budget cutbacks, it was difficult for Ruth to hide her concern that her position would be abolished.

BUT   When Ruth learned about the budget cutbacks, she found it difficult to hide her concern that her position would be abolished.

Exercise 18.6

Correct each dangling modifier.

1. Before beginning the cardiovascular portion of the workout, warmup and stretching exercises must be completed.

2. Being fascinated by the night sky since childhood, my decision was to pursue a career in astronomy.

3. At the age of ten, Don's grandfather moved in with the family.

4. Unable to see clearly in the fog, the turn-off to the farm was missed.

5. Already late for an appointment on the tenth floor, the elevator was out of order.

Exercise 18.7

Correct each dangling modifier. If the sentence is correct, write *C*.

1. After paying for the garage sale licence, the next step was to print notices and post them around the neighbourhood.

2. Listening to the radio weather report of freezing temperatures and high wind chill factors, I burrowed more deeply under the covers.

3. Unable to recognize any of the buildings or street names, it soon became apparent that Martha had taken the wrong bus.

4. After talking at length with his agent, major revisions were made to the opening and closing chapters of the novel.

5. Waiting for our guest to arrive, there was little to talk about except the weather.

6. Seeing the villain about to strike from behind the curtain, the hero's sword ran him through.

7. Uncertain of which road to take, our decision was to ask for directions.

8. Having thought the matter over carefully, Naveen agreed to work with Sharon on the project.

9. While sitting at my desk reading Poe's "The Raven," the clock struck midnight.

10. Opening the drapes, a heavy fog obscured my view of the street.

Exercise 18.8

The following paragraphs are from a personal essay describing the writer's reactions to the loss of a prized possession. Errors in the use of modifiers have been introduced. Revise the passage to correct these errors.

My gorgeous red sled was my most preciousest possession. With fast back styling, it was a beautiful 1967 fire-engine red Ford Mustang. I had only had it a few months, but it had long been an esteemed member of my family. My brother-in-law had beefed it up, who had first owned it. Then my older brother owned it before selling it to me. This wasn't my first car, but it was my first prestigious vehicle. It was the most classiest, stylish, powerful car I had ever owned, and its qualities became extensions of my own life.

One fateful night, however, while showing off and speeding around town, my faithful old sled piled into the end of an ugly street cruiser with a two-foot bumper. Unfortunately, my beautiful, sleek little car didn't come to a standstill until my radiator was wrapped around my engine block. I couldn't hardly believe that this stupid accident could happen to one of the world's best drivers, who was piloting the classiest car to come out of Detroit in the 1960s perhaps. Sitting there, head in hand, and staring in disbelief my pants were soaking up antifreeze and battery acid. That car was the embodiment of my own personality; wrecking it was like crushing my soul.

—*Bernard Doering*

18f

*Dangling
Modifiers*

269

Chapter 19

Proofreading: Verbs

Because the English verb system is quite complex, it's easy to make errors involving both verb tenses and verb forms.

19a The Principal Parts of Verbs

Each verb has four principal parts, from which all its other forms can be derived.

1. The **infinitive** form (*to* + a verb) names the verb: *to walk, to run, to think.*
2. The **past tense**: *Yesterday I **walked** to school.*
3. The **present participle**: *I **am walking** to school right now.*
4. The **past participle**: *I **have walked** to school every day this week.*

Regular verbs form the past tense and the past participle by adding ed to the infinitive: *walked, have walked; visited, have visited.*

Irregular verbs form the past tense and the past participle in a variety of ways: *drank, have drunk; brought, have brought.* If you are not sure of the principal parts of an irregular verb, check your dictionary.

19b Auxiliary Verbs

A number of verb tenses are formed by combining a participle with one or more **auxiliary verbs**:

am, is, was, were	*can, could, may, might*
be, being, been	*shall, will, should, would*
have, has, had	*ought to, have to, used to*
do, does, did	*supposed to*

19c Common Errors with Verbs

- **Using the past participle instead of the past tense**

NOT   I **seen** [*past participle*] him yesterday.

BUT   I **saw** [*past tense*] him yesterday.

- **Using an auxiliary verb with the past tense**

NOT   Ahmed **had went** to visit his parents in Manitoba.

BUT   Ahmed **went** to visit his parents in Manitoba.

OR   Ahmed **had gone** to visit his parents in Manitoba.

- **Using being *as a main verb instead of* is or was**

NOT   The reason **being** that I was already late.

BUT   The reason **is** that I was already late.

- **Using of to mean have**

NOT   He should **of** known better.

BUT   He should **have** known better.

- **Using too many couds *or* woulds *in* if... then *statements***

NOT   If you **would have asked** me, I would have helped.

BUT   If you **had asked** me, I would have helped.

19c

*Common
Errors with
Verbs*

Exercise 19.1

Revise the following sentences so that auxiliaries and principal verb parts are used correctly. If the sentence is correct, write *C*.

1. No one may enter the theatre after the first act has began.
2. If she would have tried to start the car, she would have realized that the battery was dead.
3. Someone has drank all the beer in the fridge.
4. The unconscious man laid on the sidewalk for an hour.

5. I would of came with you, but I didn't know you were leaving.

6. Make sure all the campers have brang insect repellent.

7. Maya has submitted all the term assignments, but she hasn't yet wrote her final exam.

8. Vicki Keith has swum all of the Great Lakes.

9. I seen her in class last week.

10. I would have gave you a ride if I would have known that we live so near each other.

19d Keeping Your Verb Tenses Consistent

Once you have decided on the tense—present, past, or future—of a particular piece of writing, be consistent. You may have to shift tenses to clarify time relationships, but don't do so unnecessarily. Use the present tense when you are writing about literature.

Note the use of the present tense in the following paragraph analyzing Stacey MacAindra, who is the central character in Margaret Laurence's novel *The Fire Dwellers*.

Stacey's inability to communicate with her husband and children is a manifestation of the "tomb silences" of her own parents. Again we see Laurence's concern with the past as a source of isolation, for Stacey's background does not give her the means to be fully open with others. Moreover, she is a victim not only of her own past but also of the past influences that shape her husband, Mac, who inherits his reticence and his tendency to misinterpret Stacey's remarks from a father who is himself often restrained and imperceptive. Because of their childhoods, both Stacey and Mac believe that "nice" people do not talk about fear or pain. Stacey understands the limitations of this belief, but her inability to free herself from its influence leads her to remark that everyone in her family is one-dimensional. This image conveys Stacey's feelings of dissociation from her husband and children.

Exercise 19.2

Revise the following paragraph to eliminate unnecessary tense shifts. Use the present tense. The paragraph deals with Margaret Laurence's collection of short stories *A Bird in the House*.

As a child, Vanessa expresses her imaginative concerns in the stories of "spectacular heroism" that she composes in her head to counteract the boredom of Sunday School lessons. Essentially, she rejected any ties between her fictional world and the reality she experiences growing up in a little prairie town. Although she acknowledges Manawaka in her tale of the infant swept away in its christening robe by the flooding Wachakwa River, she transformed this muddy little river into an agent of the grotesque. Beyond this, Manawaka seems hardly worthy of literary note. For Vanessa, the "ordinary considerations" of life were completely divorced from the dramatic considerations of art. Thus she abandons her heroic epic, "The Pillars of the Nation," when she learned that Grandfather Connor, with his boring stories of the past, is himself one of those pillars.

19e Active and Passive Voice

English verbs have two voices: the **active** and the **passive**. In an active construction, the subject performs the action of the verb. In a passive construction, the subject is acted upon.

Edward made the announcement. [active]

The announcement was made by Edward. [passive]

In most writing situations, it's best to use the active voice. Occasionally, however, the passive voice can be useful.

When to Use the Active Voice

In most writing situations, don't rely heavily on passive constructions, especially if you are using them merely to sound more formal. Active constructions are usually clearer, more concise, and more forceful.

PASSIVE	The homeowners were informed by the city that the weeds would have to be cleared from their lots immediately.
ACTIVE	The city informed the homeowners that they would have to clear the weeds from their lots immediately.

When to Use the Passive Voice

Sometimes the passive voice is necessary. There are two main occasions.

1. Use it when you don't know who or what performed the action.

The house was constructed of limestone from the local quarries.

2. Use the passive voice when you want to emphasize what was done rather than who did it.

The solution was heated in a beaker.

Note: Passive constructions have always been common, and often preferred, in scientific writing because they place the emphasis on what was done rather than on who did it. The use of the passive voice suggests that anyone performing the experiment would get the same results. Recently, however, passive constructions in scientific writing have become less popular as more importance has been given to the role of the researcher. Because scientific writing styles vary, check to see which voice your instructor prefers.

Being Consistent

Avoid mixing active and passive constructions in the same sentence.

19e

Active and Passive Voice

NOT   A letter was written by the homeowners saying the weeds would be cleared when they (the homeowners) were good and ready.

BUT   The homeowners wrote a letter saying they would clear the weeds when they were good and ready.

Exercise 19.3

Change passive constructions to active constructions where appropriate. If the passive voice is preferable in the sentence, write *C*. Be prepared to defend your choices.

1. The performance was thoroughly enjoyed by the audience.

2. A unanimous decision was made by the members of the housing authority to request city funds to upgrade the playground area.

3. The new carpets are being installed this week.

4. A curve ball was signalled by the catcher to the pitcher, but she threw a fast ball instead.

5. All the names in the story have been changed to protect the innocent.

6. An increased tax on cigarettes, alcohol, and gasoline will be imposed by the federal government at the beginning of the month.

7. When the cracking ice was heard by Alexa, she moved cautiously toward the edge of the pond.

8. The conclusions of the research team at McGill University on the research done when strokes and heart attacks most often occur will be presented at the fall conference.

9. Mr. Lum will be released from hospital tomorrow.

10. The swimmers were warned by the lifeguard not to go beyond the buoys because of the strong undertow.

19f Making Subjects and Verbs Agree

The principle of **subject-verb agreement** is that singular subjects take singular verbs and plural subjects take plural verbs.

> This **ornament goes** on the top of the tree. (singular)
>
> The **lights go** on first. (plural)

Making Subjects and Verbs Agree

Here are the most common causes of errors in subject-verb agreement.

• *A prepositional phrase separating subject and verb.*

The subject and verb may be separated by a prepositional phrase (*of the workers, between the houses, across the field, including all team members, along with all his supporters*). The subject of the sentence is never located in the prepositional phrase.

> **One** of the workers **has filed** a complaint with the grievance committee.
>
> **Neither** of the women **wants** to press charges.
>
> **Mrs. Murphy** along with her five noisy children **attends** mass regularly.

- *When the sentence begins with* **there** *or* **here.**

There or *here* may be the first word of the sentence, but neither will be the subject of the sentence. Look for the real subject after the verb.

> There **are** only five **bananas**, not enough for everyone.

> Here **come** the **Jackson twins**, just in time for dinner.

- *Paired conjunctions:* **either/or, neither/nor, not only/but also.**

In sentences with paired conjunctions, the subject closer to the verb makes the verb singular or plural.

> Neither Reuben nor **his cousins were prepared** to kiss the bride.

> Not only the students but also the **teacher was delighted** by the unexpected holiday.

- *Subjects that may be singular or plural.*

Collective nouns, such as *team, group, committee,* are considered singular when they refer to people or things acting as a unit.

> Our **team is** on a five-day road trip.

> The **herd has settled down** for the night.

Collective nouns are considered plural when they refer to people or things acting individually.

> The **team do** not **agree** about the need for a new manager.

> The **herd have scattered** in every direction.

Collective nouns of quantity (*number, majority, percentage*) are singular when preceded by *the*, plural when preceded by *a*.

> The **number** of unemployed people **is increasing**.

> A **number** of unemployed people **are** still **looking** for jobs.

The pronouns *all*, *none*, and *some* can be either singular or plural, depending on the noun to which they refer.

> **None** of the cake **is** left.

> **None** of the cookies **are** left.

Words joined by *and* are considered singular when they refer to a single unit or to the same person.

> **Bread and butter makes** a fine basis for a sandwich.

> My **neighbour and best friend has moved** to another city.

Exercise 19.4

Make subjects and verbs agree in the following sentences. If the sentence is correct, put *C* beside it.

1. The temptation of power and riches have always been difficult to resist.

2. The jury are listening attentively as the crown prosecutor sums up his case.

3. There goes Mrs. Mason, along with her two miniature poodles.

4. Neither the prisoners nor the warden support the changes in prison policy.

5. Each of the workers are demanding better safety procedures.

6. The number of complaints to this office has decreased over the past month.

7. Nothing printed in the newspapers seem believable to him.

8. No one in the two families remember how the feud began.

9. The committee have agreed on an agenda for the next meeting.

10. Either Maria or her daughters is coming to meet you at the airport.

Making Subjects and Verbs Agree

Chapter 20

Proofreading: Pronouns

Pronouns *substitute for nouns or other pronouns. The word to which the pronoun refers is called its* **antecedent**.

My **grandmother** goes bowling every Wednesday. Then **she** eats lunch at **her** fitness club. [*Grandmother* is the antecedent of *she* and *her*.]

We will discuss the five most common types of pronoun problems.

1. Pronoun agreement errors
2. Pronoun case errors
3. Errors with possessive pronouns
4. Pronoun reference errors
5. Shifts in pronouns of address

20a

Pronoun Agreement

20a Pronoun Agreement

Errors in pronoun agreement occur when you don't match a singular pronoun with a singular noun or a plural pronoun with a plural noun. Pronoun agreement errors occur most frequently in the following situations.

Agreement with Singular Nouns: Avoiding Gender Stereotypes

Pronoun agreement errors often involve using a plural pronoun to refer to a singular noun. Most often, the noun names a type of person (the alcoholic, the mature student, the typical worker) rather than an individual, as in the following example:

ERROR   The **alcoholic** may blame **their** drinking problem on unsympathetic family members.

There are four ways to avoid this kind of agreement error.

1. Use a singular pronoun.

   The alcoholic may blame **his** drinking problem on unsympathetic family members.

   Although this version is grammatically correct, the use of *his* is unappealing because it implies that all alcoholics are men.

2. Use the phrase *his* or *her*.

   The alcoholic may blame **his or her** drinking problem on unsympathetic family members.

   This correction works well in single sentences but becomes cumbersome when repeated frequently. Avoid using *he/she*, *s/he*, or *him/her* in any piece of writing.

3. Make the noun plural. Pluralizing is often the simplest and most effective way to ensure pronoun agreement.

   Alcoholics may blame **their** drinking problems on unsympathetic family members.

4. Alternate masculine and feminine pronouns. If you were writing about types of people, such as the teacher and his or her students or the doctor and his or her patients, you could alternate masculine and feminine pronouns by referring to the teacher or doctor as *he* in one paragraph and as *she* in the next paragraph. Alternating masculine and feminine pronouns paragraph by paragraph is much less confusing and distracting than alternating them within a single paragraph.

20a

Pronoun Agreement

Exercise 20.1

Revise the following sentences to make antecedents and pronouns agree.

1. Every parent experiences some of these problems with their children.

2. The lead runner suddenly clutched their leg and fell to the ground.

3. The typical impaired driver is confident that they are in control of their vehicle.

4. The first year college student may feel somewhat overwhelmed by their workload.

5. A dog with braces on their teeth is certainly an unusual sight.

Agreement with Collective Nouns

Collective nouns are words such as *jury, team, band, audience, group, family, committee, congregation, herd, flock* that refer to people or things taken together.

When a collective noun refers to people or things acting as a single unit, the collective noun takes singular verbs and singular pronouns.

The **jury was** unanimous in **its** verdict.

The **band was** doomed without **its** leader.

When a collective noun refers to people or things acting as individuals, the collective noun takes plural verbs and plural pronouns.

The **jury were divided** in **their** judgment of the defendant.

The **band were arguing** over **their** next number.

When a collective noun is followed by a prepositional phrase, be careful to match the pronoun with the collective noun and not with the noun inside the prepositional phrase.

A small **group** of hecklers made **its** impact on the meeting.

The stranded **herd** of horses lost **its** way.

Agreement with *Either/Or, Neither/Nor, Or, Nor*

Singular nouns joined by *either/or, neither/nor, or*, and *nor* are matched with singular pronouns.

Neither Farida nor Barbara has contacted **her** lawyer.

Either Mark or Craig will lend you **his** truck for the move.

Plural nouns joined by these conjunctions take plural pronouns.

Neither the students nor the teachers had time to collect **their** belongings when the fire alarm sounded.

When mixed singular and plural nouns are joined by these conjunctions, put the plural noun last and use a plural pronoun.

Neither the lead singer nor **the dancers** have been fitted for **their** costumes.

Exercise 20.2

Revise the following sentences where necessary to make antecedents and pronouns agree. If the sentence is correct, write *C*.

1. If you can't find your textbook before the weekend, Tom or Dick will lend you theirs.

2. The city council has made their choice of an architect for the new city hall.

3. Neither the tenants nor the landlord felt their complaints had been heard.

4. Either my aunts or my mother will express their gratitude for the flowers.

5. The pack of wolves made their first kill near the end of the day.

6. The government has made its final offer in the land claims negotiations.

7. The board of governors has appointed Jack Smart as their new chairperson.

8. A family of skunks has made their home under our front steps.

9. Susan or Megan must have left their keys on the hall table.

10. The next time your car breaks down, neither George nor Carlos will lend you his.

Agreement with Indefinite Pronouns

Singular Indefinite Pronouns

The following indefinite pronouns are always singular. They take singular verbs, and any pronouns referring to them should also be singular.

everyone	*anyone*	*no one, one*	*someone*	*either*
everybody	*anybody*	*nobody*	*somebody*	*either*
everything	*anything*	*nothing*	*something*	*each*

Here is a typical example of an agreement error with an indefinite pronoun:

Everyone in the office had put in **their** request for time off at Christmas.

281

Here *everyone*, which is singular, and *their*, which is plural, do not agree.

You could correct this error by using the strategies suggested above for singular nouns. Alternatively, you could rephrase the sentence to eliminate the pronoun altogether.

> Everyone in the office had requested time off at Christmas.

Don't be misled by prepositional phrases. If a singular indefinite pronoun is followed by a prepositional phrase ending with a plural noun (*of the children, in the houses, under the benches*) the verb and any pronouns referring to the subject are still singular.

> **Neither** of the drivers has contacted **her** insurance agent.

In this sentence, the antecedent of *her* is *neither*. Because *neither* is singular, the pronoun referring to it must be singular.

Plural Indefinite Pronouns
(Many, Few, Several, Both)

The indefinite pronouns *many, few, several,* and *both* take plural pronouns.

> **Both** of the drivers filed claims with **their** insurance companies.

Singular or Plural Indefinite Pronouns
(All, None, Some)

The indefinite pronouns *all, none,* and *some* are matched with singular pronouns when they are followed by a prepositional phrase that contains a singular noun.

> **None of the furniture** has been moved from **its** original position for years.

These pronouns are matched with plural pronouns when they are followed by a prepositional phrase containing a plural noun.

> **None of the chairs** have been moved from **their** original positions for years.

Exercise 20.3

Revise the following sentences where necessary to make antecedents and pronouns agree. If the sentence is correct, write *C*.

1. Anybody considering the egg and grapefruit diet should first consult their doctor.

2. Neither of the witnesses was willing to change their statement.

3. None of the musicians were prepared to risk that kind of damage to their instruments.

4. The special needs child is likely to make more demands on their teacher.

5. Someone has forgotten to put their name on the test.

Exercise 20.4 Pronoun Agreement Review

Revise the following sentences to make antecedents and pronouns agree. If the sentence is correct, write *C*.

1. Neither of the women who witnessed the accident has given their testimony in court yet.

2. A good sales representative learns to anticipate their customers' needs.

3. Neither Monika nor Rachel has submitted their research paper.

4. The rock group has agreed that this will be their final tour.

5. Marco was the only person who kept their wits about them during the emergency.

6. Every child will have their art work on display during Parents' Night.

7. Some of the residents have already abandoned their homes to the rising flood waters.

8. The finance committee has submitted their annual report.

9. Neither of the board members would discuss their financial interest in the company.

10. The cocaine addict may sacrifice both their job and their family to their addiction.

11. The mob forced its way through the police barricade.

12. Magda or Dorothy will lend you their notes for the lecture you missed.

13. The audience expressed their unanimous approval in a standing ovation.

14. Some of the children missed their parents intensely; others were glad to be away from home.

15. No one has let their name stand for nomination.

Exercise 20.5 Pronoun Agreement Review

Revise the following paragraph to eliminate all errors in pronoun agreement.

The parent of a deaf child typically goes through a number of stages in coming to terms with their child's condition. During the shock stage, when deafness is first discovered, the parent is often too stunned and numb to register much emotion about having a deaf child. This stage is followed by the much more emotional recognition stage, when a parent may express a good deal of anger, frustration, grief, and shame as they begin to face the implications of deafness for themselves and their child. Because this recognition stage is so painful, a parent may withdraw from it into denial, pretending that the deaf child is almost the same as their siblings and playmates and needs no special attention. A parent can be helped through this stage by learning to recognize it. When a parent begins to tell members of his extended family about his child's hearing loss and thus tries out a new role as the parent of a deaf child, they are moving towards acceptance. With acceptance comes the possibility for the final stage, constructive action, when parents begin to investigate the options for helping the child to communicate, learn, and integrate themselves into the mainstream.

20b Pronoun Case

The **subject pronouns** (*I, we, you, he, she, it, they*, and *who*) are used as the subject of a sentence or a clause. The **object pronouns** (*me, us, you, him, her, it, them,* and *whom*) are used as the object of a verb or a preposition. The most common error in pronoun case involves a confusion of subject and object pronouns.

NOT	**Her** and **I** are going to a movie tonight.
BUT	**She** and **I** are going to a movie tonight.
NOT	You can reach my wife or **I** at home after six o'clock.
BUT	You can reach my wife or **me** at home after six o'clock.

Subject Pronouns

Use subject pronouns in the subject position in the sentence. Don't be confused when the pronoun is part of a compound subject.

NOT	Frances and **me** went to the Farmers' Market on Saturday to buy vegetables.

BUT	Frances and **I** went to the Farmers' Market on Saturday to buy vegetables.

Don't be confused when the subject pronoun is followed by an explanatory noun (*we homeowners, we students, we smokers*). The pronoun is still in the subject position.

NOT	**Us** residents are presenting a petition to city council.

BUT	**We** residents are presenting a petition to city council.

Use subject pronouns after comparisons using *than* or *as*.

NOT	Peter is as tall as **me**.

BUT	Peter is as tall as **I**.

NOT	No one was more surprised than **her**.

BUT	No one was more surprised than **she**.

Use a subject pronoun as the subject of an embedded subordinate clause. Be especially careful with *that* clauses.

NOT	Ramesh said that **him** and his wife would be glad to help.

BUT	Ramesh said that **he** and his wife would be glad to help.

20b

Pronoun Case

Object Pronouns

Use object pronouns as the direct or indirect object of a verb.

NOT	The manager assigned Loretta and **she** to work a double shift.

BUT	The manager assigned Loretta and **her** to work a double shift.

NOT	Please let your mother or **I** know when you will be home.

BUT	Please let your mother or **me** know when you will be home.

Use object pronouns in prepositional phrases.

NOT	Between you and **I**, there is something strange about our new neighbour.
BUT	Between you and **me**, there is something strange about our new neighbour.
NOT	The city replied to **we** homeowners.
BUT	The city replied to **us** homeowners.

Note 1: Don't make the mistake of thinking that *me* is an informal version of *I*. *Me* is a perfectly correct pronoun, provided that you use it in the object position in a sentence.

Note 2: Don't use a **reflexive pronoun** (the pronouns that end in *self/selves*) as a substitute for a subject or object pronoun.

NOT	My family and **myself** will be going to Nova Scotia for a camping holiday.
BUT	My family and **I** will be going to Nova Scotia for a camping holiday.
NOT	Ms. Chang asked that all inquiries be directed to **herself** rather than to Mr. Morgan.
BUT	Ms. Chang asked that all inquiries be directed to **her** rather than to Mr. Morgan.

Who and *Whom*

Who is a subject pronoun. Use it to refer to a subject noun or pronoun.

Helen is the candidate. She is sure to win.

Helen is the candidate **who** is sure to win. [*Who* replaces *she*.]

Whom is an object pronoun. Use it after prepositions and to refer to an object noun or pronoun.

To whom do you wish to speak?

He is a lawyer. We can trust him.

He is a lawyer **whom** we can trust. [*Whom* replaces *him*.]

20b

*Pronoun
Case*

Exercise 20.6

Correct all errors in pronoun case in the following sentences. If the sentence is correct, write *C*.

1. All three cousins—Laurence, Edward, and him—will be spending the summer at camp.
2. They are no more likely to win than us.
3. My cousin and him are swimming in the meet on Friday.
4. Tamsin is almost as fast a runner as me.
5. King told the police that his sister and him were nowhere near the scene of the crime.
6. Now we know who to believe.
7. She is the kind of person who can make a real contribution to our cause.
8. Please contact either my husband or I if there are any problems.
9. They live across the street from my parents and I.
10. The prize money should be divided among Shelley, Saul, and she.

20c Possessive Pronouns

Use **possessive pronouns** (*mine, yours, his, hers, its, theirs, whose*) to show ownership or possession. Pay especially close attention to the following points.

Possessive Pronouns

- Don't confuse the possessive pronoun *its* with the contraction *it's* (*it is*).

POSSESSIVE   The committee has tabled **its** report.

CONTRACTION   Don't call me unless **it's** an emergency.

- Don't confuse the possessive pronoun *whose* with the contraction *who's* (*who is*).

POSSESSIVE   I didn't hear **whose** name was announced as the winner.

CONTRACTION   I don't know **who's** calling.

- Don't confuse the possessive pronoun *their* with the contraction *they're* (*they are*) or the adverb *there*.

POSSESSIVE	The Séguins are attending **their** family reunion in Regina.
CONTRACTION	**They're** staying with Cousin Denis and his family for two weeks.
ADVERB	They hope to see the whole family **there**.

- Remember to use apostrophes with indefinite pronouns.

    Everyone's assignments have been returned.

    Someone's keys were turned in to the receptionist.

- Do not use apostrophes with *hers, his, ours, yours*, and *theirs*.

    The battered canoe tied to the dock is **theirs**.

    This sweater must be **yours**.

Exercise 20.7

Correct all errors in the use of possessive pronouns in the following sentences.

1. Do you know who's briefcase this is?
2. The spruce tree in the front yard has lost half it's needles.
3. Sally makes her problems everybodys business.
4. Can that beautiful new car really be your's?
5. There's was a story of woe.

Exercise 20.8 Review of Pronoun Case and Possessive Pronouns

Correct all errors in pronoun case and possessive pronouns. If the sentence is correct, write *C*.

1. No one told Elizabeth or myself that the meeting had been cancelled.
2. Brian says that both Donato and him are trying out for the team.
3. The Steins were surprised to learn that a skunk had made its home under there porch.
4. Someone's car is parked in my spot, but I don't know whose.
5. No one was as excited about the news as him.
6. The rambling old house on the corner is our's.

7. I thought this was to be a secret between you and I.

8. The missing teenager phoned his parents to say that him and his friend were in jail.

9. Don't hesitate to ask Paul or myself if you need more help with the charity bazaar.

10. The shop supervisor fired Alice and her for smoking on the job.

Exercise 20.9 Review of Pronoun Case and Possessive Pronouns

Correct all errors in pronoun case and the use of possessive pronouns in the following passage.

A few years ago, me and my brother bought a somewhat battered 1963 Ford pickup truck, advertised as being in "good running condition." Neither of us understood at the time that this phrase was a euphemism for "on it's last legs." My father said that our mother and him doubted that we would have enough money to run it, but we assured them that we had figured it all out. Almost from the beginning, however, the truck was a major source of arguments between my brother and I. We had agreed that he would cover the costs of insurance, the licence, and gas while the cost of repairs would be borne by myself. A week after we got the truck, we woke up one morning to discover that both front tires were flat and there was no spare. A week after that, a huge puddle of oil appeared on the front driveway, and we argued about who's responsibility it was to clean up. Next the signal lights went, and we were forced to make hand signals in –20°C temperatures.

Still, us brothers did not despair. Even though the truck was just barely running, it was still all our's. But one snowy Friday afternoon in the middle of rush-hour traffic, the brakes went and we slid through a red light. My brother, always more cowardly than me, shook with fear when he saw the five-car pile-up we had caused. No one was hurt, but as we watched our truck being towed away while we talked with the police officer, we knew that our driving careers had ended, at least temporarily.

20d

Pronoun Reference

20d Pronoun Reference

When you are speaking, you can usually make yourself understood even if you use pronouns rather vaguely. When you are writing, however, you need to make the connections between pronouns and nouns clear to your reader. When this connection is unclear, you have made an error in pronoun reference.

Here are some of the most common errors in pronoun reference.

Confusing Pronoun References

This problem is most likely to occur in sentences containing indirect speech.

VAGUE   When Kevin told Ali that he was being laid off, he was very upset.

CLEAR   Kevin was very upset when he told Ali, "I'm [or you're] being laid off."

Vague Use of *They* and *It*

Avoid using *they* if it doesn't refer to a specific noun in your writing.

VAGUE   They say that a number of western democracies are shifting politically to the right.

CLEAR   Respected commentators say that a number of western democracies are shifting politically to the right.

You can see a similar problem with *it* in this sentence.

VAGUE   I spent hours working out a detailed budget, but **it** didn't solve my financial problems.

This sentence leaves your reader wondering what didn't help: the time you spent working on your budget? the budget itself? A revised sentence might read like this:

CLEAR   I spent hours working out a detailed budget, but **this effort** did not solve my financial problems.

OR   I spent hours working out a detailed budget, but **the budget itself** did not solve my financial problems.

Vague Use of *That, Which,* or *This*

In some sentences, *that, which,* or *this* refers to several different ideas.

VAGUE The cousins fought on different sides in the war, which tore their family apart.

What tore their family apart? the fact that they fought on different sides? the exploits? the war? A clearer version might read like this:

CLEAR The family was torn apart by the cousins' decision to fight on different sides in the war.

Vague References to Possessive Pronouns

VAGUE Unable to brake on the icy roads, Jesse slammed into the car's bumper that was stopped at a red light.

In this sentence, *that* refers to *the car's bumper*, an error suggesting that the car's bumper was stopped at the red light. You could revise this sentences as follows:

CLEAR Unable to brake on the icy roads, Jesse slammed into the bumper of a car that was stopped at a red light.

20d

Pronoun Reference

Exercise 20.10

Revise the following sentences to clarify vague pronoun references.

1. Volunteers are working to clean up the oil from the spill, which is why the beach has been closed.

2. Karen applied to the school of nursing, but they told her she would have to upgrade her skills in math and biology.

3. The garage with the Jaguar inside was destroyed in the fire but it isn't as bad as it seems.

4. I knew if I left home I would be broke most of the time, but I desperately needed more independence. This made me touchy and miserable.

5. The work is tedious, menial, and dangerous, but that doesn't bother Jim.

6. Rajiv told George that he had just won a thousand dollars at the races.

7. It's a mistake to run yellow lights, especially when you know the police are on the lookout for it.

8. They say that voters seldom change their minds twice in an election campaign.

9. Alan knows he should see a dentist about his sore tooth, but he doesn't have time for it now.

10. Somia thought she had taped the show, but apparently it wasn't working properly.

Exercise 20.11

Revise the following paragraph to eliminate all vague and ambiguous pronoun references. The writer is commenting on the first draft of a murder mystery.

20e

Pronouns of Address

The English country house setting of your novel provides the self-enclosed world that is often an essential element in a murder mystery. This, however, does not allow readers to focus on Dr. Hawkins' career in the way that a hospital setting would facilitate. Your astute observations of human behaviour are effective in the complex analysis you provide of his reasons for murdering the head of surgery, which gives your novel more psychological complexity. You might consider developing her character in more detail in order to set out the reasons for the rivalry between them more fully. If you do this and eliminate the rather distracting subplot of the gardener's discovery of buried treasure, you can heighten the tension in the main plot—the increasing rivalry and emotional entanglement between Dr. Hawkins and the head of surgery.

20e Pronouns of Address

You establish your relationship to your reader by the **pronouns of address** you use (or don't use) in your first paragraph. If you want your readers to focus on you—your ideas, your experiences—use first-person pronouns (*I, me, my, mine*). If you want your readers to consider how your subject relates to them directly (as in sermons, advertisements, directions), use second-person pronouns (*you, your, yours*). If you use only nouns and third-person pronouns (*he, she, it, they*), you will encourage your readers to focus on your subject.

These sentences illustrate the different relationships you might establish with your readers in an article about word processors.

FIRST PERSON | When I first began to use a word processor, I lost several files.

SECOND PERSON | When you first begin to use a word processor, you may lose a few files.

THIRD PERSON | When they first begin to use a word processor, most people lose a few files.

Once you have established the basic pronouns of address for a piece of writing, do not shift abruptly and without reason to another set of pronouns.

NOT | When **you** first begin to use a word processor, **one** may lose a few files. [*shift from second person to third person*]

NOT | When **most people** begin to use a word processor, **you** may lose a few files. [*shift from third person to second person*]

Confusing pronoun shifts may occur from sentence to sentence as well as within sentences.

NOT | When **I** began to use a word processor, **I** lost several files. **You** find it hard at first to master the sequence of commands. [*shift from first person to second person*]

These shifts disrupt your relationship with your reader.

20e

Pronouns of Address

Correcting Pronoun Shifts

In the following example, the perspective shifts from the third person, *Conrad* (*he*), to the second person, *you*.

> **Conrad** has invested **his** money wisely because, as an oil rig worker, **you** always face the possibility of seasonal unemployment.

There are two ways to correct this error.

1. Replace *you* with *he*.

> **Conrad** has invested **his** money wisely because, as an oil rig worker, **he** always faces the possibility of seasonal unemployment.

2. Rephrase the sentence to eliminate the use of the pronoun.

Conrad has invested his money wisely because oil rig workers always face the possibility of seasonal unemployment.

Exercise 20.12

Revise the following sentences to eliminate pronoun shifts. Where there are several possibilities, be prepared to defend your choice. If the sentence is correct, write *C*.

1. Silvana takes a short break after every hour of study because you can't concentrate when you are tired.

2. No matter how often you have stood before an audience, some public speakers always experience an initial few minutes of stage fright.

3. When you have replaced and tightened the lug nuts, lower the car to the ground.

4. Some primatologists claim that you are able to communicate with chimpanzees by using a computer keyboard with special symbols.

5. I dislike opening a closed door when you're not certain what's behind it.

Exercise 20.13

Revise the following paragraph to eliminate all pronoun shifts.

If athletes are prepared to put time and effort into their training, there is no need to take steroids to improve your performance. If strength and size are important factors in your sport, there are several good weight programs and diets that enable athletes to gain seven to nine kilograms and increase their strength 10 to 15%. Of course, these gains take more time than they would if you were using steroids. You would need to work out five times a week for five or six months to get these results. But following such a program gives athletes a feeling of responsibility and allows them to see that such gains are possible without chemical aids.

Chapter 21

Proofreading: Punctuation and Mechanics

21a Commas

When you are proofreading for errors in the use of commas, remember the following two principles:

1. Single commas are used to separate the items in a series of words, phrases or clauses and to set off elements at the beginning or end of the sentence.
2. Pairs of commas are used to enclose parts of a sentence.

Key Terms to Know

A **series** consists of three or more similar grammatical constructions.

> To complete grade 12, Petra needs **English, chemistry**, and **physics**. [*a series of nouns*]
>
> Before leaving for the lake, Simon needs to **buy groceries, pack the camper**, and **pick up his children**. [*a series of phrases*]
>
> **If you can meet the entrance requirements, if you can find a sponsor**, and **if you can arrange your own transportation**, you can run in this year's marathon. [*series of clauses*]

A **phrase** is a group of words without a subject and a verb (*around the corner, looking out the window, to finish the test on time*).

A **clause** is a group of words with a subject and verb.

A **main clause** can stand on its own as a sentence (*Sheila looked out the window*).

A **subordinate clause** cannot stand alone as a sentence (*After Sheila looked out the window*).

21a

Commas

295

Using Commas to Separate

Separating Items in a Series

Use a comma to separate words, phrases, or clauses in a series. Should you use a comma before the last item? Usage varies. We recommend putting a comma before the *and* or other conjunction that joins the last two items in the series, both to provide emphasis and to prevent misreading:

WITHOUT COMMA   I forgot to buy milk, orange juice, bread, peanut butter and jam. [does peanut butter and jam refer to one item or two?]

WITH COMMA   I forgot to buy milk, orange juice, bread, peanut butter, and jam.

• *Words in a Series*

I forgot to buy orange juice, milk, bread, peanut butter, and jam. [*unless you intended to buy a jar containing both peanut butter and jam*]

Note 1: Do **not** put a comma between pairs of items considered a single unit.

The Prime Minister said that full employment, regional development, and **law and order** are the chief priorities.

Note 2: Do **not** put commas between adjectives that could not be joined with *and*.

James Cook was a highly skilled eighteenth-century navigator.

• *Phrases in a Series*

The frightened puppy raced **through the door, down the hall**, and **under the bed**.

Listening to music, playing cards, and **eating peanuts** are my favourite recreational activities.

• *Clauses in a Series*

Mohammed handles the budget, Judy handles customer complaints, and Philip handles the advertising.

Exercise 21.1

Add all necessary commas to the following sentences.

1. Jeanette picked up some apples peaches pears and plums at the market this morning.

2. Moira put down the book rose from the chair and walked slowly across the room.

3. The best items on the menu are quiche baked salmon and ribs with barbecue sauce.

4. The drama instructor decided that Craig would play the male lead Iris would play the female lead and Noah would play the villain in the melodrama.

5. After falling through the ice into the muddy ditch, the cold wet bedraggled child trudged home.

Setting Off Main Clauses

Use a comma before the coordinating conjunctions *and, but, or, nor, for, yet,* and *so* when they join main clauses.

> The company sold off its unprofitable subsidiaries, **and** within six months its shares had doubled in value.

> Readers of the play may perceive Hamlet as slow to act, **but** on the stage the prince seems to rush headlong towards his death.

The comma is often omitted before *and* and *or* if the clauses are short or have the same subject.

> You stand in line and I'll find a table.

> They may achieve their goals or they may fail.

To prevent misreading, always use a comma before *for, so, yet* when used as coordinating conjunctions, since these words have other uses.

> The dog limped, **for** it was old. [coordinating conjunction]

> The dog limped **for** the door. [preposition]

21a

Commas

Exercise 21.2

Add all necessary commas to the following sentences.

1. Aunt Edna vacuumed the living room rug and Uncle Henry waxed the kitchen floor.

2. Roman makes the job look like child's play yet it is actually very difficult.

3. The premier knew that she would have to resign in favour of a more popular candidate or her party would lose the next election.

4. Audrey McLaughlin was not well known in some parts of the country before she became the NDP leader but she quickly established a reputation as a forceful speaker.

5. We have to leave immediately for we have no time to lose.

Setting Off Introductory Elements

• *After introductory subordinate clauses*

Use a comma after an introductory subordinate clause. These clauses begin with subordinate conjunctions such as *although, because, after, when, before, since,* and *while.*

> Before anyone could stop the baby, she had grabbed the edge of the tablecloth and pulled the dishes to the floor.

> Because there has been so much rain, the mosquitoes have been bad this year.

• *After introductory interjections*

Use a comma after mild interjections (*oh, well, my goodness*), and after *yes* and *no.*

> My, what a beautiful baby.

> Yes, the merchandise that you ordered last week has arrived.

• *After introductory transitional words and phrases*

The usual practice is to put a comma after transitional phrases such as *for example, on the other hand, in contrast.* Put a comma after conjunctive adverbs of more than two syllables: after *nevertheless,* but not after *thus.*

> On the other hand, many prairie grain farmers are in desperate straits.

> Nevertheless, people were optimistic that the economy would improve.

> Thus we need to work out a new system to deal with rural bankruptcies.

Note: Do **not** use a comma after a subordinate conjunction.

NOT   Although, she was desperate for a cigarette, she was too intimidated to smoke.

BUT   Although she was desperate for a cigarette, she was too intimidated to smoke.

21a

Commas

- *After introductory phrases of more than five words*

  Sitting patiently beside my neighbour's woodpile, Brutus stood vigilant guard over escaping field mice.

- *After any introductory element to prevent misreading*

  After the Smiths left, the Joneses turned out the porch light and retired for the evening.

  In the evening, darkness settled over the town.

Exercise 21.3

Add all necessary commas to the following sentences.

1. Although the clerks have been busy all day the store hasn't taken in much money.

2. During a sleepless night time seems to stand still.

3. My goodness I didn't expect to see you here.

4. Without stopping to take off his muddy boots Uncle Jeff tramped across the kitchen floor to the refrigerator.

5. On the other hand it might be better for me to work this evening and take tomorrow off.

Setting Off Elements at the End of a Sentence

Use a comma to set off a word, phrase, or clause at the end of a sentence that qualifies, contrasts with, or questions what comes before.

> A puppy is a perfect pet, if you have lots of patience. [*qualifying clause*]
>
> I ordered the chicken, not the squid. [*contrasting element*]
> You'll give me a hand, won't you? [*question*]

21a

Commas

Setting Off Direct Speech and Quotations

Use commas to set off direct speech and quotations from the rest of the sentence.

> Alice remarked, "The lights are on, but no one seems to be home."
>
> We see Hamlet's growing awareness of the burdens placed upon him when he says, "The time is out of joint. O cursed spite / That ever I was born to set it right!"

Note: Do **not** use a comma before a quotation when the structure of the sentence introducing the quotation does not call for one.

> We see Hamlet's hostility when he says that Claudius is "A little more than kin and less than kind."

Exercise 21.4

Add all necessary commas to the following sentences. If the sentence is correct, write *C*.

1. Who was it who said "The play's the thing / Wherein I'll catch the conscience of the king"?
2. Vita said that she used to live in London, Ontario not London, England.
3. Mrs. Tetley asked politely "Would you care for another cup of tea?"
4. I cannot agree with you when you say that "books are a bloodless substitute for life."
5. This yellow brick road will take us to Oz won't it?

Using Pairs of Commas to Enclose

21a

Commas

Enclosing Interruptions in the Sentence

Use a pair of commas to enclose words, phrases, or clauses that slightly interrupt the flow of the sentence. Such expressions include parenthetical remarks (*of course, indeed, for example*), transitions (*however, therefore*), interjections (*well, oh*), and nouns of direct address (*Henry, Mother*).

> I will, as I have already told you, investigate the matter fully.

> The events described in this story are true. The names, however, have been changed to protect the innocent.

> I'd say he weighs about, oh, 80 kg.

> This decision, Kevin, is for you to make.

Enclosing Nonrestrictive Phrases and Clauses

Use a pair of commas to enclose a nonrestrictive modifying phrase or clause. These clauses and phrases function as adjectives, but their presence is not essential to identifying the noun they modify. Instead, they supply additional or supplementary information.

Nonrestrictive clauses and phrases usually modify **proper nouns**—nouns that name a particular person or thing.

NONRESTRICTIVE   Bob Edward, publisher of *The Calgary Eye-Opener*, was an influential and controversial figure until his death in 1922.

NONRESTRICTIVE   Clarence's Uncle David, who is an accomplished seaman, is planning to sail around the world.

Clauses beginning with *which* are more likely to be nonrestrictive than are clauses beginning with *that*.

NONRESTRICTIVE   In the story, which is about a seemingly ordinary village lottery, the horrifying nature of the prize is not revealed until the draw has been made.

RESTRICTIVE   I've lost the book that I intended to lend you.

Note: Do **not** use commas to enclose a restrictive phrase or clause that provides essential information in the sentence.

RESTRICTIVE   Men wearing straw hats are a rare sight today. [*Only men wearing straw hats are a rare sight.*]

RESTRICTIVE   All customers who install a smoke detector are eligible for a discount on insurance premiums. [*Only customers who install a smoke detector are eligible.*]

RESTRICTIVE   The one book that I am determined to read this summer is *War and Peace*.

21a

Commas

Exercise 21.5

Add all necessary commas to the following sentences. If the sentence is correct, write *C*.

1. English mathematician Charles Lutwidge Dodgson who wrote under the pen name Lewis Carroll is best known as an author of children's books.

2. *Alice's Adventures in Wonderland,* for example is a timeless story that appeals to readers of all ages.

3. Richard Writewell whose stories appear in several anthologies will be signing autographs tomorrow at Beechwood Books.

4. My offer Ms. Wallace is final.

5. Anyone who witnessed the accident at the corner of MacLeod Road and Dorchester Avenue is asked to call police as soon as possible.

Using Commas in Conventional Places

• Use a comma to separate the day of the month from the year.

> Canada celebrated its centennial on July 1, 1967.

Note: The comma is optional when only the month and year are given.

> Canada celebrated its centennial in July, 1967 [July 1967].

• Use a comma to separate the elements in geographic names and addresses.

> Architect Douglas Cardinal designed the Museum of Civilization in Hull, Québec.

> The couple were married at St. Joseph's Basilica, 10044-113 Street, Edmonton, Alberta.

• Use a comma after the salutation in personal or informal letters and after the closing in all letters.

> Dear Aunt Margaret,
>
> Yours truly,
>
> Sincerely yours,

Exercise 21.6 Review

Add all necessary commas and delete all unnecessary commas in the following sentences. If the sentence is correct, write *C*.

1. If you drop off the suit early enough it can be cleaned pressed and ready for pickup the same day.

2. To illustrate this part of our discussion let me give you an example.

3. An actor who had begun his career as a spear carrier in Shakespearean stage productions became a highly acclaimed movie star.

4. In the dark night patrols understandably nervous paced the walkway connecting the jail with the courthouse.

5. I have never been to Tuktoyaktuk have you?

6. At the end of a long, tiring day on the rigs Jack likes nothing better than to read Homer in the original Greek.

7. Frisky, is hungry for Jim hasn't arrived home yet to feed him.

8. When the flag flies above the old soldier's eyes fill with tears.

9. Her heart may be in the right place but she has put her foot in her mouth too many times.

10. There is, of course a $15 surcharge for delivery.

11. Anyone who is caught trespassing on this property will be prosecuted to the fullest extent of the law.

12. Charlotte turned into a nervous wreck when she learned that she was suffering from lyssophobia which is an abnormal fear of becoming insane.

13. Because we knew that we would not have time for lunch we had ham and eggs toast and marmalade orange juice and coffee for breakfast.

14. The book that I wanted to lend you, seems to have disappeared.

15. Frank knew Marika was furious because, she was gritting her teeth.

16. Please forward the cheque to R. Hood 123 Sherwood Forest Lane Nottinghamshire England.

17. The exposition was opened by the Prince and Princess of Wales on May 2 1986.

18. Grandfather is fond of telling me "You can't choose your relatives but you can choose your friends."

19. You're the first person whom we thought of for the job.

20. Thank you, Mrs. Guthrie for all your help with the campaign.

21b Semicolons

Use a semicolon in the following ways.

- By itself to join two closely related main clauses

    The storm struck with a destructive fury; the ship was broken by the violent wind and waves.

303

Note 1: Never use a semicolon to join a subordinate clause to a main clause.

NOT

Although it had snowed heavily during the night; the roads were clear by noon the next day.

BUT

Although it had snowed heavily during the night, the roads were clear by noon the next day.

Note 2: Avoid using a semicolon as a kind of big comma for emphasis.

NOT

Horrified, Nelson watched the tidal wave approach; knowing that his tiny boat could never withstand its force.

BUT

Horrified, Nelson watched the tidal wave approach, knowing that his tiny boat could never withstand its force.

- With a conjunctive adverb (*nevertheless, however, otherwise, consequently, thus, therefore, then, meanwhile, moreover, furthermore*) or with a transitional phrase (*in addition, as a result, for example*) to join main clauses

  The advertisement states that applicants with a degree in a related area are preferred; **nevertheless**, applicants with a diploma and relevant experience will be considered for the position.

- With a coordinating conjunction (*and, but, or, nor, for, yet, so*) when the main clauses contain internal punctuation

  Already late for work, I dressed hurriedly, ran out of the house, and jumped into the car; but when I turned the key, I heard only the ominous clicking sound of a dying battery.

- However, if you are joining two fairly short main clauses with a coordinate conjunction, a **comma** is a better choice.

NOT

Yvette longed to escape; yet she remained passive.

BUT

Yvette longed to escape, yet she remained passive.

- Instead of a comma between items in a series when the items themselves have internal punctuation

> The lottery prize includes the dream home, custom-built by a leading home builder; custom-made draperies, professional interior decorating, and exclusive furnishings; and free cleaning for one year.

Semicolons can be useful, but too many will give your writing a ponderous tone. If you're becoming addicted to the semicolon, you're probably relying too heavily on coordination to join your ideas.

> For several years, my computer has been working fine; now I'm having major problems. Perhaps a virus has infected the command system; the computer seems to be erasing files randomly. I'll have to be more careful to duplicate my material on backup disks; I'm losing too much valuable information.

You could improve this passage by introducing more subordination.

> Although my computer has been working fine for several years, now I'm having major problems. Perhaps a virus has infected the command system; the computer seems to be erasing files randomly. I'll have to be more careful to duplicate my material on backup disks because I'm losing too much valuable information.

For more information on joining sentences effectively, see Faulty Subordination (17f).

Exercise 21.7

Add semicolons where necessary to the following sentences.

1. There has been a freezing rain as a result, people are advised to drive with caution.

2. June was three months behind in her utility payments the city therefore discontinued her service.

3. At first his story seemed very convincing however, people soon began to doubt that he was telling the truth.

4. Mr. Terakawa set out to buy a station wagon he drove home in a Maserati.

5. Because the traffic was heavy and the roads were terrible, I was already half an hour late, but I tried to stay calm and alert.

21b

Semicolons

305

Exercise 21.8

Add semicolons where necessary to the following sentences. Replace inappropriate semicolons with the correct punctuation. If the sentence is correct, write *C*.

1. I doubt that your grievance will get a fair hearing; given the makeup of the present committee.

2. A mile from our destination, we discovered that the bridge was closed because of rising flood waters; we then had to turn around and find the detour route.

3. Let's get to registration as early as possible otherwise, we'll have to spend hours waiting in line-ups.

4. The following speakers will take part in our panel discussion: Professor Moira Katz, Department of English, Dr. Lydia Lannon, Department of Classical Studies, and Mr. Gordon Rasmussen, Department of Romance Languages.

5. Isadora is the most talented and accomplished dancer in the school all of the instructors are pleased; but not surprised, that she has been awarded the scholarship.

21c Colons and Dashes

The **colon** and the **dash** can both be used to introduce a phrase or clause that explains or illustrates what precedes it.

> After the tenth day without food, the subject began to exhibit psychological debilitation: he had trouble concentrating and slept much of the time.

> I still love listening to the Beatles—they remind me of the Sixties.

The colon is more appropriate for most formal writing situations. Use the dash when you want a more informal tone.

A pair of dashes can also be used to enclose parenthetical comments that slightly disrupt the flow of the sentence. By using dashes rather than commas or parentheses, you can set off these comments more emphatically from the rest of the sentence.

> The relationship between father and son—never very good—worsened as the son began to assert his independence.

Be careful not to overuse either the colon or the dash. Too many sentences containing colons will make your writing too formal and stilted. Too many sentences containing dashes will make your writing too choppy and informal.

Colons

Use a colon in the following situations.

- To introduce a list or series preceded by a complete main clause

   You will need the following equipment: a small tent, a sleeping bag, a camp stove, and several bottles of insect repellent.

- In a sentence introducing a list of items, you can use a colon after a verb when *as follows* or *the following* is strongly implied, as in this example:

   Our report includes:

   1. background information about the problem
   2. an analysis of its causes
   3. recommendations for solutions
   4. a detailed budget

Note: Do **not** use a colon with *such as* or *for example*.

NOT	The Robinsons brought back a number of souvenirs, such as: a red plush cushion with "Visit Niagara Falls" emblazoned on it, a slightly pornographic calendar, and two incredibly ugly beer mugs.
BUT	The Robinsons brought back a number of souvenirs, such as a red plush cushion....

- To introduce a concluding explanatory phrase

   She dedicated her research to one goal: finding the link between Einstein's Theory of Relativity and the theory of quantum mechanics.

- To join main clauses when the second clause restates, explains, summarizes, or emphasizes the first

   The movie was a complete waste of time: the plot dragged, the characters were boring, and the special effects were silly.

- To introduce a formal quotation. Both the sentence introducing the quotation and the quotation itself must be grammatically complete.

   In Alice Munro's short story "Boys and Girls," the narrator gradually becomes aware of the full implications of being a girl: "A girl was not, as I had supposed, simply what I was; it was what I had to become. It was a definition, always touched with emphasis, with reproach and disappointment. Also it was a joke on me."

Note: Do **not** use a colon when the sentence introducing the quotation ends with *that* or is otherwise incomplete.

NOT	Hamlet shows a new acceptance of death when he says that: "There is a special providence in the fall of a sparrow."
BUT	Hamlet shows a new acceptance of death when he says that "There is a special providence in the fall of a sparrow."

- in biblical references (John 3:16)
- in time references: (9:45, 12:05)
- between the title and the subtitle of an article or a book
  A Harvest Yet to Reap: A History of Prairie Women

- after the salutation in a business letter:

  Dear Business Manager:
  Dear Editor:
  Dear Ms. Bennett:

Dashes

Use a dash in the following situations.

- To indicate a sudden interruption or change of thought

  I left my briefcase—I remember it distinctly—right here by the front entrance.

  And then she said—but I see you've already heard the story.

- To emphasize parenthetical remarks

  Antonia worked hard—perhaps too hard—in spite of her illness.

- After a series at the beginning of a sentence

  Sports figures, entertainers, politicians—all have been invited to the wedding.

- To set off a series that comes in the middle of a sentence

  It had everything—power, grace, beauty—that Chantal wanted in a car.

- To emphasize an expression that explains or illustrates

  Philip worked tirelessly toward his goal—an A in English.

Exercise 21.9

Add colons and dashes where appropriate to the following sentences. Where either is possible, be prepared to defend your choice.

1. You must take an elective from each of the following areas to complete your degree French, mathematics or one of the physical sciences, and one of the social sciences.

2. My Uncle Beauregard I'm sure you've met him is the most eccentric person I know.

3. The politician refuted earlier media criticism of her position "I have never agreed, and do not now agree, to the commercial development of our wilderness parks."

4. This movie takes the usual plot elements monsters, mayhem, and murder to new heights of horror.

5. The cold was intense our breath froze in our mouths before we could exhale.

Exercise 21.10

Add colons and dashes where necessary to the following sentences. Where either is possible, be prepared to explain your choice. If the sentence is correct, write *C*.

1. He hated his job the work was tedious, the conditions were dangerous, and the pay was terrible.

2. The editorial in Friday's paper stated that "city council has only itself to blame" for the uproar over the pay raises for council members.

3. And then I went shopping it's something I always do whenever I'm especially short of money.

4. We are never totally free we can never escape time or taxes.

5. Dr. Christakos as I'm sure you know is a respected community leader.

21c

Colons and Dashes

21d Parentheses and Brackets

Both **parentheses** and **brackets** serve to set apart certain information in a sentence or a paragraph, but they are used in different circumstances.

Parentheses

Use parentheses in these situations:

- To set off supplementary material that interrupts the flow of the sentence

    The council finally agreed (but only after a heated debate) to the proposed amendments.

Note 1: Parentheses, dashes, and commas can all be used to set off non-essential information. When you enclose something in parentheses, you signal to your reader that it is relatively unimportant. Dashes tend to emphasize its importance, while commas will give it approximately equal weight.

Note 2: Do **not** use parentheses to enclose important information. In the example below, the parentheses are misleading because they suggest that essential information is incidental.

    Although he was only fifteen, Victor was sentenced to nine months in a juvenile detention centre. (This sentence was the result of his fifth conviction for theft over $1000 in two years.)

- To enclose explanatory material, such as bibliographical citations, brief definitions, and pieces of historical information

    The Celsius (centigrade) thermometer was invented by the Swedish astronomer Anders Celsius (1701-1744).

For information on parenthetical citations, see Appendix B, Documentation.

- To enclose letters or numerals in a list of items

    Each oral presentation will be graded on (1) delivery, (2) voice, (3) content, and (4) language.

- In general, resist the temptation to use parentheses too often. Information enclosed in parentheses interrupts the flow and meaning of a sentence. Too many of these interruptions will make your writing choppy and hard to follow, as in the following example.

    Headhunting (often called an executive search) is the practice of seeking out (sometimes through advertising, sometimes through more direct approaches to individuals) senior, specialized employees (when no one with sufficient expertise is available within an organization) for business.

Rewritten with only one parenthetical comment, the paragraph reads much more smoothly.

Headhunting (as executive searches are often called) is the practice of seeking out specialized senior employees for business firms when no one with sufficient expertise is available within an organization. Headhunters may advertise these positions or approach prospective candidates directly.

Using Other Punctuation with Parentheses

- If the parenthetical remark is a sentence within another sentence, the parenthetical sentence does not begin with a capital or end with a period.

  The baby was sleeping (at least his eyes were closed) when I peeked into the room.

- If the parenthetical remark is a complete sentence that is not part of another sentence, capitalize the first word and put the end punctuation inside the closing parenthesis.

  After weeks of dull, cloudy weather, the first snowflakes began to fall on Christmas Eve. (The children had been convinced that Christmas wouldn't be Christmas without snow.)

- If the parenthetical construction within a sentence requires a question mark or exclamation mark, that punctuation goes inside the closing parenthesis.

  It is important for students to learn how to think (who can deny that necessity?), but they also need facts and information to think about.

Brackets

Use brackets in the following ways.

- To enclose explanatory material inserted into a quotation. These square brackets tell your reader that the material was not part of the original quotation.

  In the essay "Grace before Meat," Charles Lamb says, "I hate a man who swallows it [his food], affecting not to know what he is eating. I suspect his taste in higher matters."

Note: The punctuation of the original sentence (the comma after *it*) goes outside the material enclosed in brackets.

- To show that you have changed a word (usually a verb or a pronoun) in a direct quotation so that it will fit grammatically with your sentence

  Old King Cole [is] a merry old soul / And a merry old soul [is] he.

- With the word *sic* (Latin for *thus*) to indicate that an error in spelling, grammar, or fact is part of the original quotation

  The newspaper headline read "Affects [sic] of cutbacks not yet known."

21e Quotation Marks

The main purpose of **quotation marks** is to acknowledge that you have used someone else's words. Use quotation marks

- Whenever you quote more than three consecutive words from any printed material. (For how to document your sources, see Appendix B, Documentation.)

  According to the article, many primatologists and psychologists believe that "chimpanzees have the capacity for self-awareness, self-consciousness, and self-knowledge."

- When you include comments made by someone you have interviewed. (For how to document interviews in a research paper, see Appendix B, Documentation.)

  According to Sharon Bush, records clerk in the registrar's office, "The completion rate for this course averages about 30%."

- When you include dialogue in a personal narrative or a short story. Indent the words of each speaker as you would indent separate paragraphs.

    "Do you have any plans to publish your autobiography?" the critic asked the novelist.
    "Actually, I was saving the best till last," remarked the author. "I might even arrange to have it published posthumously."
    "The sooner, the better," replied the critic.

Note: Remember that quotation marks set off direct speech. Don't use them with indirect speech.

DIRECT SPEECH   The clerk asked the customer, "Will you pay cash, or shall I charge this purchase to your account?"

INDIRECT SPEECH	The clerk asked the customer whether she wanted to pay cash or charge the purchase to her account.

- Use single quotation marks to indicate a quotation within a quotation.

    The witness testified, "I was present when the accused said, 'She'll pay for what she did to me!'"

Other Uses of Quotation Marks

- Put quotation marks around the titles of short works that have not been published separately, such as titles of chapters, short stories, articles, and most poems.

    His favourite Poe story is "The Fall of the House of Usher."

- When you want to draw your reader's attention to a word used in a special way, you can either underline the word to indicate that it is italicized (see Italics and Underlining, 21f) or put quotation marks around it.

    It's quite acceptable to begin a sentence with "because."

- Avoid using either quotation marks or italics merely to draw attention to slang or irony.

NOT	My sister has become a real "couch potato."
NOT	Our "paperboy" is at least fifty years old.

21e

Exercise 21.11

Quotation Marks

Use quotation marks appropriately in the following sentences. If the sentence is correct, write *C*.

1. I'd like your opinion of my proposal, Jim remarked to his supervisor.

    It's worthless, Mr. Koch replied.

    I know, but I'd like it anyway, said Jim.

2. You will find Margaret Laurence's article The Greater Evil an interesting and useful resource for your essay on censorship.

3. Maria said that she would lend me her copy when she has finished reading it.

4. The driver told the police officer, The light had already turned red when the black sedan went through the intersection.

5. The expressions jumbo shrimp and airline cuisine are examples of oxymorons.

Using Other Punctuation with Quotation Marks

- As a general rule, commas and periods go inside quotation marks; colons and semicolons go outside.

  Staring in disgust at the cans of escargots in the specialty section of the grocery store, Mr. Johnson remarked to his wife, "Let's can all the snails from the garden. We'll make a fortune." [*Period is inside quotation marks.*]

  Facing Mr. Waters squarely, William replied, "That, sir, is not your concern"; he then walked resolutely out of the room. [*Semicolon is outside the quotation marks.*]

- When a quotation is a question or an exclamation, the question or exclamation mark goes inside the quotation marks.

  "Where are the snows of yesteryear?" she asked pensively.

  "Get out of my way!" the enraged customer bellowed as he pushed through the crowd.

- When the entire sentence containing the quotation is a question or an exclamation, the question or exclamation mark goes outside the quotation marks.

  What does it mean to say "A stitch in time saves nine"?

  The Great China Circus is now truly "the greatest show on Earth"!

- When a quotation ends a sentence, whatever punctuation is inside the quotation mark also ends the entire sentence. Don't add any other punctuation.

  Jane listened with growing horror as the voice from the attic screamed, "Please let me out!"

21e

Quotation Marks

Exercise 21.12

Use quotation marks appropriately in the following sentences. Be sure to punctuate each sentence correctly. If the sentence is correct, write *C*.

1. I'm writing an essay on the theme of alienation in T.S. Eliot's poems The Love Song of J. Alfred Prufrock and The Waste Land.

2. There's no such thing as a free lunch he announced, handing me the bill.

3. The term obligatory runner refers to a person whose running routine creates serious risks to his or her physical and social well-being.

4. Peter opened his bedroom door and yelled Who forgot to feed my rabbit

5. A friend of mine, now in her nineties, often says that the doors to opportunity open outward.

Exercise 21.13

Use quotation marks and other punctuation appropriately in the following sentences.

1. You'll never catch me alive shouted the outlaw as she sprang to her horse.

2. Arguing with you, he remarked, is never a complete waste of time

3. Whereas naughty is a much less negative word now than it was three hundred years ago, stupid has become much more negative.

4. Let us all sing Yes, We Shall Gather at the River the minister announced

5. Was it Shelley who wrote the line If Winter comes, can Spring be far behind

21f Italics and Underlining

Use **italic** script in typeset and word-processed material, or underlining in handwritten or typed material, for each of the following cases.

- For the titles of books, newspapers, magazines, pamphlets, plays, films, television and radio series, works of art, albums or long musical compositions

    The city library has purchased two sets of *The Canadian Encyclopedia.*

    The police drama *Homicide: Life on the Streets* steadily gained popularity during its first few years.

- For the names of airplanes, ships, trains, and spacecraft. Do not underline *the* or abbreviations that come before the name.

Captain James Cook commanded the H.M.S. *Resolution* on his second Pacific voyage.

- For foreign words and phrases that have not been accepted as English terms. Examples of these expressions include the following:

  bon vivant (a person who enjoys food and drink)
  casus belli (an event that brings about war)
  tête à tête (an intimate conversation between two people)
  weltanschauung (a comprehensive concept of the universe and the relationship of humans to it)

- For words referred to as words, letters referred to as letters, and numerals referred to as numerals.

  The one word on the test that I couldn't define was *dipsomaniac*.

  Don't forget to cross your *t*'s.

  Is this an *8* or a *3*?

- For emphasis and clarity

  I asked *who* you are, not *how* you are.

  Late papers will *not* be accepted.

Note: Be cautious whenever you are tempted to use italics for emphasis. Like exclamation marks, italics lose their force if overused.

21g Hyphens

Hyphens are used as part of some compound words (*father-in-law*, *trade-in*). Other compound words are written as one word (*hairbrush*, *stepmother*) or as two words (*lawn bowling*, *token payment*). Because there is no pattern for forming compound words, and because compound words are constantly changing, your best source of current information is an up-to-date dictionary. You may find that dictionaries disagree on compound forms. Choose one spelling and use it consistently.

Use a hyphen in the following ways.

- With two-word numbers from twenty-one to ninety-nine

  There are **ninety-nine** bottles of beer on the wall.

- With numbers used as adjectives

  Is the tank three-quarters full?

  Atsuko, a thirty-four-year-old musician, made her television debut last night.

316

- With the prefixes *self* (*self-satisfied*), *ex* (*ex-husband*), and *all* (*all-purpose*); with prefixes that come before proper nouns (*anti-Catholic*); and with the suffix *elect* (*minister-elect*).
- To avoid an awkward combination of letters or to prevent misunderstanding: *re-cover* (*cover again*)
- To indicate that two or more prefixes or words share a common root

    Both pre- and post-natal classes are available.

    This course covers eighteenth- and nineteeth-century drama.

- To join two or more words that function as a single adjective conveying a single concept: *well-written essay, reddish-brown hair*

Note 1: If these constructions come after the noun, they are **not** hyphenated.

    The essay is well written.
    Her hair is reddish brown.

Note 2: If the group of words contains an *ly* adjective, do **not** hyphenate: *poorly conceived plan, frequently used reference book.*

Hyphenating Words at the Ends of Lines

It's best to avoid dividing words at the end of a line if possible. Occasionally, however, you may not be able to squeeze all the letters on the line you are writing. Here are the guidelines to follow:

- Always hyphenate a word between syllables. The first part of the word must contain at least three letters. Try to divide the word in two approximately equal parts that convey the sense of the whole word (*butter-fly* not *but-terfly*).

- When a double consonant occurs at the end because you have added a suffix (*ing, ed*), divide between the two consonants (*let-ting* not *lett-ing*). If the root word ends in a double consonant, divide between the root word and the suffix (*bill-ing* not *bil-ling*).

- Include a single-letter syllable with the first part of the word (*regu-late* not *reg-ulate*).

- Do **not** hyphenate one-syllable words or words of five or fewer letters (regardless of the number of syllables). If possible, avoid hyphenating words of six letters.

- Do **not** hyphenate figures ($21.36, 123 000), dates (Dec. 10, 1926), abbreviations (UNICEF), or proper names (Albert Einstein, Calgary).

- Do **not** hyphenate the last word of more than two consecutive lines.

- Do **not** hyphenate the last word in a paragraph or the last word on a page.

Exercise 21.14

Add, change, or take out hyphens as necessary in the following sentences.

1. My step-mother was stupefied when she stepped on her stepson's stopwatch.
2. Only one-third of the tickets were sold in advance, but concertgoers quickly snapped up the rest at the door.
3. Well-known as a brawler, the hot tempered actor slugged one of the twenty seven everpresent reporters.
4. The President elect of the United States grinned a self satisfied grin; his allpurpose promises had swayed millions of anti government voters.
5. The recklessly-squandered lives of the ninety seven soldiers were commemorated by their ex wives.

Exercise 21.15

How would you hyphenate each of the following words if it appeared at the end of a line? If the word should not be hyphenated, write *C*.

1. druggist	6. caravan
2. drugged	7. underfed
3. sorry	8. spitting
4. sorrowful	9. alone
5. CANSAVE	10. stipulate

21h Apostrophes

Because plurals, possessives, and contractions using *s* sound the same, your ear is not a reliable guide for when and how to use an **apostrophe**. Instead, you need to know which of these forms you intend to create so that you can use the apostrophe appropriately. Remember, too, that if you're unsure of how to use an apostrophe, you are as likely to put it in the wrong place as to omit it in the right place.

- A plural noun, which is usually formed by adding *s* or *es*, indicates that more than one person, place, or thing is being discussed. Do not add an apostrophe when you wish to indicate a plural. Be especially careful with proper nouns.

PLURAL All the **Joneses** congratulate you on keeping up with them. [The plural of *Jones* is formed by adding *es*.]

POSSESSIVE The **Joneses'** car is in the garage. [The apostrophe indicates that the car belongs to the Joneses.]

- A contraction indicates that one or more letters have been omitted. The sense of the sentence will indicate whether the apostrophe signals possession or a contraction.

CONTRACTION Your **report's** already three weeks late. [*report's = report is*]

POSSESSIVE Your **report's** recommendations are out of line with current department policy. [The apostrophe indicates that the recommendations belong to the report.]

- Possessive pronouns (*yours, hers, its, ours, theirs*) do not take apostrophes. Only nouns and indefinite pronouns (*someone, something, somebody, everyone, everything, everybody, no one, nothing, nobody, anything, anybody*) take an apostrophe to show possession.

NOT These problems are **their's** to solve.

BUT These problems are **theirs** to solve.

- *Its* is a possessive; *it's* is a contraction.

POSSESSIVE The dog buried **its** bone in the garden.

CONTRACTION **It's** a serious problem.

Rules for Making Nouns and Indefinite Pronouns Possessive

1. To make an indefinite pronoun possessive, add 's.

   This is **nobody's** business.
   Everyone's assignments have been marked.

2. To make a singular noun that does not end with s possessive, add 's.

   The **child's** bike lay abandoned on the driveway.
   The **horse's** saddle is hanging on a nail in the barn.

3. To make a singular noun that ends with s or ss possessive, add 's if the word is one syllable. If the noun is more than one syllable, add only an apostrophe.

   James's gloves are lying on the hall table.
   The **boss's** instructions are on her desk.
   The next **witness'** testimony is crucial to the defence.
   The **actress'** hopes were raised by the screen test.

4. To make a plural noun that ends with s possessive, add only an apostrophe.

   All **students'** marks will be posted by the main office.
   There will be a meeting of the **girls'** hockey team on Wednesday.

5. To make a plural noun that does not end with s possessive, add 's.

   Men's suits are on sale this week.
   The **children's** story hour has been cancelled.

6. To make a compound noun possessive, add 's to the last word.

   Mario borrowed his **father-in-law's** lawn mower over the weekend.

7. To indicate that two or more people own one thing (joint possession), add 's to the last name.

   Carmen and Roberta's restaurant opened last month.

8. To indicate that two or more people own things separately (separate possession), make all the names possessive.

   Ralph's and **Howard's** cars are in for repairs.

Note: Possessive nouns do not always refer to people. They can also refer to animals or objects.

   The **sun's** rays are very strong today.

320

Today's news is better.

This **society's** children have special needs.

Exercise 21.16

Add all necessary apostrophes to the following sentences.

1. Louises and Jeremys short stories, which won first and second prizes in the literary contest, will be published in tomorrows paper.

2. William Shakespeares *The Tempest* is on our list of required reading this term.

3. The Millses new Volvo was destroyed in a garage fire set by an arsonist.

4. Both the mens construction hats are in the cab of the truck.

5. There is no agreement this year about the most fashionable hem length in womens clothes.

Other Uses of the Apostrophe

- To form the plural of letters, add 's. Italicize or underline the letter but not the s.

  Pay particular attention to the long *o*'s in this poem.

- To form the plural of words referred to as words, add 's. Italicize or underline the word but not the s.

  There are five *a lot*'s in this one paragraph.

- To form the plural of abbreviations, add 's.

  She has two **M.A.'s**, one in English and one in history.

- You have a choice in forming the plural of numerals and dates. Add 's or s alone.

  His family emigrated from Scotland in the **1920's** [1920s].

  What are the chances of rolling nothing but **2's** [2s] in a dice game?

21h

Apostrophes

Exercise 21.17

Add all necessary apostrophes to the following sentences.

1. Marc Garneau, Canadas first astronaut, is a graduate of the Royal Military College in Kingston, Ontario.

2. Joannes plane arrives at eight this evening.

3. The travel agent left a message about Sarah and Orlandos vacation package.

4. Its gratifying that Mercedes trumpet playing has improved so dramatically.

5. Someones car is parked in my spot.

6. Judy took a months leave of absence from work so that she could take a crash course in French.

7. Johns and Geraldines income tax refunds have just arrived.

8. Helenas parents house doesnt have a full basement.

9. How many *l*'s are there in *parallel*?

10. His speech is full of *likes* and *you knows*.

21i Abbreviations

Abbreviations are appropriate in scientific and technical writing and in footnotes and bibliographies. In most other kinds of writing, use abbreviations sparingly. If you wish to abbreviate a term that you intend to use repeatedly, write the term out in full the first time you use it, and then use the abbreviation.

> American Sign Language (ASL) is the first language of many deaf children. Because ASL has a different grammatical structure from English, deaf children who use ASL must learn English as a second language.

The following guidelines cover the appropriate uses of abbreviations in nontechnical writing.

Names of Dates and Times

- Write out the names of months and holidays.

> **Hanukkah** comes in the darkest part of December.

- Use a.m. (*ante meridiem*) to refer to exact times before noon and p.m. (*post meridiem*) to refer to exact times after noon. Note that these abbreviations are not capitalized.

> The meeting began at 9:07 a.m. and concluded at 5:31 p.m.

- Use BC (Before Christ) to refer to dates before the birth of Christ. Put BC after the date. Use AD (*anno Domini*) to refer to dates after the birth of Christ. Put AD before the date. Stop using AD when you can assume that your reader knows that the event did not take place before the birth of Christ, usually for any date after AD 500.

> Julius Caesar, who unified the Roman Empire under his dictatorship, was assassinated in **44 BC.**

Hadrian's Wall, completed in **AD 123**, was constructed to prevent northern tribes from invading Roman Britain.

If you prefer, use BCE (Before the Common Era) and CE (Common Era). Both of these abbreviations follow the year.

Units of Measurement

Write out metric words such as *gram, metre,* and *kilometre* when you use them without numerals.

Speed limits are now given in kilometres per hour.

Abbreviate these words when you use them with a numeral. Don't put a period after the abbreviation.

Combine 10 g flour with 1 l milk.

Scientific and Technical Terms

Some commonly known scientific and technical terms are usually abbreviated.

DNA (deoxyribonucleic acid)

DDT (dichlorodiphenyltrichloroethane)

AIDS (Acquired Immune Deficiency Syndrome)

Common Latin Terms

Although it's useful to know the following Latin abbreviations, it's usually better to omit them or replace them with English equivalents. If you use them, note where the periods go.

e.g. *exempli gratia* (for example)

i.e. *id est* (that is)

etc. *et cetera* (and so forth)

21i

Abbreviations

Be especially careful with *etc.* Using it at the end of a list suggests that you have run out of ideas. Instead, use the phrase *such as* or an equivalent expression.

NOT   The Niagara region grows apples, peaches, pears, **etc**.

BUT   The Niagara region grows fruits **such as** apples, peaches, and pears.

21j The Ampersand (&)

Never use this symbol in general writing. Use the ampersand only when you are copying the name of an organization or following APA documentation style.

> He works the night shift at the local **A&W**.

> Maccoby, E. E. **&** Jacklin, C. N. (1974) ....

21k Capitalization

All proper nouns are capitalized. A proper noun names a specific person, place, or thing.

> Meet me at the main entrance of **Eaton's**.

Use capitalization in the following way.

- For kinship terms such as mother, father, brother, sister when they are part of a name (as in *Mother Teresa, Grandfather McGregor*) or when they are used as a substitute for the proper name. Do not capitalize kinship terms preceded by a possessive adjective (*my, our, your, her, his, their*).

  > Is **Baba Kostash** going to the dance?

  > Is **Grandfather** going to the dance?

  > We are going with our father and mother.

- For titles used as part of a person's name.

  > I have a meeting with **Professor Qureshi** this afternoon.

  > I get along well with two of my **professors** this term.

- For the names of directions (*north, south, east, west*) when they are part of a proper name or a place name in themselves.

  > It has always been his ambition to travel to the **North**.

  > The house faces **north**. [*North* names a direction, not a place.]

- For the names of planets, stars, and other heavenly bodies. Do not capitalize *sun* and *moon*. Do not capitalize *earth* when it is modified by *the*.

  > The astronauts saw **Earth** from their spaceship.

  > Unless we act now, all the waters of **the earth** will be polluted.

- For the names of institutions, organizations, political parties, and branches of government. Do not capitalize words such as party, college, or university unless you are using the term as a shortened version of the full name.

  > Faryl has a **university** degree in biology.

  > Tim will complete his final year at **Capilano College** this spring.

- For nationalities, languages, religious groups, religions, sacred and religious names.

    Canadian, Cree, Protestant, Taoism, the Koran, the Bible

- For days of the week, the months, holidays, events. Do not capitalize the names of seasons.

    Monday, January, New Year's Eve, the Middle Ages, summer, winter, spring, fall

- For the names of specific courses. Do not capitalize the names of general subjects, except languages.

    Psychology 101, Chemistry 400

    I studied **English, French, drama, math, and sociology** in my first year of university.

Other Occasions for Capitalization

- Capitalize the first word in a quotation if the quotation is a complete sentence. If the quotation is not a complete sentence, do not capitalize the first word.

    The instructor turned to me and said, "Please give me your views on the opening scene in *Macbeth*."

    Susan remarked that she would rather be "poor and healthy" than "rich and sick."

- Capitalize the first, last, and all important words in the titles of books, short stories, plays, poems, articles, newspapers, magazines, movies, and musical compositions.

    *The Day the Earth Stood Still**Pride and Prejudice*
    Empire of the Sun   *Of Mice and Men*

211 Numbers

Numerals are appropriate and preferred in scientific and technical writing. In general writing, however, certain conventions determine the use of numerals or words to express numbers.

Use numerals in nontechnical writing in the following cases.

- To provide a series of numbers

    In 1986, **250** children were involved in the school lunch program. By 1987, the number had increased to **300** children. Last year, **350** children were eating lunch at school.

- To express a number that would take more than two words to spell out

    Last year the shelter for battered women helped **259** women and their children.

- To express exact times of the day and with a.m. and p.m.

  We'll begin the meeting at **9:15** sharp.

  The plane from Toronto will arrive at **8:03 a.m.**

- To express exact sums of money

  This wonderful car can be yours for only **$2999.99**.

- To express dates. Years are always expressed in numerals; centuries should be written out.

  The events between **1939** and **1945** affected the rest of the **twentieth century**.

You can use *st, nd, rd, th* with numerals in dates if you do not give the year, but these abbreviations are not essential.

- To express addresses

  2939 107 Street; #976, 10098 Elm Street; P.O. Box 12

- To express percentages and decimals

  29%, 87 percent, 3.9 cm

- To express page, line, verse, act, and scene numbers in literary works. See Appendix B, Documentation for more information.

  Act 3, Scene 2, lines 23-38 **or** 3.2.23-28

  John 1:1-5; 1 & 2 Corinthians

Use words in place of numerals in these two instances.

- For numbers that can be spelled out in one or two words

  At least **fifty** people were invited to the party.

- To express round numbers used with money, times of the day, and measurements

  Every day she gets up at **five o'clock** to do her homework.

  I used to be able to buy a huge bag of candy for **ten cents**.

  The man loitered in the alley about **two metres** from the parked car.

- When you begin a sentence with a number

  Thirty **percent** of first-year students need some form of financial assistance.

Note: Use a combination of words and numerals to prevent confusion.

NOT	He ordered **2 10 cm** pieces of wood.
BUT	He ordered **two 10 cm** pieces of wood.

Exercise 21.18

Correct all errors in the use of numerals or words to express numbers in the following sentences. If the sentence is correct, write *C*.

1. I hate to get up before 10 o'clock on the weekends.
2. In the nineteen sixties, the range of material included in children's literature changed radically.
3. 50% of her income is spent on rent.
4. If you can lend me $4.95, I can buy some paper for my art class.
5. You'll need 2 45-cent stamps for a parcel that size.

21m Commonly Misused Words

Here is a list of frequently misspelled or misused words and expressions.

A Lot

A lot is an informal expression meaning *many, much,* or *a great deal of*. Avoid *a lot* in most writing. When you use it, spell it as two words.

> I have **a lot** of work to do this weekend.

Affect/Effect

Affect is usually a verb.

> Her mood was **affected** by the cold weather and the isolation.

Effect is usually a noun.

> Extreme cold and isolation have an effect on most people's nerves.

All Right

All right should be spelled as two words. *Alright* is incorrect and should not be used.

> "**All right**," the coach agreed reluctantly, "you can miss the practice Thursday afternoon."

Allude/Elude

Use *allude* when you mean *refer to*, as in an allusion to the Bible or to Shakespeare.

In his opening comments, the guest speaker **alluded** to Hamlet's indecision.

Use *elude* when you mean to *avoid* or *escape*.

The wary old wolf managed to **elude** the hunter.

Allusion/Illusion

An *allusion* is a reference, often to literature, the Bible, or an historical event or figure.

The commander clarified his attitude towards wars of conquest with an **allusion** to the exploits of Alexander the Great.

An *illusion* can be something that deceives a person by producing a false impression. An *illusion* can also refer to the state of mind in the person who is deceived.

The mirror in the fun house gave viewers the **illusion** that they had just grown a metre taller.

Mirrie clung to the **illusion** that Dennis would always love her.

Among/Between

Use *between* when you are referring to two things.

Divide the candy **between** the twins.

Use *among* when you are referring to more than two.

Share the food **among** all the refugees at the shelter.

Amount/Number

Use *amount* to refer to things considered as a mass (*a large amount of work, a small amount of money*). Use *number* to refer to things that can be counted (*a large number of people, a small number of desks*).

A large **amount** of money is missing.

A large **number** of bills were stolen.

Bored with

Use *bored with* (never *bored of*) to mean *wearied with dullness*.

She is **bored with** her courses this year.

21m

*Commonly
Misused
Words*

Cite/Site/Sight

Cite is a verb meaning to quote from a source (usually an authority) to support an argument or to acknowledge a source of information.

Frederick **cited** recent statistics on the decline of fish stocks.

Site is a noun meaning a place.

This is the **site** of the original fort.

Sight can be a noun or a verb referring either to the sense of vision or to something remarkable to look at.

Jack recovered his **sight** after cataract surgery.

At last the weary hikers **sighted** the hostel.

The final seconds of the fireworks were an amazing **sight**.

Defer/Differ

Use *defer to* when you mean *to give respect* or *yield to*.

I'll **defer** to the experts in this area.

Use *differ from* when you mean *to be unalike*.

Your interpretation of the new tax laws **differs from** mine.

Disinterested/Uninterested

Use *disinterested* when you mean *impartial*.

The two sides in the dispute sought the advice of a **disinterested** third party.

Use *uninterested* when you mean *not interested*.

Jacob was completely **uninterested** in hockey.

Elusive/Illusory

Use *elusive* when you want to describe something that is good at escaping or difficult to express or define.

The **elusive** silver wolf disappeared into the dark forest.

The practical implications of the employment equity policy remained **elusive**.

Use *illusory* when you want to describe something that is false or unreal.

Given the decline in sales, plans to expand the business are **illusory**.

21m

Commonly Misused Words

329

Hanged/Hung

Use *hanged* as the past tense of the verb *to hang* when you are referring to a person.

The convict **was hanged** at dawn.

Use *hung* when you are referring to objects.

Her latest painting **was hung** in the city gallery.

Hopefully

Hopefully is an adverb meaning *full of hope*. It is used correctly in this sentence: The sales representative knocked hopefully at the door.

Do not use *hopefully* to mean *I hope* or *perhaps*.

NOT	Hopefully, we'll be able to meet next week.
BUT	Perhaps [or I hope] we'll be able to meet next week.

It's/Its

It's is the contraction for *it is*.

It's about time you got here.

Its is the possessive form of *it*.

The dog jealously guarded **its** new toy.

Don't put an apostrophe in *its* unless you mean *it is*.

Lead/Led

The past tense of the verb *to lead* is *led*.

Yesterday he **led** the band in the Earth Day parade.

Less/Fewer

Use *less* with mass nouns (*less unemployment, less hunger*) and fewer with countable nouns (*fewer courses, fewer assignments*).

I'm having **fewer problems** this year.

I'm having **less difficulty** this year.

Commonly Misused Words

Lie/Lay

The principal parts of the verb *to lie* (to recline) are *lie, lay, lying,* and *lain.*

The principal parts of the verb *to lay* (to place) are *lay, laid, laying,* and *laid.*

Be careful not to confuse these verbs.

NOT	She **lays** on the chesterfield all afternoon.
BUT	She **lies** on the chesterfield all afternoon.
NOT	He **laid** in the sun for half an hour.
BUT	He **lay** in the sun for half an hour.

Like/As

Use *like* as a preposition. Use *as* to introduce a clause.

She was witty and informal, **like** any good master of ceremonies.

She was witty and informal, **as** any good master of ceremonies should be.

Loose/Lose

Loose is usually an adjective or adverb (*loose change, loose clothing, let loose*).

Occasionally *loose* is used as a verb meaning *to set free* (*He loosed the dog on the intruder*). Don't confuse *loose* with *lose* (to misplace).

He often **loses** his way when he is in a strange city.

I can only give you a **loose** translation of that phrase.

21m

Commonly Misused Words

Principal/Principle

Principal means *main* or *chief.*

My **principal** objection to the new plan is the cost.

Principle means *rule* or *belief.*

What are the main **principles** underlying the pro-life position on abortion?

Take Part in/Partake of

To take part in something is *to join* or *participate.* To *partake of* is *to have a share of something* (usually a meal).

Hamlet refused to **take part in** the wedding festivities.

Would you be willing to **partake of** our simple meal?

Their/There/They're

Their is the possessive form of *they* (*their house, their mortgage*).

There is an adverb (*Put the plant over there*) or an expletive (*There were many more problems to be solved*).

They're is a contraction for they are (*They're going south for a week*).

Then/Than

Then is an adverb meaning *at that time.*

Our expectations were higher **then**.

Than is a conjunction usually found after comparative adjectives and adverbs.

In the past, our expectations were higher **than** they are now.

Your/You're

Your is the possessive form of *you* (*your book, your problem*).

You're is a contraction for *you are* (*You're late again.*)

21m

Commonly Misused Words

Exercise 21.19

Correct all the usage errors in the following sentences. Some sentences have more than one error.

1. Their were a huge amount of insurance claims after the flood.

2. The steak was laying on the barbeque, overcooked like my mother prefers it.

3. The town newspaper published a lot of gossip in it's entertainment section.

4. I'm bored of economics, so I'm completely disinterested in how the new tax laws will effect me.

5. Be careful not to loose you're money on the way home.

6. An icy fear gripped him as he laid in his cell waiting to be hung at midnight.

7. Hopefully, our conviction that we have discovered the sight of the original fort is not an allusion.

8. The principle shareholders said it was alright with them if the dividends were differed.

9. Unless we can recover from the affects of food poisoning, we won't be able to partake in the city finals.

10. I'm taking more courses this term then I was last term, but I have less assignments.

Reference Works:

The classic *Elements of Style* by Strunk and White

http://www.columbia.edu/acis/bartleby/strunk/

Webster's Dictionary

http://c.gp.cs.cmu.edu:5103/prog/webster

Roget's Thesaurus

http://humanities.uchicago.edu/forms_unrest/ ROGET.html

Research Institute for the Humanities—extensive listing of dictionaries and thesauri

http://www.arts.cuhk.hk/Ref.html#dt

University of Maine Writing Center Online Resources for Writers, including several translation dictionaries

http://www.ume.maine.edu/~wcenter/resource.html

Mr. Puddy's Reference Desk—dictionaries

http://www.sils.umich.edu/~nscherer/RefDesk.html# dictionaries

Carnegie-Mellon Online Reference Works

http://www.cs.cmu.edu/Web/references.html

21m

Commonly Misused Words

Writing Centre Handouts:

The Online Writing Centre at Purdue offers handouts on a variety of writing-related topics.

http://owl.trc.purdue.edu/prose.html

These are handouts written since 1993 by consultants at the Undergraduate Writing Center at U.T. Austin—they include information on apostrophes, documenting sources, non-sexist language, reading literature, and wordiness.

http://www.utexas.edu/depts/uwc/.html/handout.html

Grammar Guides:

An Elementary Grammar—from The English Institute in the U.K.

http://www.hiway.co.uk/~ei/intro.html

From the University of Ottawa—Hypergrammar is an online grammar handbook.

http://www.uottawa.ca/academic/arts/writcent/ hypergrammar/grammar.html

Grammar Hotline Directory 1995 (from Tidewater Community College)—a list of phone numbers or e-mail addresses that you can contact for information on proper grammatical usage

http://www.infi.net/tcc/hotline.html

Grammar and Style Notes by Jack Lynch at University of Pennsylvania—alphabetical listing

http://www.english.upenn.edu/~jlynch/grammar.html

Terminology:

Interactive English Manual—useful literary and stylistic terms

http://www.netsync.net/users/quoll/iaem/indexed.html
and

http://www.netsync.net/users/quoll/iaem.html

Dictionary of Literary Terms

http://edweb.sdsu.edu/edfirst/BellHS/Literary.Terms.html

APPENDICES

Appendix A

Quotations

A1 Using Direct Quotations

Although you will often need to cite sources of information to support ideas in any paper you are writing, you don't always need to quote your sources directly. In fact, you shouldn't include quotations unless the exact wording seems important. For this reason, you're more likely to use direct quotations in literature essays than in essays for the sciences and social sciences.

It takes skill and practice to use direct quotations effectively. The examples below come from Jane Austen's novel *Pride and Prejudice* (Oxford: Oxford UP, 1970). They illustrate some important rules to remember when using quotations.

Use Your Own Words

Make all the major points in your own words and use brief quotations to support them. Do not rely on the quotation to make the point for you; your reader may interpret the quotation quite differently from you. Often you can shorten a quotation by expressing most of it in your own words and quoting only the crucial part.

Weak Example

Charlotte's extremely practical approach to the central problem in *Pride and Prejudice*—how to catch a suitable man—is clear in the following comment:

> If a woman conceals her affection with the same skill from the object of it, she may lose the opportunity of fixing him; and it will then be but poor consolation to believe the rest of the world equally in the dark. There is so much of gratitude or vanity in almost every attachment, that it is not safe to leave any to itself. We can all begin freely—a slight preference is natural enough; but there are very few of us who have heart enough to be really in love without encouragement. In nine cases out of ten, a woman had better shew more affection than she feels (17).

Strong Example

Charlotte's extremely practical approach to the central question in *Pride and Prejudice*—how to catch a suitable man—is clearly set out in her comment that a woman should not be too cautious in showing a man that she likes him. Charlotte acknowledges that there is some risk of embarrassment if he does not return her affection, but this risk is preferable to losing him by being too cautious. After all, as Charlotte points out, most of us feel flattered by or grateful for the attention of another, "but there are very few of us who have heart enough to be really in love without encouragement. In nine cases out of ten, a woman had better shew more affection than she feels" (17).

Use Quotations in Context

Do not take quotations out of context and use them to mean something other than what the writer intended, as in this example.

Original Text

"The story line was amusing and entertaining, but it simplified the more interesting complexities of the novel."

Misleading Extract

"The story line was amusing and... interesting complexities... "

Establish the Context for the Reader

Introduce each quotation with a sentence that makes its context clear. Even a reader who is familiar with the work will appreciate a sentence identifying the speaker and the circumstances of the comment.

Weak Example

"It is a truth universally acknowledged, that a single man in possession of a good fortune, must be in want of a wife" (1). This quotation is a good example of Jane Austen's irony because single women, not single men, need to marry.

Strong Example

The irony of the opening sentence of *Pride and Prejudice* introduces the central concern of the novel—the economic necessity for women to marry: "It is a truth universally acknowledged, that a single man in possession of a good fortune, must be in want of a wife" (1).

Introduce Quotations Separately

Do not string several quotations together; introduce each one separately.

Weak Example

Mr. Bennet's lack of proper concern for the welfare of his family can be seen in his remarks to Elizabeth when she asks him to stop her wild younger sister, Lydia, from going to Brighton:

> "Lydia will never be easy till she has exposed herself in some public place or another . . ." (204).
> "We shall have no peace at Longbourne if Lydia does not go to Brighton" (205).
> "At any rate, she cannot grow by many degrees worse, without authorizing us to lock her up for the rest of her life" (205).

Strong Example

Mr. Bennet's lack of concern for the welfare of his family can be seen in his remarks to Elizabeth when she asks him to stop her wild younger sister, Lydia, from going to Brighton. Well aware that "Lydia will never be easy till she has exposed herself in some public place or another" (204), Mr. Bennet places the temporary quiet gained by Lydia's absence ahead of his family's reputation, arguing that "We shall have no peace at Longbourne if Lydia does not go to Brighton" (205). Undeterred by these excuses, Elizabeth reminds her father that Lydia's uncontrolled behaviour is likely to disgrace the whole family. But Mr. Bennet has already given up. He rationalizes his unwillingness to expend the time and energy necessary to deal with a rebellious, boy-crazy sixteen-year-old by saying that "At any rate, she cannot grow by many degrees worse, without authorizing us to lock her up for the rest of her life" (205).

Link Quotations Grammatically to Previous Sentence

- Be sure each quotation fits grammatically with the sentence that introduces it.

Weak Example

When Elizabeth criticizes Darcy for being proud, she forgets Mary's distinction "Pride relates more to our opinion of ourselves, vanity to what we would have others think of us" (*Pride and Prejudice,* 16).

Strong Example

In condemning Darcy as proud, Elizabeth ignores the distinction between pride and vanity made by her sister, Mary, who points out that "Pride relates more to our opinion of ourselves, vanity to what we would have others think of us" (16).

- If the quotation is short (not more than one sentence) and the sentence introducing it ends with *that,* do not use a comma before the quotation.

  Hamlet's intense disillusionment can be seen in his cry that "Frailty, thy name is woman" (1.2.146).

Use a comma between your sentence and the quotation if the comma fits the structure of the whole sentence.

  As Hamlet remarks to Rosencrantz and Guildenstern, "I am but mad north-north-west; when the wind is southerly, I know a hawk from a handsaw" (2.2.344–345).

Use a colon if the quotation is more than one sentence. (For more information, see Colons and Dashes, 21c)

  Hamlet's earlier belief in the ghost wavers, and he now wonders if the ghost is an evil spirit produced by his own depression: "The spirit that I have seen / May be a devil . . . and perhaps / Out of my weakness and my melancholy / . . . Abuses me to damn me" (2.2.610–615).

A2 Quotation Format

Short Quotations of Prose

- When you are quoting fewer than five lines of prose, incorporate the quotation into your paragraph. Do not change the capitalization in the original. Put the page reference in parentheses after the quotation, followed by the end punctuation for the sentence.

Elizabeth's pride in her own intelligence is obvious in her remark that she would "never ridicule what is wise and good" (50).

- Do not begin or end an obviously incomplete quotation, such as the one above, with an ellipsis (three periods in a row, to indicate words omitted).

Short Quotations of Poetry

- If you are quoting fewer than three lines of poetry, incorporate the quotation into your paragraph. Use a slash to indicate the division between the lines, with a space before and after. Do not change the capitalization or punctuation in the original. Put the line reference in parentheses after the quotation, followed by the end punctuation for the sentence.

Near the beginning of *Paradise Lost*, Milton asks God to help him in this great task: "what in me is dark / Illumine; what is low, raise and support" (Book I, 23–24).

- If you are quoting from a play with act, scene, and line numbers, give these in your reference.

Claudius, however, realizes that Hamlet is not really mad: "Love! His affections do not that way tend, / Nor what he spake, though it lacked form a little, / Was not like madness" (3.1.156–158).

Longer Quotations of Prose or Poetry

To set off long quotations of prose or poetry, triple-space before and after the quotation. Centre the quotation by indenting ten spaces from the left- and right-hand margins. Single-space the quotation. Do not use quotation marks unless the quotation is dialogue. Put the reference in parentheses on the last line of the quotation.

Claudius is intelligent enough to realize that although he can escape justice on earth, there is still a final reckoning to contend with:

In the corrupted currents of this world

Offence's gilded hand may shove by justice,

And oft 'tis seen the wicked prize itself

Buys out the law. But 'tis not so above.

There is no shuffling; there the action lies

In his true nature, and we ourselves compelled,

Even to the teeth and forehead of our faults,

To give in evidence. (3.3.57–64)

Appendix B

Documentation

B1 What to Document

Whenever you use facts or ideas from other sources in a research paper or any other kind of writing, you must clearly indicate what you have borrowed. Use parenthetical references (called in-text citations) to acknowledge your sources within your paper. Use a list of references at the end of your paper to provide more complete bibliographical information about your sources.

Documenting your sources is important for two reasons. First, it enables your reader to check statements that you have made or to look up more information on your subject. Second, it ensures that you do not take credit for information that is not your own (see Documenting Sources, 12d). For these reasons, knowing what to document is just as important as knowing how to do it.

You **don't** need to give the source of commonly known pieces of information, such as the fact that the earth is the third planet from the sun, or the source of familiar quotations, such as St. Paul's statement that it is "better to marry than to burn" or Hamlet's "to be or not to be" soliloquy, when you use them as allusions.

You **do** need to give the source of all facts, ideas, and opinions that you have taken from written sources *whether or not* you have quoted directly. Be especially careful to acknowledge the source of statistics. Don't make the mistake of thinking that you avoid having to acknowledge the source of your information if you change the wording slightly. Failure to cite your references in this situation is still plagiarism.

There are two main systems of documentation. The Modern Language Association of America (MLA) is the accepted authority for documentation in the humanities (for example, English, history, or philosophy). The American Psychological Association (APA) is the accepted authority for documentation in education, the social sciences (for example, psychology, sociology, or anthropology), and many fields in the physical sciences.

B2 MLA System: In-Text Citations

General Guidelines

Place the name(s) of the author(s) and the page number(s) in parentheses immediately after the quoted or paraphrased material (Austen 17).

- Omit the author if the introduction to the quotation makes this information clear (17).

- If you will be referring to more than one work by the same author, give a shortened version of the title and then the page reference (Austen, *Sense* 17).

The following examples demonstrate in-text citations for particular references.

- ***Quotation from primary text (author previously identified)***

For novels, short stories, and essays, give the page number (without *p.* or *pp.*) in parentheses after the quotation.

> By the time she reaches seventeen, Anne has become what Marilla wanted: "All I want is that you should behave like other little girls and not make yourself ridiculous" (89).

For short poems, give the line numbers in parentheses after the quotation. If you set off the quotation, type a space between the end of the quotation and the reference.

> John Donne begins "The Sun Rising" by complaining that the sun has awakened him:
>
> > Busy old fool, unruly sun,
> > Why dost thou thus,
> > Through windows, and through curtains, call on us?
> > Must to thy motions lovers' seasons run? (1-4)

For plays written in verse, give the act, scene, and line(s) in Arabic numerals (unless your instructor prefers Roman numerals).

> The image of the state as "an unweeded garden / That grows to seed" (*Hamlet* 1.2.135-36) appears throughout Shakespeare's plays.

- **Quotation from a critic**

As James L. Johnson points out, "Tom's world is one in which 'adventure' replaces 'experience'" (51).

- **Reference without a quotation**

Tom is not changed by his encounters with Muff Potter, Dr. Robinson, and Injun Joe, even though encounters such as these would ordinarily affect how one sees the world (Johnson 51).

B3 MLA System: List of Works Cited

General Guidelines

At the end of your paper, on a separate sheet entitled *Works Cited*, present a list of references. In most cases, your list of Works Cited should include only the works you have actually cited in your paper. If you consulted a reference, but did not cite it in your work, do not include it on the list. Make sure you include every work you refer to in a form your readers can find. If you have cited an essay in an edited collection, for instance, the bibliographical entry should appear under the author's name, not under the name of the editor.

List the entries alphabetically according to the author's last name. If there is more than one author, keep the names in the order they are given and alphabetize according to the first name in the list. If the author is not given, alphabetize according to the first word in the title (not *The, A* or *An*).

Double-space within the entry and triple-space between entries. The first line of each entry should start at the left-hand margin. Indent subsequent lines by five spaces. Do not number bibliographical entries.

In the following examples, note both the order of information and the punctuation. For a model of the name and page system of documentation, see the sample research essay, "*Tom Sawyer* and *Anne of Green Gables*: Two Models of Heroism" (12f).

Sample Citations

Print Publications

• *Article*

last name	first name	title of article	name of periodical
↓	↓	↓	↓
Fetterley,	Judith.	"The Sanctioned Rebel."	*Studies in the Novel*

volume +	year	inclusive page numbers
↓	↓	↓
3	(1971):	293–304.

If each issue in the volume starts with page one, give the issue number as well: 3.1 (1971).

• *Book*

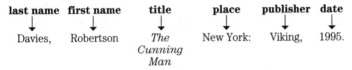

last name	first name	title	place	publisher	date
↓	↓	↓	↓	↓	↓
Davies,	Robertson	*The Cunning Man*	New York:	Viking,	1995.

Note 1: If the city of publication is not well known or could be confused with another city of the same name, add the abbreviation for the province, state, or country (Paris, TX). If several places are listed, give only the first.

Note 2: Give only a short form of the publisher's name (McClelland, not McClelland and Stewart Inc.).

• *Part of a book*

Put the editor's name (if applicable) after the title and the inclusive page numbers of the part you are citing at the end.

Cohen, Leonard. "Suzanne Takes You Down." *The HBJ Anthology of Literature*. Eds. Jon C. Stott, Raymond E. Jones, and Rick Bowers. Toronto: Harcourt, 1993. 632–33.

Whitley, John S. "Kids' Stuff: Mark Twain's Boys." *Mark Twain: A Sumptuous Variety*. Ed. Robert Giddings. London: Vision Press, 1985. 57-76.

Atwood, Margaret. "Uglypuss." *Bluebeard's Egg*. Toronto: Seal, 1984. 67-93.

• *Subsequent work by the same author*

Type ten hyphens in place of the author's name. Continue as for the appropriate entry.

––––––––––. "Unearthing Suite." *Bluebeard's Egg*. Toronto: Seal, 1984. 240-58.

- **Multiple authors or editors**

Invert the order of the first name only.

Bowles, Samuel, and Herbert Gintis. *Schooling in Capitalist America.* New York: Basic, 1976.

When there are more than three names, use only the first name and *et al.*

Gettleman, Marvin E. et al., eds. *El Salvador: Central America in the New Cold War.* New York: Grove, 1981.

- **Encyclopedia**

If the article is signed, the author's name comes first; if not, the name of the article comes first. If the encyclopedia is well known, omit the place of publication and the publisher, but include the edition (if given) and the year. If the work is arranged alphabetically, omit the volume number and the page number.

"Biological Effects of Radiation." *Encyclopaedia Britannica,* 1974 ed.

Electronic Publications

The format for citing material you access either through a portable electronic database (such as a CD-ROM) or through an online database (such as the Internet) does not differ much from other citations. You include everything you would give for the print version of your source, but you also need some additional information.

1. The publication medium. This information is important because versions of the same material published in various media (CD-ROM, diskette, magnetic tape) may not be identical.

2. The name of the vendor if the information provider has released different versions of the data to more than one vendor.

3. The date of the electronic publication. For an online database, indicate both the date of its publication and the date you looked at it, since material online may be changed or updated frequently.

You may not be able to find some of the required information. Cite what is available.

- **CD-ROMs and other portable databases**

Portable databases are electronic media that you can carry around, such as CD-ROMs, diskettes, and magnetic tapes.

1. *Periodically published databases on CD-ROM.* Many periodicals (scholarly journals, magazines, and newspapers) and ref-

erence works such as annual bibliographies are now available on CD-ROM as well as in print versions. Begin your entry by following the guidelines for citing the print version. Then give the title of the database, the publication medium, the name of the vendor (if relevant), and the electronic publication date.

Feaver, William. "Michaelangelo." *Art News* 94 (1995): 137–38.

database	**medium**	**vendor**	**electronic pub. date**
↓	↓	↓	↓
Art Index.	CD-ROM.	SilverPlatter.	1995.

2. *Books on CD-ROM.* Cite these publications as you would the print version, but add the medium of publication.

medium
↓
The Oxford English Dictionary. 2nd ed. CD-ROM. Oxford UP, 1992.

3. *Publications on diskette or magnetic tape.* Cite these publications as you would books, but add the medium of publication.

Kriya Systems Inc. *Typing Tutor III with Letter Invaders for the IBM PC.* Diskette. New York: Simon and Schuster, 1984.

• *Online Databases*

Online databases are available only through computer services (such as Dialog, CompuServe, Prodigy) or networks (such as the Internet). Give all the information you would for the appropriate print version. Then add the name of the database, the publication medium (*Online*), the name of the computer service or network, and the date you accessed the material.

Schiff-Zamano, Roberta. "The Re/membering of Female Power in *Lady Oracle*." *Canadian Literature* 112 (1987): 32–38. *MLA Bibliography 1963–1989.* Online. Dialog. 8 Aug. 1995.

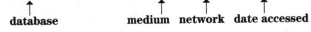

database   **medium   network   date accessed**

For further information, see Joseph Gibaldi, *MLA Handbook for Writers of Research Papers*, 4th ed. New York: The Modern Language Association of America, 1995.

Other Material

• *Film or video recording*

Include the title, the director, the distributor, and the date. Add any other information that is relevant to the discussion (such as the name of the principal actors or the costume designer) just before the distributor and the date.

> *Anne of Green Gables.* Dir. Kevin Sullivan. Perf. Megan Follows and Colleen Dewhurst. Sullivan Films, 1986.

If, instead of the film itself, you are citing the work of a director, actor, or screenwriter, begin your entry with that person's name. For videocassettes and similar recordings, give the original release date and put the medium (videocassette, filmstrip) before the name of the distributor.

• *Interview*

Give the name of the person interviewed, the type of interview (personal, telephone, e-mail), and the date.

> Brandt, Di. Personal interview. 3 Feb. 1996.

B4 APA System: In-Text Citations

General Guidelines

- As with the MLA system, place parenthetical references to your sources immediately after quoted or paraphrased material.

- If you are not quoting directly, give only the author's name and the year of publication at the end of your sentence. (Note that in the APA system, name and date are separated by a comma.)

  Japanese and Chinese immigrants, however, have the lowest rate of alcoholism of any ethnic group, while Inuit and native Indian populations have the highest. (Peele, 1986).

- If you include the author's name in the sentence introducing the reference, put the year of publication immediately after the author's name.

  In another study, McMahon and Davidson (1986) report that while depression and alcoholism are associated, it is not necessarily the depression that comes first.

- If you are quoting directly, put the page number after the year in the parenthetical citation.

  (McMahon and Davidson, 1986, 45)

- If you are citing a work that is discussed in another work, name the original work; then cite the source you consulted and give the date for that source.

Singh's study (as cited in Robertson, 1995)...

... (Singh, as cited in Robertson, 1995).

B4

- If you are repeating the same source in the same paragraph, omit the year of publication and include only the author's name in parentheses.

- If you will be referring to more than one work written in the same year by the same person, include a shortened version of the title in the reference.

Sample Citations

- *Multiple authors*

If the work has two authors, cite both names every time you refer to the work. If the work has fewer than six authors, cite all the authors in your first in-text citation. In subsequent references, include only the surname of the first author followed by *et al.* and the year. If the work has more than six authors, cite only the surname of the first followed by *et al.* and the date in all in-text citations.

- *No author*

Give a short version of the title in your in-text citation.

- *Corporate authors*

Spell out the name of corporate authors in every in-text citation (National Film Board, 1996).

- *Newspaper articles*

If the author's name is given, put the name, the date, and the year in parentheses

(Talbot, Aug. 6, 1995).

If the author's name is not given, use a short version of the title

("Hiroshima Remembered," Aug. 6, 1995).

349

B5 APA System: Bibliographical References

General Guidelines

At the end of your paper, on a separate sheet entitled *References*, present a list of all the works you have cited. Alphabetize according to the authors' last names, in the order in which they appear in the publication. If a work has no author, alphabetize by the title. Government and corporate publications are alphabetized by the name of the corporate author.

Double-space within the reference and double-space between references. Begin the first line of each reference at the left margin; indent subsequent lines 5 to 7 spaces. (In articles submitted for publication, the first line is indented and subsequent lines start at the margin.)

Capitalize only the first word of the title and of the subtitle of books and articles. Do not put quotation marks around the titles of articles.

Sample Citations

Print Publications

• *Article*

Do not use *p.* or *pp.* for page numbers of journal articles, but do use them for magazine and newspaper articles.

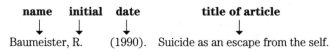

name	initial	date	title of article

Baumeister, R.   (1990).   Suicide as an escape from the self.

title of journal	volume	issue	inclusive pages

Psychological Review, 97   (1),   90–113.

• *Book*

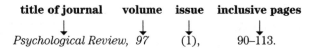

name	initial	date	title	place of publication	publisher

Katz, J. (1991). *Seductions of crime.* New York: Basic Books.

350

• *Part of a book*

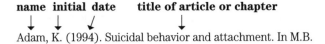

name initial date   title of article or chapter

↓   ↓   ↙   ↓

Adam, K. (1994). Suicidal behavior and attachment. In M.B.

B5

editor(s)   title of book

↓   ↓

Sperling & W.H. Berman (Eds.), *Attachment in adults*

inclusive page nos. place publisher

↓   ↓   ↓

(pp. 275–298).   New York: Guilford.

• *Subsequent work by the same author*

If you have used more than one source by the same author, arrange the works by year of publication, starting with the earliest. Arrange two or more works by the same author in the same year alphabetically by the title (disregard *A, An,* or *The*).

> Bowlby, J. (1977). The making and breaking of affectional bonds. *British Journal of Psychiatry, 130,* 201–210.

> Bowlby, J. (1980). Attachment and loss. Vol. 3, *Loss, sadness, and depression.* New York: Basic Books.

• *Multiple authors*

Give last names followed by initials for all authors, in the order in which they appear in the publication. Use a comma and an ampersand to join the last two authors in the entry.

> Bowles, S., & Gintis, H. (1976). *Schooling in capitalist America.* New York: Basic Books.

• *Encyclopedia entry*

If no author is given, begin with the title of the entry.

> Dinosaurs. (1993). *Collier's Encyclopedia.* New York: Collier.

Electronic Publications

• *CD-ROMs and other portable databases*

1. If there is a print version that's the same as the electronic version, cite the print version.

2. If there is no print equivalent, give the author, date, and title as for print versions.

3. Put the type of medium (CD-ROM, electronic data tape, computer program) in square brackets after the title.

4. If you are citing a bibliographic database, give the location and name of the producer and distributor.

B5

5. When giving retrieval information, do not end with a period. Stray punctuation will interfere with retrieval.

For materials published periodically on CD-ROM, follow this format:

Beck, C., & Stewart, S. (1996). Attention span in five-year-olds

[CD-ROM]. *Memory & Cognition*, 24, 379–394. Abstract from :

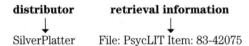

SilverPlatter   File: PsycLIT Item: 83-42075

Books on CD-ROM are cited as follows:

Statistics Canada. (1992). 1991 *Census Profiles* [CD-ROM].

Dictionary of organic compounds (Version 3.2) [CD-ROM]. (1995). Head Software International (Producer). Chapman & Hall (Distributor).

Often, publications on diskette or magnetic tape do not give an author. In such cases, begin with the title. Do not underline titles of computer languages, programs, or software.

Typing tutor III with letter invaders for the IBM PC [computer software]. (1984). Kriya Systems (Producer). New York: Simon and Schuster (Distributor).

- *Online databases*

1. Give the author, date, and title as for a print version. If the material is revised regularly, give the most recent update instead of the date of publication. If you can't determine a date, give the date you accessed the material.

2. Put the medium in square brackets immediately after the title: [Online], [Online serial].

3. Instead of the location and name of a publisher, provide an availability statement that would allow your reader to retrieve

the material, such as the computer network, the directory, and the file name: Available FTP: 137.122.136.1 Directory: pub/harnad File: psyc.93.2.33.memory.14.beck

Note: Do not end an availability statement with a period. Stray punctuation will interfere with retrieval.

Beck, C., & Stewart, S. (1996). Attention span in five-year-olds

medium
↓
[Online]. *Memory & Cognition, 24*, 379–94. Abstract from :

network   **retrieval information**
↓   ↓
SilverPlatter   File: PsycLIT Item: 83-42075

Other Material

- ***Films, videotapes, audiotapes, slides, charts, works of art***

Give the titles of the originator and primary contributors in parentheses after the name, and the medium of publication in square brackets after the title.

originator   **and/or primary contributors**
↓   ↓
Kilbourne, J. (Writer), & Lazarus, M. (Producer & Director).

medium
↓
(1987). *Still killing us softly* [Videorecording].

- ***Interview***

In APA documentation, personal communications—letters, interviews, e-mail—are cited parenthetically in the text and not given in the list of references.

For a model of the APA system of citations and references, see the sample research essay, "Whose Turn Is It to Clean Up This Garbage?" (12g).

For more information and references not covered here, consult the *Publication Manual of the American Psychological Association*, 4th ed. (Washington: Amer. Psychological Assn., 1994).

Appendix C

Format Conventions for Writing Assignments

The presentation of any writing assignment creates your reader's first impression and ensures that your ideas are clearly communicated. Take time to format your paper properly, using the following guidelines.

• *Typing*

Strive to produce a clean, professional-looking paper. Most instructors prefer papers to be typed and some insist on it (publishers accept only typed material). Make sure the print is legible. If you are planning to print the final copy on a dot-matrix printer, check that your instructor will accept it (some people find dot-matrix printouts hard to read). Avoid fonts and typographical devices that create a cluttered look. If you are allowed to submit handwritten papers, use blue or black ink.

But remember that it is the content rather than the appearance of your work that matters most. Even if someone types for you, you are responsible for any errors. Proofread and make neat corrections in ink before you hand the paper in.

• *Paper*

White 8 1/2 in. x 11 in. paper is standard. If you are handwriting, use lined paper of approximately the same size. Write or type on only one side of the page. Use plain white computer paper; separate pages and remove perforated edges.

• *Spacing*

Always type double-spaced to allow room for comments. Many readers prefer handwritten work to be double-spaced for the same reason. Others prefer handwriting single-spaced on wide-lined paper.

• *Margins*

Leave a margin of 4 cm (1 1/2 in.) on the top and left of your manuscript. Leave a 2.5 cm (1 in.) margin on the bottom and right. Besides making your text more readable, adequate margins give room for comments.

- ***Title***

Your title should make the subject of your paper and the assignment you have chosen clear to your reader. The title of an essay is often a short form of the thesis. Or it may suggest the subject and arouse interest. Never use labels such as "Essay #1" or "Personal Essay."

- ***Title page***

Place the title of your paper in the centre of the page. Write it or type it in normal-sized letters and do not put quotation marks around it or underline it. In the bottom right-hand corner on separate lines, put your name, the name of the course, and the date. You may also want to include your instructor's name (spelled correctly) and the section number of the course. See the title page of the sample research paper, "Whose Turn Is It to Clean Up This Garbage?" (12g) for an example.

- ***Pagination***

Do not number either the title page or the first page of your paper. Begin numbering on the second page (2). Place page numbers in the centre of the top margin or in the upper right-hand corner. (Some instructors ask that you include the title or your name before the page number in case pages become separated.)

- ***Bibliography***

End your paper with your list of references or Works Cited, if required. Be sure to number these pages.

- ***Fastening***

Use a staple or paper clip to fasten the pages. (Some instructors and editors object to staples; all object to straight pins and other hazardous devices.)

- ***Copies***

Keep a copy of your paper in case the original is lost.

Appendix D

Writing Essay and Short Answer Examinations

D1 Preparing for the Examination

Because a course often covers a large amount of material, you may think that your ability to do well on an essay examination depends upon luck. Not so—you can help to prepare yourself by thinking about the overall purpose and direction of the course.

- If the instructor emphasized the acquisition of one or more skills, such as the ability to analyze a piece of writing, review the terms and procedures appropriate to those skills.

- If the instructor emphasized the acquisition of a body of knowledge, such as the nature of a particular historical period or different theories of human behaviour, decide which three or four units of material seem most important and learn this material thoroughly.

You might, for example, outline the relevant chapters of textbooks or your notes, set yourself a question about each unit, and practise writing out the answer. Writing the information will help you remember it better than merely reading it over. Then think about how the less important material relates to what you've already learned.

Make notes about similarities and differences among events, theories, works of literature. Comparison questions are frequently set on exams because they cover more material and emphasize important concepts in the course.

Memorize key names, dates, facts, and so forth. The more specific information you give, the better your answer will be, as long as the information is relevant.

D2 General Tips on Writing Exams

1. Look over the whole exam paper and decide how much time to spend on each section. If one section of the exam is worth 60%, for instance, plan to spend 60% of the available time on it.

2. If you have a choice of questions or essay topics, first note any restrictions (such as not writing twice on the same subject or work) and then select accordingly.

3. Answer easier questions first. That will give you confidence. It will also allow your mind to work subconsciously on the harder questions before you tackle them.

4. Read the directions for each question carefully. Often they will suggest a focus for your response and provide directions on how to develop it. In the topic *What was Nixon's "southern strategy" and what was its impact on the policies pursued by his government?* the key terms are *southern strategy* and *policies*. To develop your answer, you would need to use both definition and causal analysis.

D2

D3 Writing an Exam Essay

1. Read the essay topics carefully. Make sure you understand exactly what is required.

2. Plan your essay before you start writing. It's a waste of time to write out a complete rough draft and then attempt to revise and copy it. Instead, use your time to plan your essay. You could begin by brainstorming on your topic (for more on brainstorming and other invention techniques, see Chapter 2, Gathering Material). Once you have some ideas on paper, you can work out an outline. Be sure that each part of your outline is directly relevant to your essay topic. (For more information on outlining, see Making an Outline, 3b).

3. Stick to the essay topic. Giving your essay a title will help you to stay on track. Asking yourself "How is this material relevant?" will remind you to connect it clearly to the essay topic.

4. Place your thesis at the end of your introduction; use topic sentences at the beginning of paragraphs to develop the points made in your thesis; and write a conclusion that summarizes what you've said.

5. Develop your ideas fully within the essay and include details and examples to support them. State your ideas clearly and precisely even if that means simplifying your normal style. Exams must often be marked very quickly. Ideas buried in elaborate sentence patterns may be overlooked.

6. Proofread carefully. Check for errors in grammar, spelling, and punctuation. These mistakes can make a negative impression on your reader.

D4   Responding to Short Answer Questions

The most common types of short answer questions include analyzing the stages of a process, the parts of a system, or causes and effects (see Analysis, 5e); making brief comparisons (see Comparison, 5f); defining terms (see Definition, 5d); identifying items; and analyzing brief excerpts of poetry or prose. We will focus on the two types not covered in the discussion of paragraph development in Part 2: identification questions and analysis of passages.

Answering Identification Questions

Identification questions generally consist of individual items or brief quotations. Answer as many of the standard questions (*who, what, when, where, why, and how*) as are relevant. Superior answers include 1) specific rather than general information about the item itself; and 2) a clear explanation of why the item is important. That importance might cover, for example, the item's causes, its effects, its role in a larger context, or its relation to the theme of a literary work.

Sample History Exam Question

Question: Briefly identify the following: War Measures Act

Superior Answer

The War Measures Act, passed in 1914, gave the federal Cabinet emergency powers to govern by decree during "war, invasion or

358

insurrection." The Act was invoked during both world wars to justify regulations that limited the freedom of Canadians, including the internment of 20 000 Japanese Canadians during the Second World War. The War Measures Act has been invoked only once during peacetime. Prime Minister Trudeau, declaring a state of "apprehended insurrection," invoked the Act during the "October Crisis" of 1970 in response to the kidnappings of British trade commissioner James Cross and Québec Minister of Labour and Immigration Pierre Laporte by the FLQ. Regulations promulgated under the Act banned the FLQ and permitted more than 450 people to be arrested or detained without charge. Although government officials defended these measures as necessary to combat terrorism, Québec nationalists and civil libertarians accused the federal government of unwarranted infringement of civil liberties. Opposition to this use of the War Measures Act contributed to the popularity of the separatist Parti Québécois, which won the Québec provincial election in 1976.

D4

Weak Answer

The War Measures Act allowed the government to use emergency powers during both world wars. It became well known when Prime Minister Trudeau used the War Measures Act against terrorists in the October Crisis. A lot of people thought Trudeau was justified at the time, but later it seemed that he might have used the Act for political purposes. There has recently been a movement to limit the powers given to the government under the Act.

In comparison with the superior answer, the weak answer contains few specific facts and no discussion of the effects of the War Measures Act.

Sample Literature Exam Question

Question: Briefly identify the following: the black box

Superior Answer

In Shirley Jackson's short story "The Lottery," the black box contains the slips of paper bearing the names of the villagers who are to take part in the annual ritual by which one of their number is stoned to death. The box's colour symbolizes death. The shabby condition of the box and casual treatment it receives during the rest of the year reinforce the theme of the story: that the force of habit and the authority of tradition can lead seemingly ordinary people into barbaric acts of violence.

Weak Answer

The name of the person to be stoned is drawn from the black box in the story "The Lottery." After Bill Hutchison draws his family's name, each member of the family has to draw again. The wife gets the X. Her little boy is given small stones to help in the killing of his mother.

The superior answer correctly identifies the author and title of the story, and explains the literal and symbolic functions of the black box and its relation to the theme. The weak answer, in contrast, omits the name of the author and merely tells what happens in the story. Telling what happens shows that you have read the material but does not show that you understand it.

Analyzing a Passage of Poetry or Prose

Most questions that ask you to analyze a brief passage require you to do three things in your response: 1) give the author and title, the speaker, and the context; 2) comment on the meaning of the passage; and 3) show how the passage relates to the work as a whole. Some questions may request you to cover other points as well, as in the example below.

Sample Literature Exam Question

Question

In a paragraph of 7-10 sentences, identify the title and author of the complete work from which this excerpt is taken (1 mark) and explain the significance of the excerpt in relation to the theme and structure of the work as a whole (9 marks). Your explanation should include relevant comments on style.

Excerpt

>   Within a month,
> Ere yet the salt of most unrighteous tears
> Had left the flushing in her galled eyes,
> She married. O, most wicked speed, to post
> With such dexterity to incestuous sheets!
> It is not, nor it cannot come to good.
> But break my heart, for I must hold my tongue.

Superior Answer

This excerpt from Hamlet's soliloquy in Act 1, scene 2 of Shakespeare's play *Hamlet* provides our first insight into the Prince's state of mind. At this point, the ghost has not appeared to him, so he does not know that Claudius has murdered his father. Yet, even without this knowledge, he is deeply disillusioned by the hasty marriage of his mother to his uncle. He describes his mother's tears as "unrighteous" and condemns the marriage as incestuous, unnatural, an idea that echoes throughout the play in suggestions that Denmark is a diseased kingdom. He accuses his mother of lust and later generalizes this accusation to include all women, even Ophelia. We see his distress in the emphasis given to the words "She married" and in the exclamation "O, most wicked speed." His awareness that he cannot openly express his opposition to the marriage intensifies the pressure he is under and prepares us for the "antic disposition" he will later assume to disguise his feelings.

D4

Weak Answer

This excerpt is from *Hamlet* by William Shakespeare. Hamlet is very unhappy with his mother for marrying so soon after his father died. He accuses his mother of committing incest because she married her husband's brother. The ghost of Hamlet's father makes the same accusation when he appears to Hamlet. We can see that Hamlet is very upset when he says that even though his heart is breaking, he must be quiet.

In comparison with the superior answer, the weak answer does little more than paraphrase the excerpt. It does not comment on style, and more important, it does not link the excerpt with the wider thematic concerns of the play.

Appendix E

Glossary of Grammatical Terms

Active Voice

A construction in which the subject performs the action of the verb.

Lightning struck the enormous tree.

In the passive voice, the sentence would read:

The enormous tree was struck by lightning.

Adjective

A word that modifies a noun or pronoun. An adjective can express quality (*red* balloon, *large* house, *young* child) or quantity (*one* apple, *many* peaches, *few* pears). Other words or grammatical constructions can also function as adjectives, including present and past participles (*skating* party, *torn* shirt) and subordinate clauses (the woman *who is chairing the meeting*).

Adjectives change form to show degrees of comparison—positive, comparative, superlative (*clean, cleaner, cleanest*).

Adverb

A word that modifies or describes a verb (run *quickly*), an adjective (*extremely* heavy), or another adverb (eat *very* slowly). Adverbs usually answer the questions *how, when, where,* or *why.* (They whispered *how*? / They whispered *quietly.*)

Phrases (walked *into a room*) and clauses (He couldn't speak *because he was angry*) can also function as adverbs.

Adverbs change form to show degrees of comparison—positive, comparative, superlative (*quickly, more quickly, most quickly*).

Antecedent

The noun to which the pronoun refers. The antecedent usually, but not always, comes before the pronoun.

The **dancers** [antecedent] are rehearsing **their** [pronoun] routine.

Appositive

An explanatory word or phrase that follows a noun or pronoun.

Martha, **my closest friend**, is visiting from Halifax.

Auxiliary Verb

A verb that helps to form the tense or voice of another verb (*have been* practising, *should have* phoned, *was* consulted).

Case

The form of a noun or pronoun that shows its relationship to other words in a sentence.

Possessive case (nouns and indefinite pronouns): **Bill's** car, **nobody's** business.

Subject case (personal pronouns): **She** and **I** left early.

Object case (personal pronouns): Give the message to **me** or **him**.

Clause

A group of words containing a subject and a verb. **Main clauses** can stand on their own as grammatically complete sentences.

He didn't finish dinner.

Some **subordinate clauses**, sometimes called dependent clauses, begin with subordinate conjunctions such as *because, although, while, since, as, when.*

Because he was in a hurry, he didn't finish dinner.

Other subordinate clauses begin with relative pronouns such as *who, which,* and *that.* These subordinate clauses function as adjectives or nouns.

The man **who didn't finish dinner** is in a bad mood. [adjective clause]

She wished **that the ordeal would end**. [noun clause]

363

Comma Fault (also called *Comma Splice*)

A sentence structure error in which main clauses have been joined by a comma alone.

The party is over, everyone has gone home.

The main clauses may also have been joined by a comma and a conjunctive adverb.

The party is over, **therefore** everyone must go home.

Complex Sentence

A sentence containing one main clause and one or more subordinate clauses. See *Clause*.

If we can't fit everyone in the car, we'll take the bus.

Compound Sentence

A sentence containing two or more main clauses. See *Clause*.

We can't fit everyone in the car, so we'll take the bus.

Compound-Complex Sentence

A sentence containing two or more main clauses and one or more subordinate clauses.

Before the storm broke, Mary put away the lawn chairs and Shistri closed the windows.

Conjunction

A word or phrase that joins words, phrases, or clauses. See *Conjunctive Adverb, Coordinate Conjunction, Correlative (Paired) Conjunctions*, and *Subordinate Conjunction*.

Conjunctive Adverb

An adverb used with a semicolon to join main clauses in a compound or compound-complex sentence. Common conjunctive adverbs include *therefore, however, nevertheless, otherwise, thus, furthermore, moreover*.

I must hurry; **otherwise**, I'll be late for class.

Coordinate Conjunction

A word used to join ideas of equal importance expressed in the same grammatical form. The coordinate conjunctions are *and, but, or, nor, for, yet, so.*

He was down **but** not out.

The weather was good, **but** the facilities were terrible.

Coordination

The stylistic technique of using coordinate and correlative conjunctions to join ideas of equal importance. See *Coordinate Conjunction* and *Correlative (Paired) Conjunctions.*

The battery is dead **and** all four tires are flat.

Neither the fridge **nor** the stove is working.

Correlative (Paired) Conjunctions

A pair of conjunctions used to join ideas of equal importance expressed in the same grammatical form. The correlative conjunctions are *either/or, neither/nor, both/and, not only/but also.*

Not only are these apples expensive **but** they are **also** of poor quality.

These apples are **both** expensive **and** of poor quality.

Dangling Modifier

A modifying phrase that is not logically connected to any other word in the sentence.

Turning green, the pedestrians crossed the street.

Definite Article

The word *the*, which specifies the noun it is describing: *the* book, *the* baby, *the* opportunity of a lifetime.

Fragment

A phrase or subordinate clause punctuated as if it were a complete sentence.

And last, but not least.

Although it seemed like a good idea at the time.

Fused Sentence (also called *Run-on Sentence*)

The error of writing two main clauses as if they were one with no punctuation between them.

> It's cold today my ears are freezing.

Indefinite Article

The words *a* and *an*, which do not specify the nouns they describe: *a* book, *a* breakthrough, *an* amazing feat.

Infinitive

To + a verb: *to run, to walk, to think.* See *Split Infinitive.*

Interjection

A word or phrase thrown into a sentence to express emotion.

> "**Oh great**, we're going on a picnic!"

> **For Pete's sake**, I knew that already.

Some interjections can stand on their own as complete sentences.

> "Wow!" "Ouch!" "Hurray!"

Misplaced Modifier

A modifying word, phrase, or clause that has been put in the wrong place in the sentence.

> **Lying in the driveway,** Mr. Jones drove over the bicycle.

Mixed Construction
(sometimes called an *Awkward Sentence*)

The error of mixing incompatible grammatical units.

> **An example of this is when** she daydreams constantly.

> The more he learns, he doesn't seem to remember much.

Modifier

A word, phrase, or clause that changes or qualifies the meaning of a noun, pronoun, or verb.

Restrictive modifiers provide essential information and are not enclosed in commas.

Teenagers **who take drugs** need help.

Nonrestrictive modifiers provide additional information and are enclosed with commas.

Susan, **who has been taking drugs for several years**, needs help.

Mood

The form of the verb that shows whether the speaker is stating a fact (indicative mood: He *wants* some food), giving a command or making a request (imperative mood: *Give* him some food), or suggesting a possibility or condition (subjunctive mood: If we *were to give* him some food).

Noun

A word that names a person, place, thing, quality, idea, or activity. A **common noun** is not capitalized and refers to any one of a class: *woman, cat, city, school*. A **proper noun** is capitalized and refers to a particular person, place, animal, thing: *Linda, Fluffy, Guelph, Westlane Elementary School*. A **collective noun**, such as *herd, flock, family, community, band, tribe*, is singular when the group is acting as a unit and plural when the group members are acting as individuals.

The band is on an extended trip.

The band are unpacking their instruments.

Object

A word, phrase, or clause that receives the action of the verb or that is governed by a preposition.

Stephen lent me his pen. [*Me* is the indirect object of the verb *lent*; *pen* is the direct object.]

She has already left for work. [*Work* is the object of the preposition *for*.]

Parallel Structure

A construction in which ideas of equal importance are expressed in the same grammatical form.

His analysis is **precise, thorough,** and **perceptive**. [parallel adjectives]

What he says and **what he means** are completely different. [parallel clauses]

Participle

A verb form that can function as a verb or as an adjective. Present participles are formed by adding *ing* to the present tense. Past participles of regular verbs are formed by adding *ed* to the present tense.

When combined with an auxiliary verb, participles become the main verb in a verb phrase (*is laughing, has been dancing, could have finished*).

As adjectives, participles can modify nouns and pronouns (*smiling* face, *running* water, *chipped* tooth, *sworn* testimony; *frowning*, he addressed the assembly).

Parts of Speech

Types of words, such as nouns, pronouns, verbs, adjectives, and adverbs. See *Adjective, Adverb, Conjunction, Interjection, Noun, Preposition, Pronoun, Verb*.

Passive Voice

A construction in which the subject is acted upon by the verb.

The water was tested for contaminants by the researchers.

In the active voice, this sentence would read:

The researchers tested the water for contaminants.

Preposition

Prepositions include such words as *by, between, beside, to, of,* and *with*. A preposition, its object (usually a noun or a pronoun), and any words that describe the object make up a prepositional phrase (*towards the deserted beach*). These phrases

E1

can function as adjectives (the man *with the red beard*) or as adverbs (walked *down the road*, tired *of waiting*).

Pronoun

A word that substitutes for a noun.

Indefinite Pronouns: *everybody, everyone, everything, somebody, someone, something, nobody, no one, one, nothing, anybody, anyone, anything, either, neither, each, both, few, several, all*

Personal Subject Pronouns: *I, we, you, he, she, it, they*

Personal Object Pronouns: *me, us, you, him, her, it, them*

Possessive Pronouns: *my, mine, our, ours, your, yours, his, her, hers, its, their, theirs*

Reflexive/Intensive Pronouns: *myself, ourselves, yourself, yourselves, himself, herself, itself, themselves*

Relative Pronouns: *who, whom, which, that, what, whoever, whomever, whichever*

E1

Pronoun Agreement

The principle of matching singular pronouns with singular nouns and pronouns, and plural pronouns with plural nouns and pronouns.

The **committee** forwarded **its** recommendations.

Everyone has made **his or her** views known to the nominating committee.

Pronoun Reference

The principle that every pronoun should clearly refer to a specific noun. See *Antecedent*.

The account that was printed in today's newspaper is completely misleading. [*That* refers to *account*.]

Pronoun Shift

The error of shifting abruptly and with no logical reason from the expected personal pronoun.

I didn't like working in the complaints department because **you** were always dealing with dissatisfied customers.

369

Split Infinitive

A form of misplaced modifier in which an adverb is placed between *to* and the verb.

to quickly run

Subject

The word or group of words that interact with a verb to establish the basic meaning of a sentence or clause. Subjects are nouns, pronouns, or constructions that function as nouns.

Costs are rising.

To argue with him is a waste of time.

Cleaning the garage is not my idea of a pleasant way to spend the weekend.

Subject-Verb Agreement

The principle of matching singular subjects with singular verbs and plural subjects with plural verbs.

He has his work cut out for him.

They have their work cut out for them.

Subordinate Conjunction

A word used to begin a subordinate clause—a clause that expresses an idea of subordinate or secondary importance. Subordinate conjunctions include words such as *although, because, before, since, while, when, if, until*. See *Clause*.

Subordination

The stylistic technique of expressing less important ideas in subordinate clauses and phrases.

Although I am angry with you, I am still willing to listen to your side of the story.

Tense

The form of the verb that shows its time (past, present, future).

Tense Shift

The error of shifting abruptly and with no obvious reason from one verb tense to another.

Hamlet **was** angry when he **confronts** his mother.

Verb

A word that indicates action (*run, jump, breathe*), sensation (*feel, taste, smell*), possession (*have, own*), or existence (*are, were, seem, become*). A verb phrase consists of a main verb (a past or present participle) and one or more auxiliary verbs. For more information on verb phrases, see *Participle* and *Auxiliary Verb*. For more information on verbs, see *Tense, Mood, Active Voice, Passive Voice*, and *Subject-Verb Agreement*.

E1

APPENDICES—Quotations, Documentation, Format Conventions

The Online Writing Centre at Purdue offers handouts on a variety of writing-related topics including quotations, paraphrases, summaries, and documentation.

http://owl.trc.purdue.edu/prose.html

The Walker/ACW Style Sheet will show you MLA documentation style including the format for electronic sources.

http://www.cas.usf.edu/english/walker/mla.html

ANSWER KEYS

Sentence Structure

Exercise 17.1

1. you will need to improve your parallel parking.
2. The car screeched to a stop
3. the Flames began to falter
4. Paula noticed the signal
5. Martin pulled himself together and tackled the first question

Exercise 17.2

1. Lockwood awoke from a fitful sleep
2. He could hear something crying and moaning...
   he was afraid to leave his bed
3. he saw the ghostlike form of a little girl
4. The window rattled... Lockwood was terrified
5. Lockwood shattered the glass

Exercise 17.3

Because sentences containing comma faults can be corrected in a number of ways, these sentences suggest only one of a number of possible revisions.

1. Visiting the SPCA can be a distressing experience because there are so many unwanted pets in need of a home.
2. Frank promised to wait for me; when I arrived, however, he had already gone.
3. As we watched, the light-air balloon drifted towards the house. We were concerned that it might not clear the large tree in the front yard.
4. Corinne pushed the door open; then she boldly entered the deserted house.
5. That joke is corny and outdated, but I still laugh every time I hear it.

Exercise 17.4

Technology is presented as much less powerful in *Dr. Jekyll and Mr. Hyde* than in *The Fly*. **While** Dr. Jekyll remains recognizably human as Mr. Hyde, Seth Brundle becomes completely non-human by the end of *The Fly*. Of course, Dr. Jekyll remains human-looking partly because special effects were more limited in the 1930s. Thus there are only minor changes in his appearance when he becomes Mr. Hyde: his hair is longer, his eyes are brighter and darker, and his jaw is larger to accommodate his bigger teeth. The focus in this movie is less on the power of science than on the evil part of Dr. Jekyll's nature when it is acted out by Mr. Hyde. Science is much more threatening in *The Fly* **because** it has the power to change not only a man's appearance but his species as well. In fact, the focus in *The Fly* is almost entirely on the horrifying changes taking place in Seth Brundle's appearance. By the end of the film, he is spitting teeth into a sink and accidentally tearing off parts of his face. His inner organs are now mostly outside his skeleton. This, the film is telling us, is what happens to scientists who do not know how to control the technology they have created. They can turn the machine on, but they cannot predict what it will do or stop it once it has started.

Exercise 17.5

1. Damion maintained a regular exercise schedule and a sensible diet; he was therefore able to lose ten kilograms.

2. Max was sorry to miss the show because he had waited all week to see it.

3. The chairlift ride to the top of hill terrified Rena; even worse was the prospect of having to ski down the hill.

4. Hearing the alarm, Linda stood up, left the room, and closed the door behind her. She then walked quickly but calmly to the nearest exit.

5. Stop talking, or you will not hear crucial instructions.

Exercise 17.6

The contrasting endings of the two films reveal very clearly the difference fifty years have made in people's attitudes towards scientific technology. In the earlier film, Mr. Hyde becomes Dr. Jekyll again as soon as the potion wears off, **but** in the later film Seth Brundle can do nothing to stop his transformation into a fly once the computer has locked him into its program. In *Dr. Jekyll and Mr. Hyde,* the focus is more on the character and intentions of the scientist than on the technology he **employs. The** implication in this film is that we have nothing to fear from science as long as it is in the hands of the right people. In *The Fly,* on the other hand, the technology is so powerful that the character and intentions of the people who use it are much less important. In this film, scientists create machines with minds of their **own; moreover,** these machines are indifferent to the wishes and best interests of their creators. In the 1930s scientists could control their creations, **so** they were responsible for them. In the 1980s no one could be sure what would happen when high-tech machinery was set into motion.

Exercise 17.7

1. The old man **wore** tattered, dirty clothes and **carried** a large shopping bag filled with bottles and odds and ends of junk.
2. At present, those people who hold boarding passes for rows fourteen through twenty-five **may board through gate eleven**.
3. **Ramon was** unable to pay his rent, for he had spent his last dollar at the race track.
4. Having filled the tank, checked the tires, and replaced the defective **headlight, Maria** was ready to leave for Jasper.
5. Pi **is** the symbol designating the ratio of the circumference of a circle to its diameter.

Exercise 17.8

1. C
2. The child **was** riding joyfully back and forth on the sidewalk, testing out her new bike.
3. The reason for the current disruption in production **is** a shortage of trained staff.
4. Unable to understand either the problem or the explanation, **she gave up** in temporary despair.
5. C
6. Although interest rates have been steady for six months, **they have now started to rise**.
7. **This is** a movie with an extraordinarily sensitive portrayal of family relationships.

8. **He wanted** to lose weight, but he rebelled against the re
   strictions of any diet.

9. C

10. **She was** always intimidated by the possibility of rejection,
    but she gathered up her courage and called him.

Exercise 17.9

There Lan stood, waving the children off to school. She always
looked the same in the morning; nothing about her ever changed.
Her blond hair **was falling** out of its rollers. Her face was covered
with face cream, **leaving** only her swollen blue eyes showing. Morning
was definitely the worst part of the day for her. A partly smoked cigarette in the corner of her mouth **gave** her a tough look. As the wind
blew against her, Lan pulled her old housecoat tightly across her
body. She wasn't fat; however, she needed to lose some weight, a
few pounds anyway. Lan shut the door and turned to walk across
the floor. Her slippers **made a scratchy sound because** Lan had always dragged her feet when she walked. "Another day," she growled.
Then she sat down at the kitchen table, reached for the newspaper,
and crossed her unshaven legs in a lady-like manner. She looked
down at her rough, chapped **hands with the** nail polish a month
old and chipping terribly. "Oh, well, there's no hurry," she thought to
herself. "There isn't much to do today anyway."

Exercise 17.10

1. Patrons are not permitted to eat, drink, or smoke in the
   library.

2. Magdalena's bedroom is bigger than her sister's.

3. The less exercise I get, the worse I feel.

4. His favourite television shows are old movies, political documentaries, and Saturday-morning cartoons.

5. Susanne was sentenced for both impaired driving and resist-
   ing arrest.

6. C

7. I have neither the time nor the inclination to clean the oven
   this afternoon.

8. A number of words have been coined by famous writers,
   including John Milton's *pandemonium* and Lewis Carroll's
   chortle.

9. C

10. The further Mario gets behind in his work, the more discouraged he feels.

Exercise 17.11

When I first entered university two years ago, I began to realize how important the human convention of keeping track of time is to day-to-day living. I found myself asking questions such as **"Will I get that essay done on time?"**, **"Can I learn to organize my time better?"**, **"Will I have time to answer all the questions on the exam?"**, **"Will I ever have some time to myself?"** I realized fairly quickly that it was almost impossible to function at university without a watch.

I have had many watches enter my life only to die shortly thereafter. The causes of their deaths have been many. Some of them drowned a week after I got them because I forgot to take them off when I showered. Two of them were fatally wounded in violent collisions: the first one against the corner of a table and the **second between the *N* and *OP* volumes of *The Encyclopaedia Britannica.*** Old age killed many more. "Old age" for these watches was, on the average, two months because every one of them was one of **those new disposable digital types, so cheaply mass-produced** that they can be sold (at a profit) for the "low, low price of $3.99."

—Sandy Block

Exercise 17.12

1. This article is a useful resource for your research paper on the influence of the mass media on public opinion.

2. Although Mr. Gertler has been out of work for fifteen months, he is not discouraged.

3. Because we have come to appreciate the high quality of your work over the past year, we are awarding you the contract.

4. After she had fed the baby, put him to bed, and washed the dishes, she went out to a movie.

5. Because Katia did not make her payment before the due date, she had to pay interest on the full amount of the bill.

   or

   Katia did not make her payment before the due date, so she had to pay interest on the full amount of the bill.

6. Dr. Margaret Choy has been invited to speak on the social systems of non-human primates.

7. Because Devon wasn't paying attention, he drove right through a stop sign.

8. Even though Susan hated math in high school, she majored in statistics at university.

9. In 1923, the Canadian doctor Frederick Banting won the Nobel Prize for medicine because he made a major contribution to the discovery of insulin, a therapy for diabetes mellitus.

or

Because the Canadian doctor Frederick Banting made a major contribution to the discovery of insulin, a therapy for diabetes mellitus, he won the Nobel Prize for medicine in 1923.

10. Although he might not have enough money to cover the rent, he wanted to buy his wife a piano for Christmas.

Exercise 17.13

1. Without a suitable organ donor, the heart patient has only a few months to live.

2. Elizabeth's refusal to marry Mr. Collins reveals her independence.

3. My report is late because I lost the graphs and had to redo them.

4. I asked whether the post office could keep my mail until I returned from Sweden.

5. The inside of the cover shows Paul wearing an Ontario Provincial Police shoulder flash.

6. Whenever he is faced with talking to a large group, he breaks out in a nervous rash.

7. The children wondered whether their grandmother would ever leave China.

8. By going to bed when you have the flu, you will get well sooner.

9. *Sunshine Sketches of a Little Town* portrays the laughable faults of the residents of a small Ontario town.

10. Because of the long hours she spent practising, Elizabeth Manley became a champion skater.

Modifiers

Exercise 18.1

1. really bad   2. more technically accomplished
3. fewer guests 4. well enough 5. softly

Exercise 18.2

1. did well   2. fewer opportunities 3. really hard
4. cold seems worse   5. did badly   6. C
7. the tallest player 8. the better worker
9. is a unique and beautiful creation   10. C

Exercise 18.3

1. I laughed when I saw the kitten tangled in the ball of string.
2. Maria has seen nearly every James Stewart movie ever made.
3. The exercise instructor advised Helen to warm up slowly . . .
4. The puck whizzed past the goalie standing just outside the net.
5. Standing at the top of the observation tower, we...

Exercise 18.4

1. There is a monument in the park...
2. I have only two dollars...
3. We waited at the restaurant...
4. When we visited Kealekekua Bay last year...
5. The candidate almost tripped on the first word...
6. Be sure to read all the instructions carefully.
7. Carrying a large bag of groceries, Doug...
8. C
9. Using a plaster model and a toothbrush, the dental hygienist...
10. When the fire broke out, the people were told to leave the building calmly but quickly.

Exercise 18.5

1. P
2. P
3. A
4. A
5. P

Exercise 18.6

1. Before beginning the cardiovascular part of the workout, you must complete the warm-up and stretching exercises.
2. Having been fascinated by the night sky since childhood, I decided to pursue a career in astronomy.
3. When Don was ten, his grandfather moved in with the family.
4. Unable to see clearly in the fog, he missed the turnoff to the farm.
5. She was already late for an appointment on the tenth floor, and the elevator was out of order.

Exercise 18.7

1. After we had paid for the garage sale licence, the next step was to print notices and post them around the neighbourhood.
2. C
3. Unable to recognize any of the buildings or street names, Martha soon realized that she had taken the wrong bus.
4. After talking at length with his agent, he made major revisions to the opening and closing chapters of his novel.
5. While we waited for our guest to arrive, there was little to talk about except the weather.

   or

   Waiting for our guest to arrive, we found little to talk about except the weather.
6. Seeing the villain about to strike from behind the curtain, the hero ran him through with his sword.
7. Uncertain of which road to take, we decided to ask for directions.
8. C

9. While I was sitting at my desk reading Poe's "The Raven," the clock struck midnight.

10. When I opened the drapes, a heavy fog obscured my view of the street.

Exercise 18.8

My gorgeous red sled was my **most precious** possession. **It was a beautiful 1967 fire-engine red Ford Mustang** with fastback styling. I had had it **only** a few months, but it had long been an esteemed member of my family. **My brother-in-law, who had first owned it**, had beefed it up. Then my older brother owned it before selling it to me. This wasn't my first car, but it was my first prestigious vehicle. It was the **classiest, most stylish,** and **most powerful** car I had ever owned, and its qualities became extensions of my own life.

One fateful night, however, **while I was showing off** and speeding around town, my faithful old sled piled into the end of an ugly street cruiser with a two-foot bumper. Unfortunately, my beautiful, sleek little car didn't come to a standstill until my radiator was wrapped around my engine block. **I could hardly believe** that this stupid accident could happen to one of the world's best drivers, who was piloting **perhaps** the classiest car to come out of Detroit in the 1960s. **I sat there, head in hand,** staring in disbelief while my pants were soaking up anti-freeze and battery acid. That car was the embodiment of my own personality; wrecking it was like crushing my soul.

—Bernard Doering

Verbs

Exercise 19.1

1. has begun
2. if she had tried
3. has drunk
4. lay
5. would have come
6. have brought
7. written
8. C

9. I saw

10. I would have given you a ride if I had known

Exercise 19.2

As a child, Vanessa expresses her imaginative concerns in the stories of "spectacular heroism" that she composes in her head to counteract the boredom of Sunday School lessons. Essentially she **rejects** any ties between her fictional world and the reality she experiences growing up in a little prairie town. Although she acknowledges Manawaka in her tale of the infant swept away in its christening robe by the flooding Wachakwa River, she **transforms** this muddy little river into an agent of the grotesque. Beyond this, Manawaka seems hardly worthy of literary note. For Vanessa, the "ordinary considerations" of life **are** completely divorced from the dramatic considerations of art. Thus she abandons her heroic epic, "The Pillars of the Nation," when she **learns** that Grandfather Connor, with his boring stories of the past, is himself one of those pillars.

Exercise 19.3

1. The audience thoroughly enjoyed the performance

2. C **or** The members of the housing authority decided unanimously . . .

3. C

4. The catcher signalled a curve ball, but the pitcher threw a fast ball instead.

5. C [The agent changing the names is unknown or unimportant.]

6. C [if you want to de-emphasize the government's role in raising taxes]
   or
   The federal government will impose an increased tax . . .

7. When Alexa heard the cracking ice, she moved cautiously toward the edge of the pond.

8. The research team at McGill University will present its conclusions on strokes and heart attacks at the fall conference.

9. C [The agent releasing Mr. Lum is unimportant.]

10. The lifeguard warned the swimmers not to go beyond the buoys because of the strong undertow.

Exercise 19.4

1. temptation/has
2. jury/is [jury acting as a unit]
3. C
4. warden/supports
5. each/is
6. C
7. nothing/seems
8. no one/remembers
9. committee/has [committee acting as unit]
10. daughters/are

Pronouns

Exercise 20.1

1. Every parent experiences/his **or** her or All parents experience/their
2. runner/his **or** runner/her
3. Typically, impaired drivers are confident that they are in control of their vehicles
4. The first-year student/his or her **or** First-year students/their
5. dog/its teeth

Exercise 20.2

1. Tom or Dick will lend you his
2. city council/its
3. Neither the landlord nor the tenants felt their complaints had been heard.
4. mother/her [**Better:** Either my mother or my aunts/their]
5. pack/its
6. C
7. board/its
8. family/its [family acting as a unit]
9. Susan/Megan/her
10. C

Exercise 20.3

1. anybody/his or her **or** a
2. his **or** her
3. C
4. the special needs child is/his or her **or** special needs children are/their
5. someone/his or her

Exercise 20.4 Pronoun Agreement Review

1. neither/her testimony
2. representative/his or her
3. Monika/Rachel/her
4. rock group/its
5. person/his
6. child/his or her
7. C
8. committee/its
9. neither/his or her
10. cocaine addicts/their job/their family
11. C
12. Magda/Dorothy/her notes
13. audience/its
14. C
15. no one/his or her

Exercise 20.5 Pronoun Agreement Review

The **parents** of a deaf child typically **go** through a number of stages in coming to terms with their child's condition. During the shock stage, when deafness is first discovered, **parents are** often too stunned and numb to register much emotion about having a deaf child. This stage is followed by the much more emotional recognition stage, when **parents** may express a good deal of anger, frustration, grief, and shame as they begin to face the implications of deafness for themselves and their child. Because this recognition stage is so painful, **parents** may withdraw from it into denial, pretending that the deaf child is almost the same as **his or her** siblings and playmates and needs no special attention. **Parents** can be helped through this stage by learning to recognize it. When **parents begin** to tell members of **their** extended families about **their** child's hearing loss and thus **try** out a new role as **parents** of a deaf child, they are moving towards acceptance. With acceptance comes the possibility for the final stage, constructive action, when parents begin to investigate the options for helping the child to communicate, learn, and integrate **himself** or **herself** into the mainstream.

Exercise 20.6

1. Laurence, Edward, and he
2. than we
3. My cousin and he
4. as I
5. his sister and he
6. whom to believe
7. C
8. or me
9. and me
10. and her

Exercise 20.7

1. whose
2. its
3. everybody's
4. yours
5. theirs

Exercise 20.8 Review of Pronoun Case and Possessive Pronouns

1. Elizabeth or me
2. Donato and he
3. their porch
4. C
5. as he
6. ours
7. you and me

8. he and his friend
9. Paul or me
10. *C*

Exercise 20.9 Review of Pronoun Case and Possessive Pronouns

A few years ago, **my brother and I** bought a somewhat battered 1963 Ford pickup truck, advertised as being in "good running condition." Neither of us understood at the time that this phrase was a euphemism for "on **its** last legs." My father said that our mother and **he** doubted that we would have enough money to run it, but we assured them that we had figured it all out. Almost from the beginning, however, the truck was a major source of arguments between my brother and **me**. We had agreed that he would cover the costs of insurance, the licence, and gas while the costs of repairs would be borne by **me**. A week after we got the truck, we woke one morning to discover that both front tires were flat and **there** was no spare. A week after that, a huge puddle of oil appeared on the front driveway, and we argued about **whose** responsibility it was to clean up. Next the signal lights went, and we were forced to make hand signals in -20°C temperatures.

Still, **we** brothers did not despair. Even though the truck was just barely running, it was still all **ours**. But one snowy Friday afternoon in the middle of rush-hour traffic, the brakes went and we slid through a red light. My brother, always more cowardly than **I,** shook with fear when he saw the five-car pile-up we had caused. No one was hurt, but as we watched our truck being towed away while we talked with the police officer, we knew that our driving careers had ended, at least temporarily.

Exercise 20.10

1. The beach has been closed because of the oil from the spill, which volunteers are working hard to clean up.

   or

   The beach has been closed, because volunteers are working to clean up the oil from the spill.
2. Karen applied to the school of nursing, but the admissions clerk...

3. ...but the situation [or the damage] isn't as bad as it seems
4. This situation [problem/dilemma] made me touchy and miserable
5. but these working conditions don't bother Jim
6. Rajiv told George, "I [you] have just won a thousand dollars at the races."
7. are on the lookout for speeders [traffic violations]
8. Experts say
9. he doesn't have time for a dental appointment
10. but apparently the VCR wasn't working properly

Exercise 20.11

The English country house setting of your novel provides the self-enclosed world that is often an essential element in a murder mystery. **This environment**, however, does not allow readers to focus on Dr. Hawkins' career in the way that a hospital setting would facilitate. Your astute observations of human behaviour are effective in the complex analysis you provide of his reasons for murdering the head of surgery, **and these observations** give your novel more psychological complexity. You might consider developing **Dr. Wong's** character in more detail in order to set out the reasons for the rivalry **between her and Dr. Hawkins** more fully. **If you make these changes** and eliminate the rather distracting subplot of the gardener's discovery of buried treasure, you can heighten the tension in the main plot—the increasing rivalry and emotional entanglement between Dr. Hawkins and **Dr. Wong**.

Exercise 20.12

1. she can't concentrate when she is tired
2. no matter how often they have stood
3. C
4. claim that it is possible
5. when I'm not certain

Exercise 20.13

If athletes [you] are prepared to put time and effort into their [your] training, there is no need to take steroids to improve [your] **their** performance. If strength and size are important factors in **a** sport, there are several good weight programs and diets that enable athletes [you] to gain seven to nine kilograms and increase their

[your] strength ten to fifteen per cent. Of course, these gains take more time than they would if **an athlete** [you] were using steroids. **An athlete** [you] would need to work out five times a week for five or six months to get these results. But following such a program gives athletes [you] a feeling of responsibility and allows them [you] to see that such gains are possible without chemical aids.

Punctuation and Mechanics

Exercise 21.1

1. apples, peaches, pears, and plums
2. Moira put down the book, rose from the chair, and walked slowly across the room.
3. quiche, baked salmon, and ribs with barbeque sauce
4. The drama instructor decided that Craig would play the male lead, Iris would play the female lead, and Noah would play the villain in the melodrama.
5. cold, wet, bedraggled

Exercise 21.2

1. rug, and [**or** no comma]
2. play, yet
3. candidate, or [**or** no comma]
4. leader, but
5. immediately, for

Exercise 21.3

1. day, the store
2. night, time
3. My goodness,
4. boots,
5. hand,

Exercise 21.4

1. said, "The
2. Ontario,

3. politely,
4. C [no commas]
5. Oz,

Exercise 21.5

1. Dodgson, who... Carroll, is
2. *Wonderland*, for example, is
3. Writewell, whose stories appear in several anthologies,
4. offer, Ms. Wallace,
5. C [no commas]

Exercise 21.6 Comma Review

1. enough,/cleaned, pressed,
2. discussion,
3. C [no commas]
4. dark, patrols, nervous
5. Tuktoyaktuk,
6. rigs,
7. Frisky is hungry,
8. above,
9. place,
10. course,
11. C [no commas]
12. lyssophobia,
13. lunch,/eggs,/marmalade,/juice,
14. The book that I wanted to lend you seems to have disappeared. [no commas]
15. Frank knew Marika was furious because she was gritting her teeth. [no commas]
16. R. Hood, 123 Sherwood Forest Lane, Nottinghamshire,
17. May 2,
18. me,/relatives, [or no comma after "relatives"]
19. C [no commas]
20. Guthrie,

Exercise 21.7

1. freezing rain; as a result, people
2. her utility payments; the city
3. convincing; however,
4. wagon;
5. late;

Exercise 21.8

1. hearing, [semicolon replaced with a comma]
2. C
3. possible; otherwise,
4. English;/Classical Studies;
5. school;/pleased, [semicolon replaced with a comma]

Exercise 21.9

1. your degree: French
2. Beauregard—I'm sure you've met him—is the most
3. position:
4. elements—monsters, mayhem, and murder—
5. intense—**or** intense:

Exercise 21.10

1. his job:
2. C
3. shopping—
4. free: [**or** free—]
5. Dr. Christakos—as I'm sure you know—

Exercise 21.11

1. "I'd like your opinion of my proposal," Jim remarked to his supervisor.

   "It's worthless," Mr. Koch replied.

   "I know, but I'd like it anyway," said Jim.
2. "The Greater Evil"
3. C

4. "The light/intersection."

5. "jumbo shrimp" and "airline cuisine" **or** *jumbo shrimp* and *airline cuisine*

Exercise 21.12

1. I'm writing an essay on the theme of alienation in T.S. Eliot's poems "The Love Song of J. Alfred Prufrock" and "The Waste Land."

2. "There's no such thing as a free lunch," he announced, handing me the bill.

3. "obligatory runner" **or** *obligatory runner*

4. yelled, "Who forgot to feed my rabbit?"

5. C

Exercise 21.13

1. "You'll never catch me alive!"

2. "Arguing with you," he remarked, "is never a complete waste of time."

3. "naughty"/"stupid" **or** [*naughty/stupid*]

4. "Let us all sing 'Yes, We Shall Gather at the River,'" the minister announced.

5. "If Winter comes, can Spring be far behind?"

Exercise 21.14

1. stepmother

2. one third/concert-goers

3. well known/twenty-seven

4. President-elect/self-satisfied/all-purpose/anti-government

5. recklessly squandered/ninety-seven/ex-wives

Exercise 21.15

1. drug-gist

2. C [no hyphen]

3. C [no hyphen]

4. sorrow-ful

5. C [no hyphen]

6. cara-van

7. under-fed

8. spit-ting

9. C [no hyphen]

10. stipu-late

Exercise 21.16

1. Louise's, Jeremy's, tomorrow's

2. Shakespeare's

3. Millses'

4. men's

5. women's

Exercise 21.17

1. Canada's

2. Joanne's

3. Orlando's

4. It's/*Mercedes'*

5. Someone's

6. month's

7. John's and Geraldine's

8. Helena's parents'/doesn't

9. C

10. "like's" and "you know's"

Exercise 21.18

1. ten o'clock

2. 1960s *or* 1960's

3. Fifty per cent

4. C

5. two 45-cent stamps

Exercise 21.19

1. **There were** a huge **number** of insurance claims after the flood.

2. The steak was **lying** on the barbeque, overcooked **as** my mother prefers it.

3. The town newspaper published **a great deal** of gossip in **its** entertainment section.

4. I'm **bored with** economics, so I'm completely **uninterested** in how the new tax laws will **affect** me.

5. Be careful not to **lose your** money on the way home.

6. An icy fear gripped him as he **lay** in his cell waiting to be **hanged** at midnight.

7. **I hope** our conviction that we have discovered the **site** of the original fort is not an **illusion**.

8. The principal shareholders said it was **all right** with them if the dividends were **deferred**.

9. Unless we can recover from the **effects** of food poisoning, we won't be able to **participate** in the city finals.

10. I'm taking more courses this term **than** I was last term, but I have **fewer** assignments.

Index

used with participles of regular verbs, **19b**, 270
in verb phrases, **19b**, 270; **19c**, 271

"Back to the Basics: A Step Backwards," sample position paper, **11e**, 146-147
bad/badly, **18c**, 261
Biblical references
capitalization of, **21k**, 325
colons with, **21c**, 308
Bibliographies
abbreviations in, **21i**, 322; **B3**, 344-348; **B5**, 350-353
in APA style (sciences and social sciences), **B5**, 350-353
MLA works cited, **B3**, 344-347
in proposals, **15e**, 208
in note-taking and drafting, **12a**, 154-55
working, compiling, **12a**, 154; **12b**, 155-156
See also APA system of documentation; MLA system of documentation
Books
citing: APA system, **B5**, 350-351; MLA system, **B3**, 345
finding, for working bibliography: **12a**, 154; **12b**, 155-156
reviewing, **11h**, 150; sample, **11i**, 151-152
both...and: see Correlative (paired) conjunctions
Brackets, **21d**, 311-312
to indicate error in original text, **21d**, 312
to indicate grammatical changes in quotations, **21d**, 312
around material inserted into a quotation, **21d**, 311
Brainstorming
as method of gathering material, **2a**, 8-9
for expository essays, **9a**, 101-102
Business Letters
audience and purpose, **4**, 180-181
checklist for revising, 178-179
format, **13b**, 182-183
guidelines, **13a**, 180-181
sample (general), **13c**, 183
sample, **13i**, 188
types of: application, **13h**, 187;

sample, **13i**, 188; complaint, **13e**, 184; sample, **13g**, 186; request; **13d**, 184; sample **13f**, 185
Web links, 216
See also Letters to the Editor

Capitalization, **21k**, 324-325
in APA styles of documentation, **B5**, 350
of courses, **21k**, 325
of days of the week, months, holidays, events, **21k**, 325
of directions, **21k**, 324
of institutions, organizations, political parties, branches of government, **21k**, 324, misuses of, **21k**, 324-325
of kinds of terms, **21k**, 324
of nationalities, languages, religions, **21k**, 325
of parenthetical sentences, **21d**, 311
of plants, stars, other heavenly bodies, **21k**, 324
in quotations, **21k**, 323; **A2**, 339-340
of titles of people, **21k**, 324
in title of works, **21k**, 325
Case: *see* Pronoun case
Catalogues, on-line, **12b**, 155-156
CD-ROMs
citing, APA system, **B5**, 351-352; MLA system, **B3**, 346-347
reviewing, **11h**, 150
using, for doing research, **12b**, 155-156
Checklists
for proofreading, 240-241
for revising; business letters, 178; business reports, 179; business writing, 178; essays, 66-67; paragraphs, 18; resumes, 179
Citations: *see* Documentation
Classification, **5c**, 34-36
choosing a general category for, **5c**, 34
choosing subcategories for, **5c**, 34-35
in expository essays, **9a**, 101
as method of developing a paragraph, **5c**, 34-35; sample, **5c**, 36
in plot summaries, **10c**, 131
(Exercises, 56, 36-38)

comparison essays: block
method, **7c**, 82-83; point by
point method, **7c**, 83-84
essays beginning with thesis, **7a**,
74-79
essays leading to thesis, **7b**, 79-82
Essays
audience for, **1b**, 6-7; essays analyzing literature,
9c, 106-107; essays analyzing
nonfiction, **9e**, 114; personal
essays, **8a**, 85-86; persuasive
essays, **11a**, 137-138; research papers, **12a**, 154
checklist for revising, 66-67
conclusions in: essays analyzing
literature, **9c**, 109; essays beginning with thesis, **7a**, 78-
79; sample; **7a**, 79; essays
leading to thesis, **7b**, 80, 81,
82; how-to articles, **10d**, 135
defined, **6a**, 68
on examinations, writing, **D3**, 357-
358; format, **Appendix C**, 354-355
formulating a thesis for, **6b-6c**,
68-73
gathering material for: descriptive
essays, **8c**, 91; essays analyzing
literature, **9c**, 109-110;
essays analyzing nonfiction, **9e**,
115-117; expository essays,
9a, 101-102; narrative essays,
8a, 85-86; position papers,
11d, 142-145; reflective essays, **8e**, 95; research papers,
12a, 154-156
introductions in: essays analyzing
literature, **9c**, 108; essays analyzing nonfiction, **9e**, 115; essays beginning with thesis,
7a, 76; sample, **7a**, 77;
essays leading to thesis, **7b**, 80,
81; how-to articles, **10d**, 135
middle paragraphs in: essays analyzing literature, **9c**, 108-109;
essays analyzing nonfiction **9e**,
115; essays leading to thesis,
7b, 80, 81, 82; essays beginning
with thesis, **7a**, 77-78; expository essays, **7a**, 103;
how-to articles, **10d**, 135
outlines for, **3b**, 13-14;
comparison essays, **7c**, 83, 84
paragraph sequence in: essays
beginning with thesis, **7a**, 76-
78; essays leading to thesis, **7b**,

80, 81, 82; expository essays,
9a, 103; how-to articles,
10d, 135; letters to the editor,
11f, 147-148; narrative essays,
8a, 86; persuasive essays, **11a**,
138-139; reviews, **11h**, 150-151;
summaries, **10c**, 133
purpose of: essays analyzing literature, **9c**, 106; expository essays, **1a**, 3; 9, 100; personal
essays, **1a**, 4; 8, 85; persuasive
essay, **1a**, 3-4; 11a, 137;
structure, **7a-7c**, 74-84; comparison, organizing, **7c**, 82-84; essays beginning with thesis, **7a**,
74-79; essays leading to thesis,
7b, 79-82; topic sentences in,
7a, 75-76, 77-78 thesis and topic
sentences as framework for,
7a, 75-76, 77-78
types of: see Essays analyzing literature; Essays analyzing nonfiction; Expository essays;
Personal essays; Persuasive
essays; Research papers
Essays analyzing literature, **9c**, 106-
110
audience for, **9c**, 106-107
conclusions, **9c**, 109
discovery questions, **9c**, 109-110
documenting, **12d**, 158-160;
B2-B3, 343-348
examples for, **9c**, 109
focus for, **9c**, 107
gathering material for, **9c**, 109-110
instructor as audience for, **9c**, 107
integrating secondary sources, **9c**,
110
introductions, **9c**, 108
methods of development for, **9c**,
107
middle paragraphs, **9c**, 108
organization of, **9c**, 108-109
purpose for, **9c**, 106
quotations in: as evidence, **9c**,
108; format, **A2**, 339-341; integrating, **A1**, 336-339; punctuat-
ing, **21e**, 312, 314
research papers as, **12f**, 162-168
samples, "The Theme of
Description in Alice Munro's
'The Office,'" **9d**, 111-113; "*Tom
Sawyer* and *Anne of Green
Gables*: Two Models of
Heroism," **12f**, 162-168

401